The *Odyssey*

The *Odyssey*

Structure, Narration, and Meaning

BRUCE LOUDEN

THE JOHNS HOPKINS UNIVERSITY PRESS
Baltimore & London

© 1999 The Johns Hopkins University Press
All rights reserved. Published 1999
Printed in the United States of America on acid-free paper
2 4 6 8 9 7 5 3 1

The Johns Hopkins University Press
2715 North Charles Street
Baltimore, Maryland 21218-4363
www.press.jhu.edu

Library of Congress Cataloging-in-Publication Data will be found
at the end of this book.
A catalog record for this book is available from the British Library.

ISBN 0-8018-6058-x

To Donna

꧁꧁꧁

Contents

~~~

Acknowledgments

This book, the result of several years' meditation on the structure and meaning of the *Odyssey*, grows primarily out of an article, "An Extended Narrative Pattern in the *Odyssey*," which first appeared in the journal *Greek, Roman, and Byzantine Studies* 34 (1993): 5–33. At the time I intended that piece as a self-contained article, and I was eager to move on to a book on *Paradise Lost* and Homeric epic. I soon found, however, that I could not stop thinking about other implications raised by this initial study. The larger shape of the project began to come together when I attended a National Endowment for the Humanities Seminar, "Oral Tradition," conducted by John Miles Foley, in the summer of 1994, at the University of Missouri. There I fleshed out an early version of the third chapter and made an initial sketch of what would become the fifth. In 1996 I was a Summer Fellow at the Center for Hellenic Studies in Washington, D.C., in which Skherian surroundings I wrote an early version of the fourth chapter, a draft of the introduction, and sketched out the second chapter. I wish to thank both the directors and my fellow colleagues on both of these occasions for providing an invaluable and stimulating environment. In addition to those portions of chapter 1 which earlier appeared in the article in *Greek, Roman, and Byzantine Studies* referred to above, a shorter version of much of chapter 3 first appeared in *Phoenix*, Journal of the Classical Association of Canada, 51 (1997): 95–114. I thank the editors of both journals for permission to reprint parts of those articles and for their comments on earlier drafts, as well as the comments of anonymous referees.

I also made yearly (1993–97) visits every May to the classics and graduate libraries of the University of California at Berkeley, which were vital to keeping abreast with current research. I thank the staff of the classics department for facilitating access to the library and my own languages and linguistics department here at the University of Texas at El Paso for providing funds for travel. I also thank my generous hosts on these visits,

Dana and Mary Smith and Mark Leon and Diane Torkelson, who offered truly Homeric hospitality. In terms of day-to-day research I have also benefited greatly from the quick and efficient staff of the interlibrary department of my library here at UTEP.

I was also aided by generous feedback I received from several scholars kind enough to read drafts of parts of the project. Terry Bell and John Miles Foley commented on early drafts of the third chapter. Richard Janko did the same for early drafts of the third and parts of the fourth and fifth chapters. Robert Charles Schmiel also read an early version of parts of the fifth chapter. I further thank audience members for some helpful observations at various meetings of the American Philological Association and the Classical Association of the Middle West and South, at which I presented as papers parts of the first, third, fourth, and fifth chapters.

I wish to express special gratitude to my parents, Anne and Bob Louden, for providing me, over the years, with many essential reference works, lexica, concordances, and commentaries, volumes that Prospero would have prized—the crucial tools for an enterprise such as this.

ᔐᔐᔐ

Introduction

This is a study of structure in the *Odyssey*, of the narrative components around which its plot is organized. Though centrally concerned with the form through which the poem presents its rich and complex plot, this study is not exclusively, or even primarily, formalistic. Any interpretation of the poem, if it is to be persuasive, must depend upon close awareness of the structures that serve to convey whatever meaning the poem is thought to convey. Accordingly, this book, especially in the fourth chapter, ventures into broad areas of interpretation based upon the narrative structures under investigation.

An analysis of structure in Homeric epic is, to a large extent, a study of repetition, as the *Odyssey* depends upon all manner of repetitive elements, at the level of the word, line, type-scene, and larger units.[1] Homerists have accounted for such repetitions in a number of ways. By comparing the repetitive elements of Homeric composition with those in a (then) living oral epic tradition in (the former) Yugoslavia, Milman Parry argued that the elements repeated in the *Odyssey*, verbal fomulas and repeated lines, allow a bard to improvise performances of traditional song. The Parry-Lord theory of oral composition offers the most persuasive account for the relentless presence of various repetitive elements in the *Iliad* and the *Odyssey*.[2] However, since we will never know for certain the means by which Homeric texts reached the form in which we have them, in this book I view the *Odyssey* as an oral-derived text, following Foley's definition and argument.[3] The present study can be seen as offering support for the oral view, though I have not undertaken it with any such goal in mind, nor do I primarily intend it as such. However, the presence of a single extended narrative pattern underlying the bulk of the poem's plot, as described here, makes it far more likely that a single bard could perform *ex tempore* a work as lengthy and intricate as the *Odyssey*. The hope is that students of the *Odyssey* will find something of value and interest here, regardless of theoretical orientation.

This work is especially concerned with narrative units of considerable magnitude, strings of interconnected type-scenes extending over several books. Studies of Homeric epic rarely focus on larger narrative structures. As a consequence of Parry's original exposition of his theory of oral composition, post-Parry Homeric research has been largely dominated by concern with small, discrete structures, a tendency which his own writing established.[4] While Lord, almost fifty years ago,[5] pointed to a method for the study of Homeric epic's larger compositional units, few have followed it. Lord suggested that the narrative rests on a succession of underlying themes, or type-scenes, some expanded or developed with ornamentation, some not. Though I disagree with some of his interpretations and the relative value he assigns some units,[6] his method is a useful one. While the study of smaller structures has been important, from the ground-breaking work of Parry and on, it is through study of the larger patterns and structures of Homeric epic that we can best appreciate interrelations of one part of the plot with another, and provide contexts for analyzing those passages argued as narrative inconsistencies by oralists or as problematic in other ways by analysts. For instance, if a passage which has been attacked as an interpolation is found to be part of a pattern that repeats three times, perhaps commentators have overlooked pertinent information by which to assess its authenticity. Awareness of such larger structures is invaluable for interpreting the poem's overall meaning.

Scholars have made particularly significant contributions by analyzing specific type-scenes, revealing both the generic components of these scenes and the overall employment of that type-scene throughout one or both of the epics.[7] Fenik and M. W. Edwards, in particular, have substantially forwarded the understanding of Homeric epic in this regard.[8] Structures and patterns larger than the type-scene, however, remain curiously unexplored, though Fenik effectively analyzes some reasonably large sequences in both poems.[9]

When commentators do note possible evidence of larger structures and patterns in the *Odyssey* they disagree considerably over how to interpret such phenomena. Consider Odysseus' address to the Phaiakians, when, provoked by Euryalos, a rude athlete, the hero competes in the games, winning the discus throw.[10] He comments on his prowess in other events, including archery:

> I am not bad in any of the contests where men strive.
> I know well how to handle the polished bow, and would be

first to strike my man with an arrow aimed at a company
of hostile men.[11]

(8.214–7)

Hainsworth reports, but discounts, the ancient suggestion by the *scho-
lia* that the passage foreshadows the slaughter of the suitors in book 22:
"Schol. suggest that the present passage προοικονομεῖ the massacre of
the suitors, but that episode does not need the support of so distant and
incidental a comment as this."[12] Are thematic parallels such as this the result of coincidence or design? This is one of the great divides in current
Homeric scholarship, especially between different schools of oralists.[13]

I would first supply a larger context to consider more carefully whether
there might be more to the argued connection between Odysseus' comment about archery and the later slaying of the suitors by bow. As is
often noted,[14] there are many correspondences between Odysseus' situation on Skheria and the state of affairs on Ithaka. In each case Odysseus
is verbally abused by a group of young men, the Phaiakian athletes / the
suitors. There is a parallel-name formation for one of the men instigating
the abuse: Euryalos/Eurymakhos. The abusive band competes in athletic
events: the games on Skheria / the bow contest on Ithaka. Odysseus bests
the entire band in the event in which he takes part. This series of correspondences, each of which can be fleshed out in considerably greater
detail, strikes me as too great a number to be easily dismissed.[15]

But a great deal more can be added. Many of the same correspondences
recur a third time, in the friction between Odysseus and another sometimes abusive band of young men, his crew. Again a character with the
same parallel-name formation, Eurylokhos/Euryalos/Eurymakhos, leads
the band's malcontents into a troublesome course of action against Odysseus. No, the slaying of the suitors "does not *need* the support of so distant
and incidental a comment as this," but just the same, this type of patterned
correspondence is pervasive in the *Odyssey*, and deserves closer attention.[16]

When confronted with a series of correspondences between one section of narrative and another, many commentators insist that all details
of a given episode are locally motivated. That is, correspondences exist
only because of the demands of the moment, an improvising poet's need
to flesh out one particular episode, or the reflex of his habitual compositional tendencies, without the possibility of larger design.[17] In a sense, this
is a modern restatement of Homer as "the noble savage," a consummate
craftsman of intricate small structures but with little awareness of events
happening more than a few pages away, a prisoner of the present moment. This study takes the opposing view, arguing that large-scale design

is pervasive in the *Odyssey*'s plot, the final layer in the poem's overwhelming tendency toward thematic organization.[18]

Perhaps those scholars who discount the possibility of such design in the *Odyssey* hold to too limited a notion of the possibilities present in an oral tradition,[19] underestimating what may be possible for performer and audience. When oralists insist on tightly limiting interpretative possibilities, they may be depending on too strict an idea of performance (adhering too tightly to Parry's Yugoslavian model), resulting in an overemphasis on the genesis of the text, the moment of performance, rather than addressing those possibilities that the text itself actually presents.[20] Lord, however, addresses the importance of allowing greater sensitivity to meaning in traditional oral poetry: "It cannot be treated as a flat surface. All the elements in traditional poetry have depth, and our task is to plumb their sometimes hidden recesses; for there will meaning be found" (46). As we can never know with any certainty the dynamics that governed the performance of oral Greek epic poetry, we should remain open, so as not to unnecessarily close off significant meaning that is to be found in our text.

A rich and complex narrative achieves its effects on a number of levels. An ancient performer may have performed the *Odyssey* over and over for a period of decades, allowing for considerable familiarity with the plot and, therefore, with its construction. Commentators may have too monolithic a conception of an archaic Greek epic audience, simultaneously overprivileging the idea of an oral audience but underestimating its actual ability and expertise. That is, if one scholar argues for previously unnoted subtleties of construction in Homeric epic, another responds that this particular subtlety is unlikely because it is too acute to be grasped by a listening audience. But would not some listeners have heard versions of the poem performed at different stages throughout their lives, and thus themselves be sophisticated listeners, capable of perceiving intricacies not perceived by most other audience members? Other listeners at the same given performance would necessarily be neophytes, able to follow the story well enough, and with enjoyment, but less aware of fine points of construction and meaning. To deny meaning in such correspondences may underestimate the richness and complexity of the tradition itself.[21] The poem's overall thematic structure is in many ways like that of a piece of symphonic music.[22] In a symphony, when we hear a new restatement of a theme, do we write it off merely as a matter of technique, as a compositional habit on the part of a composer? Perhaps on some occasions. But other times we see such thematic restatements as highly significant, the repetition invoking a previous context, adding to its new setting, gaining momentum with restatement.

Furthermore, all aspects of narrative construction do not exist solely for the audience's perception. Some devices are present as aids to the composer/performer, whether or not an audience perceives them. Fenik remarks on this inevitability: "Certain resemblances are unmistakeable—not to a listening audience, of course, or even to a reader. One has to search to find them, a fact which strengthens my own conviction that this technique of large-scale structuring is not there for aesthetic reasons as much as to serve as an outline for the poet himself—a framework on which to arrange his story and keep himself oriented" (182). While I allow greater potential both for competence in the audience and for aesthetic motivations in the poem itself, his point is well taken.

This study, then, argues for larger design in the *Odyssey* than previously recognized by most scholars. If large-scale design is present, how then to interpret it? The repetition evident in the design helps drive home some of the poem's central, primarily ethical thrusts, particularly the importance of self-control and the ability to observe the gods' behests in the face of adversity.[23] Chapter 4 suggests a new classification for the subgenre of myth to which the *Odyssey* belongs.

What then is our methodology for examining the *Odyssey*'s structure? Throughout the *Singer of Tales,* Lord makes many observations pertinent to an investigation of the *Odyssey*'s larger structures. He speaks of a succession of themes (type-scenes) as the singer's notion of the skeletal structure of a song: "The poet thinks of his song in terms of its broader themes" (95). As the singer envisions the broader outlines of his song in terms of type-scenes, he is able to keep the larger design of the song before him: "The theme is always at hand when the singer needs it; it relieves his mind of much remembering, and leaves him free to think of the plan of the song itself" (86). The singer shapes the overall form of the song through manipulation of individual scenes or type-scenes and through concatenation of groups of them: "Themes can be expanded and contracted . . . they are joined together to form the final product which is the song" (4). As a singer manipulates a complex of type-scenes, he keeps the individual components together: "A strong force . . . keeps certain themes together. . . . It pervades his material and the tradition. He avoids violating the group of themes by omitting any of its members" (98). Clusters of type-scenes cohere: "Some themes have a tendency to cling together, held by a kind of tension, and to form recurrent patterns of groups of themes" (112). There are various reasons behind such clustering: "These complexes are held together internally both by the logic of the narrative and by the consequent force of habitual association. Logic and habit are strong forces, particularly when fortified by a balancing of elements in recognizable patterns" (96–97).

The *Odyssey* itself, in book 8, perhaps the single book of Homeric epic most concerned with the conventions of epic poetry,[24] suggests a technical term for the importance of sequence in epic narrative. After Demodokos performs two songs, Odysseus asks him to sing of the Trojan horse, promising reward: αἴ κεν δή μοι ταῦτα κατὰ μοῖραν καταλέξῃς, "if you should narrate these things for me in good order."[25] Finkelberg argues that κατὰ μοῖραν, when the final α of κατὰ is long, reflecting the actual earlier form of μοῖρα (originally σμ-, making the final α of κατὰ long by position), retains its earlier meaning, which "connoted an ordered succession" (135–38). Accepting Krischer's formulation of καταλέγειν as "to relate the subject point by point" (135), Finkelberg concludes that the combined phrase, κατὰ μοῖραν καταλέξῃς, suggests that correct epic performance consists of a point-by-point narrative succession (138). In that part of the *Odyssey* that serves as a segue into Odysseus's own bardlike performance, the narrative emphasizes sequence as a central index of epic competence and performance.

Hainsworth offers a similar interpretation for κατὰ κόσμον, used seven lines earlier as Odysseus compliments the orderliness of Demodokos' earlier song, λίην γὰρ κατὰ κόσμον Ἀχαιῶν οἶτον ἀείδεις (8.489): "In an oral tradition the *sequence* of themes that identifies a song is easily disordered not merely by the incompetence of poor performers but also the ambition of good singers to expand and ornament their work" (378, emphasis mine). Twice, then, in his comments on Demodokos' poetic performances, Odysseus singles out sequence as a fundamental criterion of performance and composition.[26]

I argue that a large sequence of successive type-scenes or motifs, which I call an "extended narrative pattern," underlies the bulk of the *Odyssey*. The full extended pattern occurs three times in the poem, single instances of which I refer to as "sequences." This pattern in its three full versions provides the underlying skeletal structure of some 90 percent of the poem's plot. The present study thus attempts to analyze the structure of almost the entire narrative, whereas many structural analyses of the *Odyssey* largely confine themselves to explorations of the Apologue,[27] only one-sixth of the poem.

If I am correct in my analysis of the pattern, why has the structure not been recognized before? Several factors combine to hinder recognition of the pattern. Lord noted early on that themes/type-scenes do not necessarily exhibit verbal correspondence: "The theme, even though it be verbal, is not any fixed set of words, but a grouping of ideas."[28] The lack of verbal parallels has no doubt hindered recognition of the pattern. In the three different sequences, though the connected type-scenes with rare exceptions occur in precisely the same order, there is occasional intervening material less directly related to the pattern and its components. Specific details may receive more or less expansion or ornamentation in one sequence than another, impeding recognition of their basic equivalence. Furthermore, the three large sequences are in interlocked ring-compositional order, A1, B1, C1, C2, B2, A2, again hindering recognition.

Lord offered a caveat to the scholar attempting a new analysis: "It would be a brave man who would undertake another analysis of them [repeated themes in Homeric epic], unless he were convinced that there are really new and significant grounds for so doing, and that the analysis would bring decisive results" (1960: 145). I do feel my analysis yields substantive results in a number of contexts, affecting our understanding of the poem's overall structure and meaning. The recurrence of the narrative patterns suggests greater attention should be paid to some specific subgenres of myth, especially theoxeny,[29] and key motifs, notably divine interdictions and divine wrath, around which the poem has centered the sequences of this narrative pattern. The selectivity the poem exercises in emphasizing one type of mythic vehicle over another is one of the best hermeneutic tools for eliciting meaning from the poem.

Chapter 1 sets out the single extended narrative pattern, its three principal sequences and several minor variations. Subsequent chapters discuss additional features of the narrative pattern common to two, but not all three sequences. For instance, further specific parallels exist between the crew and suitors but are absent in the Phaiakian athletes (chapter 2). Parallel male escort figures who act as conduits between Odysseus and the respective powerful females exist on Skheria and Ithaka, but not on Aiaia (chapter 3). Chapter 4 argues that the proem refers to the concluding motifs of the narrative pattern, and employs the verb $\pi\lambda\acute{a}\zeta\omega$ as a key index of divine hostility, especially as a vehicle to express Poseidon's anger at Odysseus. Chapter 4 also posits that the mythic subgenre to which the *Odyssey* belongs is that of a local, contained apocalypse, resulting from a deity's anger at mortals' impiety, in which the "one just man" in the community's midst survives. Chapter 5 notes the singularity of book 5, and that Kalypso, though like Kirke in many respects, is not part of the pattern, but is an antitype to the parallel females Odysseus encounters in Kirke, Arete, and Penelope.

My method throughout is to let the evidence of the *Odyssey* itself point to an analysis of its form and structure and possible interpretation thereof. In this respect Fenik (1974) is perhaps the closest precursor to the present study, though our differences are many. I should also like to cite Lowenstam's recent formulation of his methods and goals: "The work as a whole is intended not only to confirm Austin's formulation that the Homeric poems indeed act as 'one vast and joyful paean to correspondence' but also to provide a new demonstration that it was this technique of repetition that allowed Ancient epic poets to explore a variety of complex ideas."[30]

The *Odyssey*

෴෴෴

CHAPTER ONE

The Extended Narrative Pattern
in the *Odyssey*

The architectonics of thematic structure are wondrous to observe.
— A. B. LORD

Many studies argue that the *Odyssey* is a highly thematic narrative,[1] and any serious analysis of the poem's structure needs to proceed from this cardinal observation. I have undertaken what can be called a thematic analysis of the structure of the *Odyssey*, as I think we can better appreciate the *Odyssey*'s larger structure by concentrating not on specific themes or type-scenes, as is usually done, but by recognizing the existence of a lengthy complex of interwoven motifs or type-scenes. Consideration of such clusters of motifs offers a more accurate understanding of the overarching devices of Homeric epic, in terms of its larger components, than the more usual analysis by theme. I employ the term *extended narrative pattern* to refer to the particular lengthy recurring complex of themes and type-scenes under investigation.[2] As ring composition is known to be a pervasive organizing device in Archaic Greek poetry, and has often been found present in numerous small contexts, we shall also keep in mind the possibility that a large-scale ring compositional structure helps organize the *Odyssey*'s plot.[3]

A useful body of scholarship has uncovered significant parallels between Odysseus' stay on Skheria and his later adventures on Ithaka.[4] We note for now only some of the broad overall motifs: Odysseus comes alone to each island, disoriented, uncertain of his whereabouts. He proceeds to the palace, his identity unknown, receiving an uncertain reception, but slowly acquiring some status, and comes into friction with a band of abusive young men (the Phaiakian athletes, the suitors), led by Euryalos/Eurymakhos. Odysseus perseveres, receiving the blessing of a powerful female figure (Arete, Penelope), and attains what he desires, access to the next phase of his homecoming—the band of young men having been destroyed. However, apart from the most general features, it has escaped notice that the many details replicated on Skheria and Ithaka also have close parallels in the Apologue, in the large section of narrative centering on Kirke and her island, Aiaia. Perhaps the reason that correspondences between events at Aiaia and those at Ithaka and Skheria have not been as well established as those between Ithaka and Skheria is that Odysseus narrates the Apologue, while the principal narrator narrates the other two sections, resulting in less responsion in diction and formula than found between the Skherian and Ithakan sequences. Let us first, then, consider a basic statement of the narrative pattern.

Stated most simply, the narrative pattern is as follows: *Odysseus, as earlier prophesied, arrives at an island, disoriented and ignorant of his location. A divine helper appears, advising him how to approach a powerful female figure*[5] *who controls access to the next phase of his homecoming and pointing out potential difficulties regarding a band of young men. His identity a secret (as approach to the female is perilous), Odysseus reaches her, finding a figure who is initially suspicious, distant, or even hostile toward him. She imposes a test on him, whereupon Odysseus, having successfully passed the test, wins her sympathy and help, obtaining access to the next phase of his homecoming. Their understanding is made manifest in her hospitable offer of a bath. Furthermore, Odysseus is now offered sexual union and/or marriage with the female. However, conflict arises between Odysseus and the band of young men. The young men abuse Odysseus in various ways and violate a divine interdiction. The leader of each band has the parallel name of Eury___; the band's consequent death, earlier prophesied, is demanded by a wrathful god. A divine consultation limits the extent of the death and destruction.*

The *Odyssey* develops three extensive multiforms of this narrative pattern, and occasionally offers smaller treatments of the same.[6] The principal figures in the three extended multiforms are, on Aiaia, Odysseus, Kirke, and the crew; on Skheria, Odysseus, Nausikaa/Arete,[7] and the Phaiakian athletes; on Ithaka, Odysseus, Penelope, and the suitors. I will refer to the three multiforms as sequences, named for the islands on which they take place, that is, the Aiaian, Skherian, and Ithakan sequences. In each sequence, a particular element or motif may receive greater development and attention, have a greater or slightly different function than in the other sequences. In this first chapter I am most concerned with establishing the similarities between the corresponding elements of the three sequences. Subsequent chapters will deal more with significant differences between the corresponding elements. By comparing the three sequences, however, we can better understand individual details in each narrative unit, some of which have received widely varying interpretations as they occasionally constitute significant cruxes in the poem. The Ithakan sequence, the most expansive, is the goal toward which the other two sequences aim. They are rehearsals or anticipations of what later unfolds at greater length. As such, they offer valuable comparative indications of Odysseus's interactions both with the suitors, the final abusive band of young men, and with Penelope, the last of the partly inscrutable females who exercise so much control over his destiny.

Before noting other tendencies, let us turn to a fuller investigation of the structure, proceeding diachronically through the three sequences in their chronological order of Aiaian (bks. 9–12), Skherian (bks. 6–8, 11.333–84, 13.1–187), and Ithakan (bk. 13.187), and synchronically tracing Odysseus's progress through each of the three multiforms. As we are dealing with substantial sections of the poem, discussions of some areas and the relevant secondary literature are necessarily brief.

Odysseus, as earlier prophesied,[8] arrives at an island, disoriented and ignorant of his location. Though Odysseus names Kirke's island, Aiaia, in his narration to the Phaiakians (10.135), his knowledge of the name is clearly retrospective.[9] Upon arrival he and the crew are literally disoriented as to where they are, ignorant of the island's name and location: "We do not know where the darkness is nor the sunrise, / nor where the Sun . . . rises, nor where / he sets" (10.190–92). Kirke is able to recognize Odysseus because Hermes had told her he would come: "Argeiphontes / of the golden staff was forever telling me you would come / to me, on your way back from Troy with your fast black ship" (10.330–32). Hermes' telling her that Odysseus would come is a divine form of speech we can equate with prophecy.[10]

Similarly, though the narrative earlier mentions Skheria and the Phaiakians,[11] Odysseus on arrival at Skheria has no knowledge of his whereabouts: "Ah me, what are the people whose land I have come to this time?" (6.119). Alkinoös later reveals to Odysseus that his father, Nausithoös, had said that Poseidon would one day severely punish the Phaiakians for ferrying men home (8.564–70). Odysseus is not named, nor does Alkinoös yet understand that his father's declaration applies to Odysseus, but the prophecy, as effected in book 13, clearly applies to him, both his arrival and circumstances attendant upon his departure.

In a typical Odyssean irony, Odysseus cannot recognize Ithaka when first waking there in book 13: "But now great Odysseus wakened / from sleep in his own fatherland, and he did not know it, / having been long away" (13.187–89). His first words, identical to those uttered when he woke on Skheria, occur only in these two instances (13.200–202 = 6.119–21).[12] Theoklymenos offers the most important prophecy of Odysseus's return. Having been brought to the palace just as Odysseus himself is actually headed there with Eumaios, Theoklymenos, descended from an illustrious family of prophets,[13] correctly prophesies that Odysseus is already on Ithaka, plotting revenge (17.152–61).

⤳

A divine helper appears, advising him how to approach a powerful female figure who controls access to the next phase of his homecoming and pointing out potential difficulties regarding a band of young men. On Aiaia, Hermes encounters Odysseus after Eurylokhos and the half crew fail to complete scouting the island. The god appears, assuming the form of a young man.[14] "There as I came up to the house, Hermes, of the golden / staff, met me on my way, in the likeness of a young man [νεηνίη ἀνδρὶ ἐοικώς] / with beard new grown, which is the most graceful time of young manhood" (10.277–79). In a somewhat playful[15] speech, Hermes advises Odysseus that the crew have been transformed and confined in pens. Then, counseling Odysseus how to approach Kirke safely, he predicts a hostile reception. Armed with Hermes' drug and advice, Odysseus is to proceed, offering the threat of violence in his drawn sword, and make no agreements with her until she swears an oath that she will devise no further harm.

Odysseus begins to have difficulties with his crew during the stay on Aiaia. Earlier episodes foreshadow what develops on Aiaia and, later, on Thrinakia, into the threat of open violence and hostility. The first stop on the voyage home, Ismaros, foregrounds this tendency in a summary miniature. After successfully sacking the Kikones' city, the crew ignore Odysseus' suggestion of a quick departure, preferring to indulge themselves. "They were greatly foolish and would not listen, / and then and there much wine was being drunk, and they slaughtered / many sheep on the beach" (9.44–46). As a consequence, the Kikones have time to gather allies and counterattack Odysseus and crew, turning a previously successful raid into a disaster claiming six crewmen from each ship (9.60–61). This first episode of the Apologue thus establishes a general pattern of the crew's insubordination and inability to control themselves.[16] Rebellion continues when, sailing home from Aiolos' isle, an unnamed crew member suggests that the crew open Aiolos's bag, which subsequently blows them back to his isle (10.34–35). In effect, minor mutinies have transpired in both episodes. Only on Aiaia, however, as the sequence centers on Kirke, does the poem begin to assign distinct personalities and names for the crew. Eurylokhos, deputized to lead half of the crew to investigate this island, does not fully carry out Odysseus's orders (10.208–73), conforming to the established pattern of behavior suggestive both of lack of self-control and, sometimes, mutiny, which will climax on Thrinakia.[17] It is worth emphasizing that Odysseus makes his approach to Kirke alone, unaided by his crew, conforming to the solitary state he will be in on Skheria as he approaches Arete, and on Ithaka even later.

On Skheria, Odysseus prays to Athene that he come among the Phaiakians φίλος and ἐλεεινός, "loved and pitied." Having heard his prayer, the goddess appears: "there the gray-eyed goddess Athene met him, in the likeness / of a young girl [παρθενικῇ ἐϊκυῖα νεήνιδι], a little maid, carrying a pitcher" (7.19–20). As with Hermes in book 10, the divine helper takes a youthful form, forms of the same word, νεηνίη/νεήνιδι, being used in both contexts. When Odysseus asks her for directions to Alkinoös' palace, the disguised Athene warns him that the Phaiakians are not hospitable to strangers ("nor do they hospitably entertain the man come from elsewhere," οὐδ' ἀγαπαζόμενοι φιλέουσ' ὅς κ' ἄλλοθεν ἔλθῃ, 7.33). The narrator earlier describes her covering Odysseus in a mist so that no Phaiakian would taunt or provoke him (7.15–17). The warnings about possible Phaiakian hostility[18] point ahead not only to the delays Odysseus will be subject to in the palace but especially to the rude taunts he will receive from the young men during the games in book 8 (which parallel the abusive violations of hospitality in which the suitors will engage). When he reaches the palace, Athene recommends that Odysseus advance boldly (much as Hermes advises for the approach to Kirke).[19] Surprisingly, she bids him to approach not Alkinoös, the king, but queen Arete, whose importance is emphasized in the lengthy expansion that follows on her ancestry and stature among the Phaiakians (7.54–75). The goddess concludes emphasizing that a successful homecoming depends on Arete's good will:[20] "So if she has thoughts in her mind that are friendly [φίλα φρονέῃσ] to you, / then there is hope that you can see your own people, and come back / to your house with the high roof and to the land of your fathers" (7.75–77).

Having awakened on Ithaka in book 13, and suspecting treachery on the part of the Phaiakian rowers, Odysseus is again approached by a disguised Athene: "now Athene came near him / likening herself in form to a young man [ἀνδρὶ δέμας ἐϊκυῖα νέῳ], a herdsman / of sheep, a delicate boy, such as the children of kings are" (13.221–23). As on Aiaia and Skheria, the divine helper takes a youthful appearance. Though we noted above (note 14) that Hermes' youthful form in book 10 has provoked considerable debate, it is clearly part of the basic structure of all three episodes.[21] Why? In each encounter the respective deity has come specifically to offer advice and aid. As a result of this function the god assumes an emphatically nonthreatening guise with which to approach and assure Odysseus.[22] I suggest, therefore, that Hermes' youthful form of Aiaia is not modeled on *Iliad* 24.347, but is better understood as an element in the *Odyssey*'s own repeated pattern.

In the ensuing dialogue, Athene teases and manipulates Odysseus, much as Hermes does in book 10. She withholds the name of the land, for which Odysseus has specifically asked (13.233), until the end of her reply (13.248), noting that even a fool knows the name of Ithaka: "You are a fool, oh stranger . . . if you ask the name of this land" (13.237–38).[23] Her advice, however, strongly contrasts with the advice given in the earlier sequences. She counsels an initially passive approach (13.306 ff) as opposed to the bold advance he makes against Kirke and his direct approach to Arete. He is to endure the suitors' abuse in silence, while plotting their destruction. She also notes that he is to test Penelope (336). This different course of action allows the suitors more room to display their outrageous behavior and places more emphasis on Penelope's dilemma. Neither Kirke nor Arete has any real stake, by comparison with Penelope, in Odysseus' agenda.

The Ithakan sequence is greatly expanded compared to those on Aiaia and Skheria. Odysseus' meeting with Athene, for instance, is almost four times as long as the two earlier divine encounters (13.221–440 vs. 10.275–308 and 7.18–81). Part of the Ithakan sequence's expansion involves indirection. Athene bids Odysseus first visit Eumaios, not Penelope.[24] Athene's Ithakan consultation also differs from the two earlier scenes because only here does the deity assume her proper form (13.288 ff), while in books 10 and 7 Hermes and Athene retain their youthful guises throughout. The biggest difference, however, is that on Ithaka Athene counsels disguise and indirection, whereas on Aiaia and Skheria Odysseus approaches the female directly.[25]

His identity a secret (as approach to the female is perilous), Odysseus reaches her, finding a figure who is initially suspicious, distant, or even hostile toward him. When Odysseus first arrives, Kirke does not know who he is (10.325–29), but the narrator leaves no doubt as to her hostile intent. She drugs the drink she offers him, a grave violation of hospitality, the narrator noting her ominous intent, "with evil thoughts in her heart," κακὰ φρονέουσ' ἐνὶ θυμῷ (10.317). Furthermore, the crew, transformed into pigs, are kept in a pen, apparently intended for eating.[26] Well armed by Hermes' warning, however, Odysseus withstands Kirke, and briefly threatens her himself. He rushes forward, his sword drawn, as if to kill her. Startled and panicked, the goddess grabs him by the knees in supplication, asking the standard question between strangers, "What man are you and whence? Where are your city and parents?", τίς πόθεν εἶς ἀνδρῶν; πόθι τοι πόλις ἠδὲ τοκῆες; (10.325).[27] Quickly recovering, she now recognizes him as Odysseus. Though not analyzed as such by commentators, the encounter is a recognition scene.[28] What distinguishes it from most recognitions is Kirke's status as a goddess. Armed with Hermes' earlier prediction of Odysseus' arrival, she immediately deduces his identity.[29]

On both Skheria and Ithaka the approach to the female is significantly more complex. As I suggested earlier, the functions found together in Kirke and Penelope are on Skheria separated into Nausikaa and Arete, Nausikaa embodying the erotic and marital element, Arete suggesting a more powerful but less intimate figure.[30] Odysseus must first approach Nausikaa before he can advance further. In terms of her prior position in the narrative, Nausikaa serves to anticipate Arete (as well as the other females in the pattern), Odysseus' earlier coming to terms with her prefiguring his later success with Arete. Furthermore, the narrative suggests particularly close parallels between Odysseus' encounter with Nausikaa and his later encounters with Penelope.[31]

As with Kirke, divine prompting engineers Nausikaa's meeting with Odysseus. Where Kirke received direct warning from Hermes (10.330–31), Athene sends Nausikaa a dream causing her to view Odysseus as a potential husband (6.25–40). Nausikaa, and the episode itself, dwell almost obsessively on the possibility of marriage with Odysseus.[32] The encounter is imbued with a subtle erotic potential,[33] partly owing to Odysseus's uniquely naked circumstances, the *locus amoenus* where they meet, and Nausikaa's own focus on marriage.

Alone among the female multiforms, Nausikaa displays none of the suspicion or hostility prominent in the others. As Odysseus approaches her, the serving maids flee, but Nausikaa remains to face him, Athene having put daring into her heart (6.139–40). Supplication is again part of the initial approach to the female, as with Kirke, though here roles are reversed as Odysseus tactfully supplicates Nausikaa, asking the way to the city, and the identity of the people but chiefly flattering her (149–69), implicitly deducing and playing on her interest in marriage (180–85). Odysseus' own identity remains undisclosed. His deft ability to communicate with her will reappear in his encounters with Arete and Penelope, and broadly recalls his coming to terms with Kirke.

In Odysseus' initial approach to Arete, supplication and surprise are again central ingredients. He startles Arete as he had Kirke, since Athene's mist of invisibility breaks only when he embraces Arete's knees. Athene emphasizes that the approach to Arete is dangerous, as this is her motivation for supplying the cloud of mist (7.15 ff).[34] Unlike Kirke and Nausikaa, Arete makes no response, nor do any of the Phaiakians until Ekheneos admonishes them for failing to receive the stranger hospitably (7.155–66). Proper hospitality initiated, Arete still refrains from answering Odysseus until Alkinoös first questions him, with Odysseus repeating his plea for an escort home. Only when all the others retire for the night does Arete, alone with Alkinoös and the mysterious stranger, enter into discourse with Odysseus (as Penelope will do with her mysterious guest in book 19), considerable time having already elapsed since Odysseus' initial supplication of her.

Arete addresses him with the same half line uttered by Kirke in the Aiaian sequence (10.325), as will Penelope on Ithaka (19.105), but she tacks on a different ending referring to the clothes Odysseus is wearing: "What man are you and whence? And who was it gave you this clothing?", τίς πόθεν εἰς ἀνδρῶν; τίς τοι τάδε εἵματ' ἔδωκεν; (7.238). Her long hesitation in offering any response to the man who specifically supplicated her is indicative of the various retardations that typify the Skherian sequence, but also can be seen to signify caution and suspicion on her part.[35] She has waited until the other Phaiakians have left (just as Odysseus' first interviews with Kirke and Nausikaa were also conducted in private, 10.310 ff, 6.138–99) before discussing a topic that must have been on her mind the entire time, that Odysseus is wearing royal clothing last seen in her daughter's possession. In reply, Odysseus evades revealing direct information about himself, other than his most recent whereabouts, instead finding an opportunity to praise Nausikaa's conduct.[36]

On Ithaka, Odysseus encounters direct physical violence and verbal abuse as he approaches the palace, conforming to the perilous approaches to Kirke and Arete. He first sees Penelope when she makes her appearance before the suitors in book 18 (208–89). Penelope's appearance has been criticized as unmotivated, a narrative inconsistency.[37] However, the sequence closely parallels Athene's provoking Nausikaa to encounter Odysseus, which resemblances, I suggest, are better indications of the scene's validity and evidence of its intentions.[38] Penelope earlier asked to speak with the stranger after hearing Eumaios' account of his guest (17.529 ff). Odysseus, however, suggests delaying the meeting until the suitors go home for the night (17.560 ff).

As a prelude of sorts to the first interview, postponed until book 19 (just as Odysseus' first interview with Arete was postponed), Athene motivates Penelope to appear, much as in book 6 she motivates Nausikaa to encounter Odysseus. Critics have noted that Penelope gives one reason for now appearing before the suitors (declaring that she wishes both to appear before them and to dissuade Telemakhos from associating with them), but claims a different motivation when she speaks before them (chastising Telemakhos for allowing shoddy treatment of the stranger and them for their ignoble attempts at wooing her).[39] The narrative displays a parallel discrepancy, however, between Nausikaa's stated motivation for taking the wagon out (to wash the family's clothes) and her actual intention (interest in marriage).[40] Both appearances are provoked by Athene in order to bring Odysseus together with the respective females for the first time, both females masking their true motives for their encounter. Furthermore, this scene directly highlights Penelope's sexuality to a degree unique in the poem,[41] while we have already noted the sexual modality in Nausikaa's role on Skheria.[42]

By so appearing before them in this way, Penelope is able to manipulate the suitors into offering her substantial gifts (18.275–303), as an admiring Odysseus observes her deception.[43] We might compare Arete's manipulation of the Phaiakian nobles in the Intermezzo, as she arranges for further gifts for her ξεῖνος (11.338–41). Though this element occurs in different order in the two sequences, and with Penelope ignorant of Odysseus's presence, both queens nonetheless use their own power to obtain gifts as part of a coming to terms with Odysseus.

In all three sequences Odysseus's first encounter with the female is the most overtly sexual. When Penelope descends before the suitors (and Odysseus), "Their knees gave way, and the hearts in them were bemused with passion, / and each one prayed for the privilege of lying beside her" (18.212–13). Odysseus's first encounter with Kirke is the only explicitly sexual scene described between the two, and we have already noted the essential sexual and marital element in Odysseus's encounter with Nausikaa.[44]

In his first conference with Penelope (bk. 19) and the arrangements that bring it about, Odysseus acts much as Arete had, cautious, unwilling to converse until he is alone with Penelope.[45] This is just as Athene directs in their initial meeting on Ithaka (13.336), that Odysseus will test his wife rather than openly reunite.[46] However, in their second interview, positions will be reversed as Penelope will conform to the pattern of the suspicious, distant female, already encountered in Arete, and to a lesser extent, Kirke.

∽

The female imposes a test on him, whereupon Odysseus, having successfully passed the test, wins her sympathy and help, obtaining access to the next phase of his home-

coming. *Their understanding is made manifest in her offer of a bath. Furthermore, Odysseus is now offered sexual union and/or marriage with the female.*[47] On Aiaia, Odysseus passes a test, in no uncertain terms, as he remains neither enchanted nor transformed by Kirke's spell. Kirke's subsequent behavior (how often does a goddess supplicate a mortal?) underscores the unique and unexpected nature of Odysseus' success. Nonetheless, the goddess quickly recovers her composure, suggesting that they make love as a token of faith and trust (10.333–35).

The *Odyssey* is rather discreet as to the sexual relations between Odysseus and Kirke, one line serving to describe their lovemaking: "I mounted the surpassingly beautiful bed of Kirke" (10.347).[48] Note, however, that though Odysseus will delay eating with Kirke out of concern for his crew, no such concern delays their sleeping together.[49] However, this behavior is in accord with Hermes' earlier decree, expressed as a command not to "resist and refuse the bed of the goddess" (10.297). Hermes had further declared that she would release the crew after they made love (298). Four servants then prepare a luxuriant bath for him, and a banquet for Kirke and her guest. The bath, while a standard element of hospitality scenes,[50] in these three sequences conveys, I suggest, a greater than usual intimacy, bordering on the erotic.

On Skheria Odysseus implicitly passes a test in the way he negotiates the delicate encounter with Nausikaa. Her test would seem to be that of determining his suitability as her husband. Her doubts answered by his speech, Nausikaa bids her servants bathe Odysseus, but in the subsequent narrative they do not do so (6.211–16). Instead they provide him with the necessary implements that he may bathe himself. Commentators have thus posited an inconsistency.[51] Odysseus' uniquely naked circumstances may provide a partial reason for an apparent aloofness on their part. Facing a nude adult male in a room intended for bathing may be one thing, facing him in the wild—a not infrequent locus for rape in classical myth—may be another.[52] Yet in terms of the narrative pattern, their aloofness serves to anticipate the shoddy treatment Odysseus will receive from Penelope's maids and conforms to the well-supported depiction of the Phaiakians as distant to strangers.

After Odysseus bathes, Athene pours grace, χάρις, on him, prompting Nausikaa's admiration (6.242–44). She bids her servants offer him food and drink, in effect, granting him hospitality. Lacking a hearth, or οἶκος, however, Odysseus is not yet officially accepted into a family or city. Nonetheless, Nausikaa's actions foreshadow the hospitality that Arete and Alkinoös will bestow. In all three sequences, Odysseus' reception of hospitality is closely tied to his coming to terms with the powerful female figure.[53]

Nausikaa now guides Odysseus to the next phase of his homecoming, as Athene specifically intended,[54] by directing him to Arete. Subsequently, Alkinoös offers Odysseus her hand in marriage (7.313).[55] As with Kirke, and later with Penelope, Odysseus comes to terms with Nausikaa and she is offered to him (7.311–14), though acceptance of the offer remains outside the range of narrative possibilities.

Instructed by Nausikaa (6.289–315) and Athene (7.48–77), Odysseus sets forth to win over the aloof Arete. In an indication of the complexity of this part of the narrative pattern, both Arete and Penelope will require two tests of Odysseus. In Arete's first meeting with him, the explicit test she imposes is an accounting of the court clothing he wears, as well as an explanation of who he is and, perhaps, what his motives are. In his lengthy response (7.241–96), Odysseus carefully addresses both issues, clearly satisfying her on the former but deliberately providing only the most recent information as to his identity, merely stressing that his desire is to return home, and that not even a goddess, Kalypso, was able to restrain him permanently. Having passed Arete's initial test through this account, Odysseus wins preliminary acceptance in the palace.

However, Arete still makes no response to Odysseus' supplication, specifically addressed to her, in accordance with Athene's own instructions (7.75–77). Athene earlier utters what we can view as a technical term for the process through which Arete goes in her relations with Odysseus, the goddess noting that he will obtain his homecoming "if she [Arete] has thoughts in her mind that are friendly to you," εἴ κέν τοι κείνη [Arete] γε φίλα φρονέῃσ' ἐνὶ θυμῷ (7.75). Elsewhere in Homer this term (and its opposite κακὰ φρονέων) usually describes a deity's attitude toward a mortal.[56] In the narrative pattern φίλα φρονέουσα, "having friendly thoughts," describes the powerful female after Odysseus has reached an accommodation with her. Kirke is first described as the exact opposite. When Odysseus initially approaches her she is κακὰ φρονέουσ', "having evil thoughts" (10.317). Though never described as φίλα φρονέουσα, Kirke evidences such an attitude in her intimacy, hospitality, and subsequent aid offered to Odysseus.[57] Arete becomes φίλα φρονέουσα when, in the Intermezzo, she proclaims that Odysseus is her ξεῖνος, her guest.[58] Why she does so, however, has been a matter of considerable debate. As she was not present at Odysseus' triumph in the athletic games, only his overall demeanor and tact and particularly his narratives in the first half of the Apologue could account for her shift in position.[59]

The narratives Arete hears about Odysseus in the Apologue offer her substantial cause, on two accounts, for coming to terms with Odysseus. The Apologue continually depicts an Odysseus focused on returning home, even leaving two goddesses who desired him as their husband (which point he clearly foregrounds right at the outset: 9.29–33). In effect, Odysseus establishes a thesis, which much of the Apologue supports: "So it is / that nothing is more sweet in the end than country and parents / ever, even when far away one lives in a fertile / place, when it is in alien country, far from his parents" (9.33–36). Odysseus' assertion is rhetorically similar to that which closed his earlier, brilliant speech to Nausikaa, "for there is nothing better than this, more steadfast / than when two people, a man and his wife, keep a harmonious / household" (6.182–84). With a parallel use of comparatives, Odysseus in each case claims an ideal, aimed at a specific audience. The priority of marriage (with no mention of children,[60] hence a *young* married couple) is aimed at the young, marriage-minded Nausikaa; the priority of parents and homeland is aimed at his hosts, parents themselves and, as rulers, an embodiment of Skheria itself. Much of Odysseus's subsequent narrative demonstrates his desire to return home in spite of formidable obstacles which would have defeated a man with less self-control.

Second, Odysseus tailors his narrative of the Nekuia so that it focuses almost exclusively on women, until the Intermezzo rechannels a more traditional focus on the heroes who died at Troy. Sent explicitly to consult with Teiresias, Odysseus sees his mother, Antikleia, approach (84–89), driving him to tears, though he keeps her at a distance until meeting with the prophet. When he has completed his assigned consultation with the Theban (90–151), during which he kept his mother alive as a topic (141–44), Odysseus enters into a dialogue with her (152–225), one lengthier than that he held with Teiresias. Antikleia concludes with the admonition, "but remember / these things for your wife, so you may tell her hereafter" (11.223–24), further depicting Odysseus as a man concerned about his wife and sensitive to women's reactions. There follows the Catalog of Women (225–332), after which Arete proclaims, "Phaiakians, what do you think now of this man before you / for beauty and stature, and for the mind well balanced within him? / And again he is my own guest" (11.336–38). Arete is now φίλα φρονέουσα, in effect answering Odysseus's supplication from 7.146–52, and fulfilling the role earlier forecast by Nausikaa and Athene.[61] Odysseus has now passed a second test. Further, she advises (commands?) the others at court to bestow additional gifts upon Odysseus (11.338–41). Odysseus' final words in Skheria are to Arete (13.59–62), a further acknowledgment of her central role. As his first words at court were also to her (7.146–52), his focus on Arete encapsulates the entire Skherian sequence after the initial meeting with Nausikaa (Tracy 1990: 80).

The process by which Odysseus comes to terms with Penelope is similarly involved. Odysseus has three encounters with Penelope, her appearance before the suitors (18.158–303, discussed above), their lengthy interview (19.53–604), and the recognition scene (23.85–343). The first interview (19.53–604) offers numerous parallels with the encounter with Arete.[62] As with Arete, clothes form a significant topic in the first interview with Penelope. Penelope begins with the same formulaic line asked by Kirke and Arete (19.105 = 10.325 = 7.238a). As before, Odysseus avoids revealing any particulars of his identity. His initial response (19.107–14), praise of her reputation and stature, thematically parallels Athene's description of Arete (7.66–74). However, when he claims to have hosted Odysseus, Penelope requires proof. To test him, as she explicitly states is her purpose (19.215), she asks what clothes Odysseus wore on that occasion. As with Arete, Odysseus is able to reach an understanding on the basis of his account about clothes of central interest to his female interlocutor. In each case, his answer contributes to the temporary identity he is establishing. Her test satisfied, Penelope notes, "Stranger, while before this you had my pity, you now / shall be my friend and be respected here in my[63] palace" (19.253–54), equivalent to Arete's declaration in the Intermezzo (11.336–41).

Having passed her test, Odysseus now prophesies his own return, but finds an incredulous Penelope. Much as on Skheria, the Ithakan sequence now postpones a full coming to terms between Odysseus and Penelope, a parallel in the lengthy delay between Odysseus' initial supplication of Arete and her eventual proclamation of him as her ξεῖνος. Penelope does, however, offer Odysseus a bath (19.317), a sign of his being accorded full hospitality. The bath as well, however, will remain incomplete (being here limited, at Odysseus' request, to a footbath) until resumed in the second full interview between Odysseus and Penelope in book 23.

Though Odysseus's coming to an understanding with Penelope occurs after other elements in the pattern we have yet to consider, it nonetheless deserves a brief analysis here, as it supplements the book 19 interview. Penelope refuses to believe Eurykleia's report of the slain suitors (23.10 ff, 63 ff). Descending into the μέγαρον, "She sat a long time in silence" (23.93), much as had Arete. Odysseus turns his attention to Telemakhos, laying plans for the eventual battle with the suitors' relatives, and suggesting that they bathe and dress. As many have noted, Odysseus then emerges from his bath, described in the same words as those following his bath from Nausikaa's servants (6.230–35 = 23.157–62).[64] Still apparently unmoved, Penelope poses the test of the bed, and, unique among the poem's characters, she temporarily outwits Odysseus, causing him to lose his characteristic self-control (23.182–204). Only now, after an aloofness worthy of Arete and an apparent distance suitable to Kirke, does Penelope, satisfied in multiple tests, come to an agreement with Odysseus. Shortly thereafter, husband and wife make love. As in the Aiaian sequence with Kirke, we note the close proximity of the bath and the lovemaking.

⤳

However, conflict arises between Odysseus and the band of young men. The young men abuse Odysseus in various ways and violate a divine interdiction. The basic equation of the three groups—crew, Phaiakian athletes, and suitors—has been made, if little discussed, since the time of Horace.[65] While the Ithakan sequence offers the most direct conflict between Odysseus and the young men, with the hero himself slaying the band of 108, both of the other sequences offer significant suggestions of tension and conflict. While on Ithaka the conflict is centered on Penelope, in all three sequences much of the conflict is due to the opposite natures involved, as Odysseus more often than not is capable of exercising considerable self-control, whereas the three bands of young men, the suitors and crew in particular, are significantly lacking, and, in these cases, are prey to the kind of excessive consumption against which the poem sounds numerous warnings.

We earlier noted a pattern of insubordination evident in the crew and centered in Eurylokhos in particular. Elpenor, the only other crew member developed as a distinct personality, also becomes a problem on Aiaia. Though Elpenor may seem harmless enough though having had too much to drink (οἰνοβαρείων 10.555), the only other characters described by Homer as οἰνοβαρείων are Polyphemos (9.374) and Eurytion the centaur (21.304), both notorious violators of hospitality and other social norms, both involved in violent encounters. Furthermore, Elpenor's other qualities, that he is "not terribly / powerful in fighting nor sound in his thoughts" (10.552–53), as well as his drinking to excess, are emblematic of much of the crew's behavior.[66] Elpenor falls to his death, startled out of a drunken sleep by the crew's loud noises, "when his companions stirred to go, he, hearing their tumult," κινυμένων δ᾽ ἑτάρων ὅμαδον καὶ δοῦπον ἀκούσας (556). While ὅμαδος occurs only here in the *Odyssey*, ὁμαδεῖν occurs five times, always to describe the suitors and the ruckus they raise in Odysseus' palace.[67] In Elpenor and the crew the narrative thus describes behavior quite similar to that of Penelope's wooers. The ἑταῖροι, as the suitors, have been taking part in a non-stop feast, their stay capped by Elpenor's drunken death. Elpenor is thus the poem's embodiment of the excessive, even fatal consumption to which the crew, as highlighted in the opening proem (1.7–9), is susceptible.[68]

Eurylokhos embodies a more active, overtly disobedient side of the

The *Odyssey:* Structure, Narration, and Meaning

crew. He repeatedly leads the equivalent of mutinies, the next of which almost breaks out into violence. After Odysseus comes to terms with Kirke, persuading the goddess to restore the crew and accepting her hospitality, Eurylokhos again rebels, arguing that in staying with Kirke they go to their doom (10.429–37). Odysseus reacts strongly:

> I considered in my mind whether
> to draw out the long-edged sword from beside my big thigh
> and cut off his head and throw it on the ground, even though
> he was closely related to me by marriage.
>
> (10.438–41)

This scene parallels and foreshadows the violence that will erupt between Odysseus and the suitors. That this occurs on Aiaia suggests an implicit friction between Odysseus and his crew with regard to Kirke, perhaps in that only Odysseus has any intimacy with Kirke, just as he, not the suitors, will win Penelope.

The conflict with the crew culminates on and around Thrinakia, an episode closely linked to events on Aiaia. Helios figures prominently from the beginning of the Aiaian sequence. Kirke's lineage, as daughter of Helios (10.137–38), suggests alignment between events on Aiaia and Thrinakia, as do earlier events before Odysseus even meets the goddess.[69]

Uttered by Kirke (and Teiresias), the prohibition against eating Helios's cattle (12.127–41, 11.105–13) is a divine interdiction, comparable to that in Genesis 2–3. Fully aware of the interdiction, as Odysseus informs the crew that both Kirke and Teiresias warned them of certain disaster if they stopped on Thrinakia (12.271–76), the crew, led by Eurylokhos, are nonetheless, for landing on Thrinakia, since they are weary and fear death at sea as a consequence, or so claims Eurylokhos (12.279–93). Eurylokhos' own later speech (12.340–51) demonstrates that he and the crew are, in fact, completely informed as to the divine interdiction against slaughtering any of Helios' cattle, and of the dire consequences in store for them if they do. Odysseus observes the effected mutiny: "So spoke Eurylokhos, and my other companions assented. / I saw then what evil the divinity had in mind for us" (12.294–95). Noting that Eurylokhos has the numbers, and even force on his side, "you force me to it as I am only one man," ἦ μάλα δή με βιάζετε μοῦνον ἐόντα (297), Odysseus has the crew swear an oath that they will not slaughter the oxen (12.298–304). However, when Kirke's provisions are exhausted, Eurylokhos once again leads a revolt, now arguing, with perverse logic, that the worst of all deaths is to die of starvation (340–51). His reasoning is perverse because he argues for the exact opposite of his earlier speech (279–93), in which, implicitly, death at sea was to be avoided at all costs, now suggesting that death at sea is preferable to dying on land.[70] Furthermore, he foolishly diminishes the consequences of violating the divine interdiction.

As Crane has suggested, Thrinakia constitutes a test, and an unusual one: "[Thrinakia] is unusual . . . it demands that Odysseus remain passive and idle . . . nevertheless [it] serves the underlying purpose of every heroic task: it elicits from the hero those qualities that set him apart from ordinary men" (148). Odysseus, here as elsewhere, survives both because he is πολύτλας, "much enduring," and has learned to respect the gods, much as Zeus emphasizes in the opening scene.[71]

On Skheria conflict between Odysseus and the band of young men remains largely implicit and potential, flaring up on one brief occasion.[72] As earlier noted, Nausikaa and Athene suggest the possibility of friction.[73] Nausikaa raises the possibility of conflict between Odysseus, as her suitor, and the potentially rejected Phaiakian suitors.[74] And indeed in the athletic games, themselves Alkinoös' attempt at creating a diversion for his guest, who has been moved to tears by Demodokos' singing, conflict does erupt in the form of Euryalos' rude insults directed at Odysseus. The provocations, being a clear violation of hospitality, instantiate the earlier warnings of both Nausikaa and the disguised Athene that some of the Phaiakians were less than hospitable. As on Aiaia, the possibility of violence between Odysseus and the band of young men is suggested, if only dimly. In reply to Euryalos' abusive response when Odysseus declines to participate in the athletic games, the hero observes, "Friend, that was not well spoken; you seem like one who is reckless [ἀτασθάλῳ ἀνδρὶ ἔοικας 8.166]." The adjective by which Odysseus characterizes Euryalos, ἀτάσθαλος, is highly censorious, and related forms are used to describe members of all three bands: the crew (1.7, 10.68), the suitors (22.416), and here, the most antagonistic of the Phaiakian youths.[75] Provoked by the insult, Odysseus does compete, after the fact, surpassing the others in the discus. He also claims other athletic prowess, especially in archery: "I know well how to handle the polished bow, and would be / first to strike my man with an arrow aimed at a company / of hostile men" (8.215–17). Since antiquity commentators have rightly seen connection between this passage and the μνηστηροφονία, as Odysseus' declaration here not only prefigures the slaying of the suitors but occurs at the same point in the extended narrative pattern in both the Ithakan and Skherian sequences, when friction between Odysseus and the abusive young men has reached a climax.[76] I suggest it also parallels the episode discussed above when Odysseus considers slaying Eurylokhos (10.438 ff).

The specific type of friction Odysseus encounters at the games in the form of Euryalos' violation of hospitality conforms to a widespread pattern throughout Greek myth, one the *Odyssey* briefly hints at outside of the narrative pattern. The hero in Greek myth, when abroad, often comes into contact with an oppressive figure who compels guests to compete in an athletic event, an ἄγων (cf. ἄεθλος), usually slaying the defeated guest in a typically outrageous violation of hospitality. The visiting hero, however, is triumphant, slaying the evildoer and restoring the conventions of hospitality. Numerous examples exist, especially in the careers of Herakles and Theseus (and the Argonauts' encounter with Amycus, king of the Bebrycians, who forces guests to box with him, *Argonautica*, 2.1–97). The *Odyssey* establishes this common myth type as a theme in Menelaos' brief reminiscence of how once, in Lesbos, Odysseus had wrestled and defeated Philomeleides (4.341–44, repeated by Telemakhos, 17.132–35). Eustathius and Hellanicus supplement the account by noting that Philomeleides was a king of Lesbos who challenged every passerby to a wrestling match until Odysseus and Diomedes killed him, establishing an inn for ξεῖνοι at his tomb.[77] Significantly, Menelaos connects the exploit with present affairs, plugging it into the narrative pattern, as it were, when he wishes that "such an Odysseus would come now among the suitors" (4.345 = 17.136).

Brief though it is, the account of Odysseus's defeating Philomeleides in wrestling informs the encounter between Odysseus and Euryalos, and the parallels in the other two sequences. Though the sport in which Odysseus competes on Skheria is the discus, the tradition solidly claims him as a wrestler, not only in the anecdote under discussion but in the funeral games for Patroklos in which he wrestles Aias Telamonian to a draw (*Il.* 23.700–739).[78] In the athletic games on Skheria, Euryalos, before he insults Odysseus by pressing him to compete, is victorious in wrestling (8.126–27). As the victorious wrestler who rudely challenges a guest to compete in athletic games, Euryalos now plays the same role in this scene as that played by Philomeleides in Menelaos' anecdote. Were Odysseus to compete in wrestling he would defeat Euryalos, who is no Aias. Instead he performs in the less confrontational discus throw, besting the previous mark of Elatreus, who has no further role in the poem. Nonetheless, Euryalos appears to meet the same fate as Philomeleides, as we see in the conclusion of the episode.

The Skherian sequence contains a further conflict, far more fatal though less directly involving Odysseus, who will be offstage when it reaches its telos. As a consequence of Odysseus' visit, Poseidon will take the lives of the crew who ferry Odysseus to Ithaka (13.125–64). Though the crew's identities are never specified, I suggest that they largely consist of the athletes participating in the games in book 8, among them Euryalos.[79] Fifty-two young men are selected, "who have been the best before" (ὅσοι πάρος εἰσὶν ἄριστοι, 8.36, cf. 8.48). Having finished preparations for the voyage, the crew then enter Alkinoös' palace for the feast (8.55–56). When Alkinoös proposes the games, he leads the way and "all the other best men of the Phaiakians went" (8.107–8), necessarily including the crew, again specified by the designation οἱ ἄριστοι, "the best." There follows a catalog of the best athletes, in which thirteen are named, all with nautical etymologies, names eminently suitable for members of a ship's crew. Of the entries in the catalog, Euryalos is most prominent (8.115–17). The crew are referred to as ἑταῖροι (8.151), the word most often used by Odysseus of his own crew.[80]

Though the Skherian sequence does not offer an explicit divine interdiction, implicitly Poseidon intends limits on the Phaiakians' power to convoy people across the seas. This is apparent both in the prophecy threatening the Phaiakians in this respect (quoted below) as well as Poseidon's manner of punishing them. Implicitly, Poseidon would seem to intend "do not ferry everyone home with ease (and certainly not Odysseus, object of my wrath)."[81] Poseidon articulates his own version of the implicit divine interdiction in a later consultation with Zeus, "so that they may stop and give over conveying / people" (13.151–52).[82]

In the Ithakan sequence conflict between Odysseus and the suitors is overt and omnipresent. Initially revolving around hospitality, as the suitors and their party seek to prevent the disguised Odysseus from taking part in the feasts in his own palace, ultimately the conflict focuses directly on the wooing of Penelope. The poem, in the opening books, foreshadows the eventual conflict in the increasingly tense and hostile relations between Telemakhos and the suitors. It is perhaps significant that Telemakhos repeats Menelaos' anecdote about Odysseus' defeating Philomeleides (17.132–36) immediately before actual hostilities break out between the suitors' party and Odysseus, the encounter with Melanthios coming only eighty lines later and the footstool hurled by Antinoös, toward the end of the same book (17.462).

In terms of transgressing divine interdictions, the suitors repeatedly violate the basic tenets of Zeus, Ξείνιος, as the poem repeatedly demonstrates. As uninvited guests who have forcefully taken over the palace, they have inverted and perverted the norms of hospitality, a sacred institution most central to Archaic Greek culture. It is precisely this kind of inversion of the laws that underlie not only human society but the cosmos itself (cf. the role of dharma in Hindu religion) which the gods find most offensive and which prompts them to extreme measures, manifest in subsequent wraths. Secondly, the suitors' wooing of Penelope violates a pattern of behavior earlier articulated by the gods. In Zeus' programmatic first speech (1.31–43), in which Aigisthos prefigures the behavior of the suitors,[83] the ruler of the universe emphasizes that Hermes pronounced two divine interdictions to Aigisthos, μήτ' αὐτὸν κτείνειν μήτε μνάασθαι ἄκοιτιν, "not to kill him [Agamemnon] and not to woo his wife" (1.39). The suitors openly and intentionally woo Penelope, directly violating the second interdiction. In so doing the suitors parallel Aigisthos, whose behavior Zeus finds offensive, and whose slaying, by Orestes, receives the gods' sanction.

Just as Aigisthos was not to be persuaded, even by divine messenger, to alter his course, the suitors similarly resist persuasion. In a role which probably parallels that played by Hermes in Zeus' account (we will see below that in the later stages of the Ithakan sequence Odysseus often plays a role which in the other sequences is filled by a god), the disguised Odysseus twice offers implicit warning to the suitors of danger to come if they continue to act abusively. In the first such speech (17.419–44), he offers an exemplum from his life of how the gods punished him for reckless acts. Instead of offering him the hospitality he seeks, Antinoös' response to this highly relevant and potentially instructive narrative is to hurl a footstool at the disguised hero. In the second speech (18.125–50), serving to parallel the warning Hermes gave to Aigisthos, the disguised Odysseus makes an even plainer connection, noting that he had once been prosperous, but is no more because of the violent, reckless acts he committed. The word he uses for reckless acts which implicitly provoke divine punishment is ἀτάσθαλα (18.139), the same root which, as noted above, is used to describe the excessive behavior of all three bands of abusive young men (1.7, 8.166, 10.68, 22.416). Odysseus now makes an explicit connection with the suitors, noting that he sees them engaging in similar reckless behavior, again using ἀτάσθαλα (18.143) to denote their offensive behavior. He further specifies the nature of their recklessness: "how they show no respect to the wife, and despoil the possessions / of a man" (18.144–45), a formulation which partly recalls the terms of Zeus' divine interdictions to Aigisthos. However, his audience, Amphinomos, does not alter his behavior as a result of the warning, again conforming to the pattern set by Aigisthos.[84]

The leader of each band has the parallel name of Eury__. Eurylokhos's name, probably a possessive compound, may mean "having [a] wide ambush."[85] In effect, he ambushes Odysseus in the series of conflicts and mutinies he leads against him. Ironically, however, Odysseus himself is the figure in all of Greek mythology most adept at plotting and surviving ambushes.[86] I suggest that the meaning of the name Eurylokhos is, to an extent, thematically operative for the similar sounding Euryalos and Eurymakhos as well.

Both *ambush* Odysseus, Euryalos in the games and Eurymakhos on Ithaka, their names specifying the contexts in which their conflicts occur. As do many of the Phaiakian names, Euryalos, perhaps "broad sea" or "having [a] broad sea," signifies his identity with his people, and, perhaps, the location and manner of his death at the hands of Poseidon.[87]

In the case of the suitors, the largest and most fully characterized of the three bands, Antinoös and Eurymakhos act as virtual co-leaders,[88] Antinoös, conspicuous for his speaking ability and display of power, Eurymakhos, smoother, a flatterer, a ladies man.[89] Though Eurymakhos is capable of greater subtlety, he is just as aggressive as Antinoös. It is Eurymakhos, not Antinoös, who inquires after the identity of Telemakhos' mysterious visitor in book 1 (400–411). He is described as the suitor with the best chance of winning Penelope (15.17–18), and he is the first to address her when she appears to the suitors (18.245–49). He helps offer an ambush not only for Odysseus but for Telemakhos as well.[90] The second element in his name may look ahead to the μνηστηροφονία, Odysseus's last heroic exploit in the poem, and thus ironically helps glorify the protagonist.[91]

~

The band's consequent death, earlier prophesied, is demanded by a wrathful god. The poem offers several indications that the death of the crew is of the utmost importance for understanding the greater plot. Of all the events in all three sequences of the narrative pattern, the only episode singled out for mention by the proem is how the crew die on Thrinakia. In terms of our structural analysis, the event forms the climax and conclusion of the Aiaian sequence, the earliest and innermost of the three sequences. As a final indication of the central importance of the episode, we note that Zeus, who rarely leaves Olympos to take action in either Homeric epic, and only here in the *Odyssey*, is the divine avenger for the transgression on Thrinakia, destroying the ship with a storm, though Helios is the injured party, the deity concerned with loss of respect.[92]

Teiresias prophesies the death of the ἑταῖροι in no uncertain terms (11.112–13), a prophecy afterwards restated by Kirke (12.139–40).[93] The crew clearly die as a result of transgressing the divine interdiction against violating Helios' cattle. As noted above, the crew have been fully informed of the consequences of their act, as Eurylokhos makes clear (12.348–52), even if Odysseus' narrative does not fully depict the incident. In any case it is a clear-cut breaking of a divine interdiction, one in which the hero does not take part, conforming to the pattern earlier established in the proem, and visible at Ismaros, the Lotus Eaters, the return from Aiolos, and on Aiaia. An outraged Helios appeals to Zeus, the father of gods and men, to himself punish the offenders with death.

In the Skherian sequence, Alkinoös' father, Nausithoös, is the source of the relevant prophecy, given twice by the Phaiakian king:

> and told me how Poseidon would yet be angry [ἀγάσεσθαι]
> with us, because we convoy without hurt to all men.
> He said that one day, as a well-made ship of Phaiakian
> men came back from a convoy on the misty face of the water,
> he would stun it, and pile a great mountain over our city to hide it.
>
> (8.565–69 = 13.173–77)

No specific mention is made of the crew, but their death is a necessary consequence of the prophecy. According to our analysis, the slain crew include the abusive Euryalos. In this sequence, Poseidon, the wrathful deity, exacts his own vengeance. Unlike Helios, who is specifically angered by the crew's violation, Poseidon is the thematically angry god throughout the poem, angered at Odysseus, angered at the Phaiakians for conveying him home. We will return in chapters 4 and 5 to a fuller consideration of the role Poseidon's anger plays in the greater plot.

Of the several prophecies of the suitors' deaths, most important is that of Theoklymenos in book 20. His prophecy, preceded by a series of eerie events,[94] suggests the suitors' proximity to Hades:

> Poor wretches, what evil has come upon you? Your heads and faces
> and the knees underneath you are shrouded in night and darkness;
> a sound of wailing has broken out, your cheeks are covered
> with tears, and the walls bleed, and the fine supporting pillars.
> All the forecourt is huddled with ghosts, the yard is full of them
> as they flock down to the underworld and the darkness. The sun
> has perished out of the sky, and a foul mist has come over.
>
> (20.351–57)

While the imagery of the opening lines is common enough,[95] it is not generally recognized that the concluding details belong to a specific subgenre of prophecy: the wrath of god on the day of judgment. The book of Isaiah (13.9–13) offers an example thought to be roughly contemporary with the *Odyssey*,

The day of the Lord is coming, that cruel day of wrath and fierce anger, to reduce the earth to desolation and destroy all the wicked there. The stars of heaven in their constellations will give not light, the sun will be dark at its rising, and the moon will not shed its light.

The book of Joel offers a close parallel: "The sun will be turned to darkness and the moon to blood, before the coming of the great and terrible day of the Lord" (2.31).[96] All three passages depict celestial bodies failing to provide light as an angry god punishes mortals for their transgressions. The suitors' own response to the (accurate) prophecy is highly abusive, a further depiction of their impiety. As in the other two sequences, then, we should expect an angry deity, in accord with the prophecy, to destroy the suitors.

While the gods have expressed their outrage at the suitors' offensive behavior, witnessed firsthand by Athene in book 1, Odysseus himself fulfills the role of the divine avenger who punishes wrongdoing in the Ithakan sequence. As Kearns in particular has noted, the depiction of Odysseus' homecoming contains many elements of a theoxeny, in which a disguised god visits mortals testing their hospitality.[97] Typically a god will then reward those who have passed the test and destroy those who did not offer hospitality. A theoxenic myth implicitly demonstrates the sanctity of hospitality: always be hospitable in case your guest is a disguised deity. While perhaps the best-known instance in Greco-Roman myth is the tale of Baucis and Philemon, the pattern is frequently visible in the Bible (cf. the angels appearing to Abram, Genesis 18, and Lot, Genesis 19, Hebrews 13.1–2, and the like). The *Odyssey* firmly introduces theoxeny as a key shaping device in the poem's structure from the beginning, when Athene, a goddess, visits Telemakhos disguised as Mentes, a mortal. Telemakhos passes the test, demonstrating exemplary hospitality. He will be rewarded with her careful aid and occasional attendance for the remainder of the poem. She complains of the suitors' behavior, however, in strong terms:

> How insolently they seem to swagger about in their feasting
> all through the house. A serious man who came in among them
> could well be scandalized, seeing much disgraceful behavior.

> ὥς τέ μοι ὑβρίζοντες ὑπερφιάλως δοκέουσι
> δαίνυσθαι κατὰ δῶμα. νεμεσσήσαιτό κεν ἀνὴρ
> αἴσχεα πόλλ᾽ ὁρόων, ὅς τις πινυτός γε μετέλθοι.

> (1.227–29)

Among a number of strong terms, ὑβρίζω, perhaps the strongest, is used exclusively of the suitors and Melanthios.[98] If we view Athene's remarks under the rubric of a theoxeny, the failure to observe hospitality's conventions has already provoked the divine displeasure which will result in the deaths of the suitors. But, as noted, in the Ithakan sequence it is Odysseus, Athene's protégé, who carries out the role exercised by Zeus and Poseidon in the other sequences, the destruction of the abusive band of young men.

Though not a god, Odysseus carries out an agenda directed by Zeus and Athene, in effect carrying out their intentions. Though he is not a god, many on Ithaka mistake him for one, including some rather astute observers.[99] The suitors themselves so intimate when, in a declaration amounting to the poem's clearest statement of a theoxeny, one criticizes Antinoös's violence against the disguised Odysseus:

> Antinoös, you did badly to hit the unhappy vagabond:
> a curse on you, if he turns out to be some god from heaven.
> For the gods do take on all sorts of transformations, appearing
> as strangers from elsewhere, and thus they range at large through the cities,
> watching to see which men keep the laws, and which are violent.
>
> (17.483–87)

When he has slain the suitors, and Eurykleia exults in triumph, Odysseus downplays his own role, assigning responsibility to the gods:

> These were destroyed by the doom of the gods and their own hard actions,
> for these men paid no attention at all to any man on earth
> who came their way no matter if he were base or noble.
> So by their own recklessness [ἀτασθαλίῃσιν] they have found a shameful death.
>
> (22.412–16)

As earlier noted, Athene herself designs and sets in motion Odysseus's course against the suitors,[100] enjoying Zeus' full support (24.478 ff). Events suggest a parallel, reinforcing divine avenger in Apollo,[101] on whose holiday the μνηστηροφονία occurs and through whose medium, the bow, it is effected.

⌒

A divine consultation limits the extent of the death and destruction. When Helios learns of the violation of his cattle, he consults with Zeus (12.375–88), demanding the deaths of the crew and threatening greater destruction if this does not occur:

> Father Zeus . . . punish the companions of Odysseus . . .
> for they outrageously killed my cattle . . . Unless
> these are made to give me just recompense for my cattle,
> I will go down into Hades' and give my light to the dead men.
>
> (12.377–83) [102]

Zeus willingly assents to the former option (384–88), averting Helios' greater threat. Consequently he destroys Odysseus' crew, but spares the hero, as he did not transgress the interdiction.

In the Skherian sequence, as at Thrinakia, the angered divine party, Poseidon, consults with Zeus to air his complaint (13.127–59). Much like Helios, Poseidon offers a second, more destructive threat:

> This time, I wish to stun that beautiful vessel
> of the Phaiakians . . . so that they may stop and give over conveying
> people. And I would hide their city under a mountain.
>
> (13.149–52)

Zeus talks Poseidon out of the second more destructive option, hiding the city under a mountain, and grants him free rein to fulfill the first, much as in the sequence with Helios.[103]

In the Ithakan sequence, after Odysseus has slain the suitors, their relatives threaten further fighting. As before, the interested deity, Athene, consults with Zeus, considering two options:

> Son of Kronos . . . What does your mind have hidden within it?
> Will you first inflict evil fighting upon them, and terrible
> strife, or will you establish friendship between the factions?
>
> (24.473–76)

As in the other sequences, the more threatening option is avoided. This consultation again underlies Athene's responsibility in the μνηστηροφονία, as she, like Helios and Poseidon, here appears in the role of the injured divinity.

The three episodes under discussion have been criticized on a variety of grounds. Helios' consultation with Zeus (12.375–88) has been attacked as an interpolation since Alexandrian times.[104] Poseidon's consultation has been criticized as "a flat copy of similar Olympic scenes in the *Iliad*,"[105] the same criticism directed against Athene's consultation with Zeus in book 24.[106] Such criticisms reflect the bias of an *Iliad*-centered view of Homeric epic. The three scenes exhibit very close parallels *with each other*, exhibiting the same essential dynamic of a private consultation between Zeus and an offended, angered god, with Zeus restoring the god's sense of respect through his agreeing with the less destructive of the god's two suggested courses of action. Not only do the scenes exhibit these similarities with each other, but all three occur at the same place in their respective sequences. Consequently, regardless of the language and motifs the scenes may have in common with divine councils in the *Iliad*, they make better sense when analyzed as the concluding element in the *Odyssey*'s recurring narrative pattern. We also note that the three scenes are in fact a type-scene evident as early as *Gilgamesh*. As will be discussed in chapter 4, the same essential dynamic occurs when Ishtar (VI iii–iv), enraged at her rejection by Gilgamesh, goes to Anu and demands that he give her the reins of the Bull of Heaven, or else she will descend to the underworld and release the dead into the world above. Anu instead talks her into accepting a less destructive option. I take the antiquity of the type-scene as further evidence that in book 13 Zeus talks Poseidon into accepting the less destructive option, and only destroying the ship instead of the city.

Having established the overall trajectory of the narrative pattern in some detail, we may now consider how a few sections of the *Odyssey* function with respect to the pattern. We have seen how the suitors are an integral component of the narrative pattern in the second half of the poem, functioning as the most fully developed multiform of the entity *band of young men who abuse Odysseus in various ways*. We now consider how their appearance in the poem's first four books serves to introduce the Ithakan sequence, though Odysseus himself remains offstage.

I have argued above that in some particulars of the Ithakan sequence Odysseus fills the role played by a god in the other two sequences, being the agent who punishes and kills the band of abusive young men (as do Zeus and Poseidon in the Aiaian and Skherian sequences). Conversely, in the opening scene on Ithaka (1.96–323), after the first divine council, Athene, in the form of Mentes, plays the role later taken on by Odysseus. She comes among the suitors in disguise, lies about her identity, implicitly testing their hospitality and Telemakhos' fidelity, and refraining from meeting with Penelope.

In the identity she assumes as Mentes, she conjures up a character much like Odysseus himself, and, in many of her remarks, sketches out a scenario that consistently looks ahead to Odysseus' slaying of the suitors. The narrator suggests the parallel even as Athene first enters the palace:

> Now far the first to see Athene was godlike Telemakhos,
> as he sat among the suitors, his heart deep grieving within him,
> imagining in his mind his great father, how he might come back
> and all throughout the house might cause the suitors to scatter.
>
> (1.113–16)

On first seeing Athene as Mentes, Telemakhos simultaneously thinks of his father, and of the slaying of the suitors. After Telemakhos dutifully receives her with proper hospitality, several of Athene's subsequent comments conjure up a context like that of the μνηστηροφονία. She voices her disgust with the behavior of the suitors (1.227–29), in what amounts to a theoxeny, as noted above, with serious consequences for the inhospitable suitors. She continues with a wish to see Odysseus before her in full battle gear:

> Oh, for shame. How great your need is now of the absent
> Odysseus, who would lay his hands on these shameless suitors.
> I wish he could come now to stand in the outer doorway
> of his house, wearing a helmet, and carrying shield and two spears.
>
> (1.253–56)

Her narrative reaches a climax of sorts as she improvises a lie about how Odysseus came to her father to seek poison for his arrows, "in search of a poison to kill men, so he might have it / to smear on his bronze-headed arrows" (1.261–62). Of all the details Athene could have improvised about Odysseus, she selects a jarring particular calling attention to him as an archer who may use his arrows to kill men, a detail which emphatically looks ahead to the μνηστηροφονία. She concludes the "reminiscence" about Odysseus by again invoking his presence in the palace as an armed warrior: "I wish that such an Odysseus [i.e., with bow and poisoned arrows] would come now among the suitors. / They all would find death was quick, and marriage a painful matter" (1.265–66). In a typical instance of small-scale ring composition, Athene's two visions of an armed Odysseus scattering the suitors in his palace (1.255–56 and 1.265–66) frame and highlight the significant detail about the lethal arrows. The meeting concluded, Telemakhos reacts accordingly to the relevant character Athene has conjured up: "My guest, your words to me are very kind and considerate, / what any father would say to his son" (1.307–8). As the goddess departs, a germ of what is to come has been planted.

In terms of overall structure and the narrative pattern, then, book 1, until Athene departs, functions as a brief startup of the Ithakan sequence with Athene in Odysseus's own later role: the disguised stranger taking offense at the suitors' outrageous behavior in the palace. Though Odysseus' palace is busy throughout the poem, largely due to the suitors' continual uninvited presence, the only guests entertained in the palace in the entire poem are the disguised Athene and the disguised Odysseus,[107] adding to the natural, if subtle parallels between the two narrative sections. Given the tight teamwork Athene and Odysseus demonstrate—most prominently in the book 13 dialogue (13.221–439; note especially the dual participle expressing their joint deliberation: βουλεύσαντε: 13.439) and the slaying of the suitors (22.205–309)—their partly reciprocal roles in the pattern itself should not be a complete surprise. The parallels between Athene's arrival disguised as Mentes and Odysseus' eventual disguised approach increase the richness of the closing theoxeny in which Odysseus occupies the role of the offended god; the opening theoxeny points to and initiates the closing one.

After the goddess departs, however, Telemakhos, prompted into action by her visit, begins to step into the role similar to that which Odysseus will later occupy. For the remainder of book 1, and through the assembly in book 2, and on into his voyage to encounter Nestor and Menelaos, Telemakhos is concerned with acquiring power over the band of young men, entering into increasingly open conflict with them. Though he is initially unable to gain the upper hand, evident in the ineffective assembly in book 2, he takes steps which will eventually ensure the defeat of the band of abusive young men. Though in both instances, Athene's circumstances in book 1 and Telemakhos's thereafter, certain details of the pattern might be less relevant, such as the approach to the powerful female, there are, nonetheless, traces of this in Telemakhos' own struggles with Penelope, as he, in his own way, is also concerned with being recognized by the powerful female (as is Odysseus when the Ithakan sequence is resumed in the second half of the poem), though with the sexual/marital element, key to Odysseus' own circumstances, entirely lacking.

If we accept that books 1 through 4 serve to introduce the Ithakan sequence, which is then resumed in the middle of book 13, when Odysseus returns to his island, we can now appreciate one of the most significant features of the *Odyssey*'s use of the extended narrative pattern. Typical of the sense of form and composition in Archaic Greek poetry, the poem develops the three sequences in a large-scale instance of ring composition.[108]

The *Odyssey* opens focusing on Telemakhos, the suitors, and Penelope (bks. 1–4). Books 6 through 8 focus on Nausikaa, Arete, and the young Phaiakian athletes, while the Apologue depicts the crew and their destruction.[109] The narrative continues with the Phaiakians' escort of Odysseus and the destruction of their ship. The remainder of the poem concerns the destruction of the suitors and Odysseus's coming to terms with Penelope. We have, then, in narrative sequence, the Ithakan sequence (1–2, 4.625–847), the Skherian sequence (5.282–bk. 8, beginning with Odysseus's approach to Skheria), the Aiaian sequence (9–12, other than the Intermezzo: 11.333–84), resulting in the destruction of the crew, resumption of the Skherian sequence (13.1–187), and resumption of the Ithakan sequence resulting in the μνηστηροφονία (13.188–end). We might represent the narrative order of the sequences as shown in figure 1.

We can discern various progressions in some of the differences between the three sequences. The Aiaian sequence is the most fantastic and heroic (most fantastic in locales and beings, Odysseus' crew, a band of warriors). It features a successful descent to and return from the underworld, one of the highest designations of heroism in ancient myth. Odysseus successfully upholds the divine interdiction, again a sign of similar heroic caliber. The Skherian sequence is somewhat less fantastic, the least heroic, and most civilized (no physical violence between Odysseus and the Phaiakians), which may be another way of saying the same thing. The Ithakan is the least fantastic, both more heroic than the Skherian but less heroic than the Aiaian sequences. The Aiaian sequence has the least amount of delay or indirection, while the Ithakan has the most, the Skherian falling in between. We have, then, chronologically from Aiaia to Skheria to Ithaka, a progression from the most to the least fantastic, from the least to the most retarded.

These distinctions are reinforced and others emerge if we note how the powerful female figures differ proceeding through the sequences. Kirke is a goddess, to whose motivations the narrative is denied access, and Aiaia

A1: Ithakan Sequence, book 1 through book 4
B1: Skherian Sequence, end of book 5.282 through book 8
C1: Aiaian Sequence: book 9 through book 11.332
Intermezzo: 11.333–82
C2: Aiaian Sequence: book 11.383 through book 12
B2: Skherian Sequence, book 13.1–187a
A2: Ithakan Sequence, book 13.187b through book 24.

Fig. 1

is the mysterious abode of a goddess.[110] On Skheria, however, we are privy to Nausikaa's workings, though perhaps denied deep insight into Arete. The Ithakan sequence offers a still deeper exploration of Penelope's dilemma and emotions. The *Odyssey* as a whole thus offers something of a parallel to the ascending scale of affection Kakridis recovered in the Meleager story and its parallel in Akhilleus and Patroklos (11 ff). Though temporarily swayed by Kirke, Odysseus forms a lasting agreement only with the last, most intimate of the females, rejecting the offer of being Nausikaa's husband. The pattern thus further demonstrates how Skheria mediates between boundaries and spheres of action in the *Odyssey*.

The different roles that Kirke and Penelope play with regard to the deaths of the crew and suitors (see chap. 2) present a further significant distinction in the powerful females. The suitors die in conflict centered on Penelope; she is in the next room as Odysseus slays them. The crew die far from Aiaia, though Kirke is linked to their death by having relayed the divine interdiction they go on to violate. She is, however, central to their descent to the underworld. Thus there are considerable parallels between the crew's descent to Hades and the slaying of the suitors, the Aiaian sequence implying several key motifs in the descent which the Ithakan sequence employs in the slaying of the suitors.

Though the narrative pattern forms the skeletal structure of much of the *Odyssey*, its influence is not confined to these three sequences. The poem contains additional shorter multiforms organized around the same elements. Perhaps the two most notable brief versions are Zeus' opening account of Agamemnon, Klytemnestra, and Aigisthos, and Demodokos' song of Hephaistos, Aphrodite, and Ares.[111] At somewhat greater length, Telemakhos' visit with Helen and Menelaos explores many of the same elements.[112]

Recognition of the pattern reveals much about the structure of the *Odyssey*. The sequence offers evidence of an intricate level of design in the poem, though interpretation of that design may remain a subjective matter.[113] Why does the pattern exist, and how conscious is the composer of such a pattern? The answer depends upon one's point of view concerning oral composition. Clearly such a structure is of great aid to an improvising composer, consciously or unconsciously. While improvising a performance, a poet aware of the pattern can more easily concentrate on the distinct characterizations of the three females, the different motivations in the three bands of young men, differences between the three instances of divine wrath, the different levels of response called for in Odysseus, and so forth. I do not think it unreasonable that a bard was aware of the narrative pattern. Oral literature is an essentially conservative medium, retaining and manipulating inherited motifs and type-scenes. It may very well be that the pattern itself is older than our *Odyssey*.[114]

I thus argue that we can better understand the *Odyssey*'s structure not as a collection of separate themes but as a complex of themes which should not be so easily separated. Awareness of the narrative pattern helps clarify reputed narrative inconsistencies such as Hermes' youthful appearance at 10.277, the role of Arete, the emphasis placed on Odysseus's winning her favor and her delay in answering his initial request, Penelope's appearance to the suitors at 18.206 ff, the role of Theoklymenos,[115] the parallels between Athene preventing further hostilities among the Ithakans and Zeus talking Poseidon out of further harming the Phaiakians,[116] the authenticity of at least parts of book 24, among other issues. While one element may function more smoothly in one sequence than another, as some have suggested with regard to parallels between events on Skheria and Ithaka,[117] the pattern persists, reflecting the essential conservatism of oral literature: why discard a useful motif?

As for the existence of *three* sequences of the narrative pattern, we might consider Lévi-Strauss' formulation: "The question has often been raised why myths, and more generally oral literature, are so much addicted to duplication, triplication or quadruplication of the same sequence . . . the answer is obvious: repetition has as its function to make the structure of the myth apparent" (105). In this pattern the repetition helps emphasize the qualities essential to Odysseus, his cunning, perseverance, and piety, setting him apart from the young men in their lack of self-control and piety, making him attractive to the female figures. Such an Odysseus engages the three different females, three different bands of young men. While possessing their own identities, these characters have in common primarily their intersection with Odysseus and the pain or profit that thereby results. Furthermore, there is particularly significant emphasis in the repetition of the endings of each sequence, the divine wrath and subsequent destruction of the abusive band of young men, the only episode singled out by the proem. We return to this topic in chapter 4.

$\sim$$\sim$$\sim$

Elpenor and Leodes
Desire and Limitless Wine

Having established the constants in the three sequences of the narrative pattern, locating those most stable elements of the poem's plot, we now concentrate on the variations that exist on those constant elements. Such variations provide crucial aid not only in noting key differences between one sequence and another but also in providing a lens through which some central interpretive issues can be considered. In the second and third chapters we analyze further elements of the narrative pattern which occur in two, but not all three, of the sequences. As each sequence has its own distinct modality and context, and somewhat different priorities, on occasion two of them will necessarily share a significant feature which is absent in the third.

A central constituent of the narrative pattern in all three sequences is the band of abusive young men with which Odysseus must content— his crew, the Phaiakian athletes, and the suitors. Each band (or members thereof) not only acts abusively toward the hero but commits acts offensive to the gods, all members dying as a result of both conditions. The parallels extend further, in some cases, to specific members of each band. All three groups have a leader, given a parallel name formation, Eurylokhos, Euryalos, and Eurymakhos (co-leader with Antinoös). This figure aggressively confronts Odysseus, is verbally abusive, and is responsible for provoking the band of young men to commit reckless acts.[1]

A further parallel figure exists, common both to the crew and the suitors (but absent among the Phaiakian athletes), in the persons of Elpenor and Leodes.[2] As Eurylokhos and Eurymakhos function as leaders of the two parallel bands, aggressively opposed to Odysseus, so Elpenor and Leodes embody an opposite pole of behavior, a passive figure characterized by a lack of heroism, a wistful outlook, and excessive consumption of wine. While there are differences between the two characters, demanded by the considerable differences in their contexts, in terms of their central functions they play the same essential role in their respective bands. They serve to summon up a figure opposite in many ways to Eurylokhos/Eurymakhos, a passive character, content to overindulge in alcohol, an idle dreamer not a leader. As such the figure is essentially nonthreatening, a danger only to himself. In this respect he represents another aspect of the bands' negative qualities. Eurylokhos/Eurymakhos actively promotes rebellion and insubordination, leading other members of the band to their doom. Elpenor and Leodes belong to the band but, because of their passivity, neither promote nor take part in their groups' more rebellious activities. As a result they are both capable of provoking sympathy in some readers. Their shortcomings are more subtle. They are the embodiment of each band's tendency toward excessive consumption, especially with regard to alcohol. Furthermore, they implicitly represent a further violation of hospitality, not the forceful perversion of that institution as figured in the suitors' takeover of Odysseus' palace, but a violation of the decorum on which true hospitality must rest.[3] They violate a norm more than once on Odysseus' lips, οὐ κατὰ κόσμον (8.179 to Euryalos, cf. οὐ κατὰ μοῖραν 9.352 to Polyphemos), not through force but through excessive consumption and their passive acceptance of their band's reckless behavior.

Parallels in the Crew's Descent to Hades and the Slaying of the Suitors

To prepare for an analysis of the parallels between these two characters, we first must consider a number of structural parallels between the two larger contexts in which they appear, the crew's descent to the underworld in book 11 and the slaying of the suitors in book 22. These are not treated as corresponding scenes in terms of our analysis according to the narrative pattern, nor have they been seen as such by other scholars, who logically associate the actual *deaths* of the two groups, as well as drawing a parallel between the crew's impious feasting on Helios' cattle (12.394 ff) and the perverse final day of banqueting by the suitors (20.345 ff).[4] There are, nonetheless, key differences between the deaths of the two abusive bands in their respective sequences. In the Aiaian sequence, the crew die in a remote setting far from any other mortals, far from Kirke, far from Teiresias who predicted their death. In the Ithakan sequence, the suitors perish in Odysseus's palace, with Penelope in the next room, and with Theoklymenos having been a short time ago in their midst.

Conversely, there are a considerable number of motifs or constituent elements common to the crew's descent and the suitors' slaying. In effect, both the crew and the suitors each have two episodes involving death. Each band has a descent to the underworld (bk. 11 for the crew, bk. 24 for the suitors), each also having a scene in which they actually die (the end of bk. 12 for the crew, bk. 22 for the suitors). In both cases, however, they are separate, distinct scenes. This is somewhat surprising in the suitors' case, as the *Odyssey* could easily have presented their descent to Hades following immediately upon their slaying, but has chosen not to do so. We are dealt a mixture, then, so that in the Aiaian sequence the poem forms the crew's descent with a number of the same elements which in the Ithakan sequence are used to depict the slaying of the suitors. We should not find this overly surprising, as both types of scenes are centrally concerned with death, one scene depicting the band of men in the place of the dead, the other scene accounting for why they must die and thus go permanently to that place.

The settings in which the two episodes, crew's descent and suitors' slaying, take place are themselves closely parallel. Of all the places visited by the crew in the wanderings, the only one suggestive of the suitors' later activities on Ithaka is Aiaia. The crew spend a year, feasting lavishly in a palace presided over by Kirke. This image, more than any other depiction of any of the crew's activities, most closely prefigures and parallels the suitors' existence in Ithaka, where they feast daily in the palace and are enthralled by Penelope.[5] There are key differences, to be sure. The suitors are uninvited guests, squandering resources to which they have no claim, offending the gods by their behavior. Odysseus and crew are invited guests in Kirke's palace, specifically commanded by the goddess to feast in her palace (10.460–63), consuming "limitless meat and sweet wine" (10.468) day by day for a year.[6] We have, then, as parallel contexts in the crew's descent and the suitors' slaying, the similar day-to-day existence of endless feasting by the respective bands in the court of an enchanting, powerful female figure.

Teiresias and Theoklymenos, multiforms of the figure who prophesies the deaths of the respective bands of young men, are a key instance of the Aiaian sequence employing an element in the crew's descent which the Ithakan sequence uses for the slaying of the suitors. Odysseus and crew encounter Teiresias in Hades, Kirke having sent them there to hear him. Odysseus and the suitors, however, hear Theoklymenos' climactic prophecy in Odysseus' palace. Penelope, much like Kirke with Teiresias, is well acquainted with Theoklymenos, having herself conversed with him (17.152–65) and heard him prophesy the coming destruction of the band of young men (17.152–59). Theoklymenos' prophetic speech (20.351–57, 364–70)[7] virtually depicts the suitors in Hades, though they are still alive. Teiresias' prophecy, though made from Hades, correctly predicts the destruction of the crew at Thrinakia, if they harm the cattle of Helios (11.112–13). Theoklymenos, in his prophecy of the suitors' fast-approaching death, himself draws pronounced parallels between their present circumstances and Hades:

> Oh wretches, what is this evil you suffer? Your heads and faces
> and the knees underneath you are shrouded in night;
> wailing has broken out, your cheeks are covered with tears,
> and the walls are sprinkled with blood, and the fine pillars.
> All the forecourt is full of ghosts, the yard is full of them
> as they flock down to the underworld under the darkness. The sun
> has perished out of heaven, and a foul mist has come over.
>
> (20.351–57)

Theoklymenos's prophecy, prompted by the suitors' perverse feasting (20.345 ff), suggests that he foresees the suitors as they will soon be, disembodied souls in the underworld, and/or that he sees the underworld superimposed upon their present setting.

Several terms in his prophecy are prominent in the vocabulary used to describe the *Nekuia*. Theoklymenos' word for the ghosts he sees, εἰδώλων (20.355), is used of Elpenor in the underworld (11.83) and of several other shades Odysseus encounters there (11.213, 11.476, 11.602). It will be used again to describe the underworld in book 24 as the suitors' own descent is described (24.14).[8] Theoklymenos uses one of the specific names for the underworld, ἔρεβος (20.356), which occurs twice in the *Nekuia* (11.37, 11.564). His word for the darkness of Hades, ζόφον (20.356), also occurs twice in the earlier episode (11.57, 11.155).

Kirke, something of an authority on life and death, suggests common ground between the crew's descent and death itself: Σχέτλιοι, οἳ ζώοντες ὑπήλθετε δῶμ' Ἀΐδαο, / δισθανέες, ὅτε τ' ἄλλοι ἅπαξ θνῄσκουσ' ἄνθρωποι, "Wretches, who, while alive, have descended to the house of Hades, / twice-dead, when the rest of humanity dies once" (12.21–22). Both scenes depict the bands of men, crew and suitors, finishing a sumptuous feast to arrive in a "place of death." Odysseus "leads" both groups to this place of death, personally guiding the crew to Hades, personally sending the suitors to their death. Kirke herself sends Odysseus and crew to the underworld, while Penelope draws the suitors, through their own desire, to the palace, the place in which they will be slain. We now turn to a final link between the crew's descent and the suitors' slaying in the persons of Elpenor and Leodes, two characters present only in these two scenes.[9] The abundant feasting common to each episode, offering the presence of abundant wine, is an essential prerequisite for both characters. On the last day of this year-long feast Elpenor makes his first and last appearance as a living man (10.552). On the last day of the suitors' feasting in the palace, Leodes makes his first appearance, also dying later in the day (21.144–62), never seen except for the suitors' last day of feasting.[10]

Elpenor and Leodes as Misfits

Though the immediate context for each character is a large, lavish feast, Elpenor and Leodes both exhibit behavior quite distinct from that of the other members of their bands. Both are uniquely unqualified for martial activities. While the crew are warriors, who participated in the sack of Troy and, more recently, of Ismaros, Elpenor is sharply singled out from the other members as "neither terribly / valiant in his fighting, nor composed in his thoughts," οὔτε τι λίην / ἄλκιμος ἐν πολέμῳ οὔτε φρεσὶν ᾖσιν ἀρηρώς (10.552–53). Equally evident in the Ismaros episode, however, is the crew's predilection for insubordination. Odysseus narrates that after the successful sack of the city, he advised an immediate departure. But the crew would not listen, preferring a lavish feast (9.43–46). The result of the crew's decision is disastrous. The Kikones, having time to summon allies, organize a counterstrike, slaying seventy-two of the crew. The Apologue develops a regular pattern of such insubordination, locating it in Eurylokhos in particular, culminating in the crew's desecration of Helios' cattle on Thrinakia (12.278–97, 339–52), an episode in which Eurylokhos persuades and leads the crew. Elpenor, then, does not appear to share the insubordination which will eventually hold sway over and destroy the majority of the remaining crew members.

In what I argue is a parallel depiction, given the different circumstances that prevail in Odysseus' palace, Leodes is unable to string Odysseus' bow (21.150–51). While it turns out that, in fact, none of the suitors is able to string the bow, Leodes draws considerably more attention in his failure than any of the others, and, like Elpenor, evidences a fundamental lack of aptitude for the pursuits of a warrior. Leodes is prominent in being the first suitor to attempt to string the bow. The narrative emphasizes his initial position through a brief instance of ring composition: "Leodes was the *first* to arise, the son of Oinops. . . . He was the *first* to take up the bow and the swift arrow now," Λῃώδης δὲ πρῶτος ἀνίστατο, Οἴνοπος υἱός . . .

ὅς ῥα τότε πρῶτος τόξον λάβε καὶ βέλος ὠκύ (21.144–48). As the first of a series, then, his failure to string the bow is all the more prominent.

The reasons given for Leodes' failure are quite specific and implicitly suggest his character's essential lack of heroic potential. When he tries to string the bow, the narrator pointedly remarks, "but he could not string it; before that he wore out his soft, delicate / hands, pulling at the strings," οὐδέ μιν ἐντάνυσε· πρὶν γὰρ κάμε χεῖρας ἀνέλκων / ἀτρίπτους ἁπαλάς (21.150–51). In failing to have hands accustomed to the task, Leodes reveals his unfamiliarity with basic warrior training and conditioning, and his isolation from the rest of the suitors in this regard. Antinoös suggests as much: "You were not such a one, when the lady your mother bore you, / as ever to be able to manage the bow and arrows," οὐ γάρ τοι σέ γε τοῖον / ἐγείνατο πότνια μήτηρ / οἷόν τε ῥυτῆρα βιοῦ τ᾽ ἔμεναι καὶ ὀϊστῶν (21.172–73). The doubly modified hands, soft and delicate, suggest an upbringing, and/or regimen quite unlike that of his group, who are elsewhere portrayed exercising with spears (4.625–27 = 17.167–69). In his failure at even being able to handle the bow properly, Leodes occupies among the suitors a parallel to Elpenor's lack of martial qualities and heroic possibilities.

But there is more to it than that. An implicit ranking underlies the sequence of the suitors as they attempt to string the bow.[11] After Leodes' failure, while Odysseus goes outside to reveal his identity to Eumaios and Philoitios (21.188–244), most or all of the other suitors try their hand at the bow, excepting Antinoös and Eurymakhos, all without success (21.184–87). As Odysseus and his retainers reenter the hall, Eurymakhos tries and fails (21.245–47). Antinoös then declines the attempt, claiming that it would be inappropriate to do so on a day sacred to Apollo.[12] We have a clear suggestion, then, that as the leaders and most powerful suitors, Eurymakhos and Antinoös, were to go last, so he that went first, Leodes, is regarded as the least powerful, least likely to succeed in stringing the bow. Dimock similarly concludes, "We now can see that Leodes represents one end of the spectrum of the suitors' characteristics, with Antinoös representing the other. Leodes is the least hostile, least violent, least aggressive, as well as weakest physically, whereas Antinoös is the opposite" (283).

Elpenor and Leodes are further distinguished from their groups in other particulars of their behavior, standing apart as extremes of sorts. Elpenor is the youngest, νεώτατος (10.552), perhaps a censorious term in a poem that privileges Odysseus, a mature hero, married and with offspring. He is further described as physically isolated, alone on Kirke's roof (10.554). His peculiar position on the roof points not only to the extent of his excessive consumption and consequent intoxication, but subtly suggests a violation of the decorum and camaraderie normally expected at a heroic banquet. Leodes is also first described with emphasis on an isolated location. Though in the same room as the suitors, "he always sits in the corner / beside the fine mixing bowl," παρὰ κρητῆρα δὲ καλὸν / ἷζε μυχοίτατος αἰεί (21.146). In his habitual proximity to the wine bowl, there is a suggestion of overindulgence in alcohol and, if true, a possible violation of the spirit of the feast which in its own way offers a parallel for Elpenor's behavior. While in each case the character's isolation and excessive drinking can be said to spring from a different motivation—Elpenor's youthfulness being no doubt a contributing factor in his behavior and Leodes' role as θυοσκόος probably entailing responsibility for leading the suitors in libations but perhaps shading into his taking advantage of his position—nonetheless, within their respective bands the two characters behave in a manner apart from their comrades and, though not mirror images of each other, display correspondingly soft tendencies.

Leodes is further depicted as distinct from the suitors in much of his overall attitude and behavior. Like Elpenor, a nonwarrior amid a warrior band, he appears not to take part in his group's dominant activities. The narrator's initial description asserts that Leodes alone refrains from some of the suitors' more excessive actions: "To him alone their recklessness / was hateful, and he disapproved of all the suitors," ἀτασθαλίαι δέ οἱ οἴῳ / ἐχθραὶ ἔσαν, πᾶσιν δὲ νεμέσσα μνηστήρεσσιν (21.146–47). Leodes himself, face to face with Odysseus, reiterates how different his behavior has been from that of the other suitors (22.313–15),

> For I claim that never in your halls did I say or do anything
> wrong to any one of the women, but always was trying
> to stop any one of the other suitors who acted that way.

> οὐ γάρ πώ τινά φημι γυναικῶν ἐν μεγάροισιν
> εἰπεῖν οὐδέ τι ῥέξαι ἀτάσθαλον· ἀλλὰ καὶ ἄλλους
> παύεσκον μνηστῆρας, ὅτις τοιαῦτά γε ῥέζοι.

Both characters, then, while exhibiting somewhat offensive behavior, are less involved with the confrontational actions and insubordination which characterize the rest of their bands. They do not take part in their group's most violent activities[13] and represent less direct challenges to Odysseus' authority than do such suitors as Antinoös and Eurymakhos, or, among the crew, Eurylokhos.

Their Excessive Drinking

Among the crew, warriors who spent ten years at Troy and who sacked the city of the Kikones, Elpenor is marked by a peculiar passivity. The same holds true for Leodes among the suitors, who are also trained in warfare and are depicted exercising themselves in related pursuits (4.626–27 = 17.168–69). The poem implies a partial explanation for why these two characters differ from their comrades in behavior and motivation. Though both the crew and the suitors exhibit various forms of excessive behavior and are seen as opposite to the self-control usually found in Odysseus, Elpenor and Leodes are the sole members of each band singled out for emphasis in excessive consumption of alcohol. Elpenor, we recall, went up on Kirke's roof in the first place, because he, "in search of cool air, had lain down drunkenly to sleep," ψύχεος ἱμείρων κατελέξατο οἰνοβαρείων (10.555). The participle, οἰνοβαρείων, is a most negative term in Homeric epic, used elsewhere in the *Odyssey* only of Polyphemos (9.374), as he belches and vomits in a drunken sleep, and of the Centaur, Eurytion, singled out as "the first who found his evil in heavy drinking" (21.304), and who incited the battle with the Lapiths. Elpenor himself, when Odysseus is surprised to encounter him in the underworld, ascribes his demise largely to his excessive consumption of alcohol: "The evil destiny of the god and prodigious wine ruined me," ἆσέ με δαίμονος αἶσα κακὴ καὶ ἀθέσφατος οἶνος (11.61).

Though less explicit regarding Leodes, the poem nonetheless closely associates him with excessive drinking through two suggestive techniques. The text is problematic, but his patronymic appears to be Οἴνοπος υἱός (21.144), "The son of Oinops."[14] Most commentators take the father's name literally as "Wine-Face,"[15] as Homeric epic is quite fond of significant names and wordplay based on proper names.[16] Greek myth in general demonstrates a tendency toward children's inheriting their parents' dominant traits. Thus the patronymic, whether taken as "Wine-face" or "Wine-colored," is quite suggestive of Leodes' own association with drink. With less ambiguity, the narrative emphasizes that Leodes' regular seat always places him closest to the wine bowl: "and [he] sat always in the corner / beside the fine mixing bowl," παρὰ κρητῆρα δὲ καλὸν / ἷζε μυχοίτατος αἰεί (21.145–46). Whereas his duties as θυοσκόος, diviner, might entail a role in pouring libations for the rest of the suitors, the passage, with the combined forces of αἰεί, the imperfect of ἷζε, and the superlative, μυχοίτατος, subtly suggests Leodes' close association with drinking, alone of the suitors' party.

Excessive consumption of alcohol by both the suitors and crew is thematic throughout the poem. In the assembly in book 2, Telemakhos complains that the suitors "drink the gleaming wine / recklessly," πίνουσί τε αἴθοπα οἶνον / μαψιδίως (2.57–58). In the first episode in which the crew is involved they are described as drinking "much wine," ἔνθα δὲ πολλὸν μὲν μέθυ (9.45).[17] This is the same feast they insist on holding, against Odysseus's advice, which results in the death of seventy-two men as it allows time for the Kikones to summon allies and counterattack. On this occasion, then, the narrative draws a connection between inappropriate drinking and resultant death. On Aiaia, earlier in the day on which Elpenor dies, the crew are described as "feasting on unlimited meat and sweet wine," δαινύμενοι κρέα τ' ἄσπετα καὶ μέθυ ἡδύ (10.477), which last detail, as Heubeck notes, "prepares indirectly for the fall of Elpenor" (10.477).

On the last day of the suitors' existence (occupying 20.91–23.299), the only day in which Leodes is depicted, the drinking appears to be even heavier than usual, reaching a peak in book 21. This particular day is designated as a public festival (ἑορτή) for Apollo (20.156, 20.276–78, 21.258), which may prompt more libations than usual. The narrator describes the suitors' entourage mixing wine and passing out goblets early in the day (20.252–55). When Penelope brings the bow out and places it before them she refers to their "incessant drinking," πινέμεν ἐμμενὲς αἰεὶ (21.69). After all the suitors except Antinoös have tried to string the bow and failed, Antinoös asks the steward to pour yet another round of wine for everyone (21.263). The narrator then describes, more wine being mixed, goblets filled and passed, until "they had drunk as much as they wanted," ἔπιόν θ' ὅσον ἤθελε θυμός (21.273), this last passage (21.270–75) being the poem's most extensive description of the suitors' drinking.

Antinoös narrative about the Centaur offers the most telling instance of book 21's treatment of the motif of excessive drinking. When the disguised Odysseus asks if he might handle the bow, Antinoös responds, "The honeyed wine has hurt you, as it has harmed / others as well, who gulp it down in excess," οἶνός σε τρώει μελιηδής, ὅς τε καὶ ἄλλους / βλάπτει, ὃς ἄν μιν χανδὸν ἕλῃ μηδ' αἴσιμα πίνῃ (21.293–94). As exemplum Antinoös recalls the story of Eurytion, the Centaur, who, from drinking too much wine, went mad and started the battle with the Lapiths. Although some analysts have sought to athetize the passage because of incongruity between Antinoös' argument and his own behavior,[18] such an interpretation does not take into account the *Odyssey*'s tendency toward the ironic. Antinoös, a hypocrite, cannot see that his exemplum best applies to himself,[19] one of the most emphatic instances of a tendency regular throughout the poem. Book 21, then, in which Leodes, son of Oinops, makes his first appearance, sustains a thematic association of heavy drinking on the part of the suitors. Serving as climax to the excessive drinking on this final day for the suitors, Antinoös, the first suitor to be killed, is slain by an arrow through his throat as he reaches for his goblet (22.9–11). The poem would thus imply Elpenor and Leodes' association with heavy drinking as a partial explanation for their passivity.

Their Wistful Natures

In Elpenor's case further explanation may be found in the meaning of his name,[20] a transparent formation from that root from which ἐλπίς and ἔλπω derive.[21] His actions are in accord with the meaning of his name. Elpenor is a character of strong desires, but whose desires and hopes are incongruous with his position and behavior. In the series of events leading up to his death, he is described as "*desiring* cool air," ψύχεος ἱμείρων (10.555). As the only description that the poem offers of Elpenor while alive, the passage is noteworthy in assigning desire as his motivation. It is this act of desire, a consequence of his drinking, that leads to his death, a linkage emphasized in dark wordplay: "Desiring *cool air*, he lay down, heavy with wine . . . and his *soul* went down to Hades," ψύχεος ἱμείρων, κατελέξατο οἰνοβαρείων . . . ψυχὴ δ' Ἄϊδόσδε κατῆλθεν (10.555–60).[22] While ἱμείρων and ἔλπω are not necessarily equivalent, there is a broad semantic overlap between the two roots, both delineating a subject's relation to future actions, both suggesting selection based on emotion and emotional appetite, rather than assessment of fact, likelihood, or need. Both, if a character's sole motivation, may suggest a figure rooted more in wistful thought than decision or action.

Elpenor continues to be motivated by hope and desire in the afterlife. He entreats Odysseus, as a suppliant, to return to Aiaia and grant him a burial with full heroic honors. While Odysseus grants his request, and, having returned to Aiaia, dutifully carries out the ceremony, observers have commented on the gulf that exists between Elpenor's fundamental lack of heroism and the full, heroic funeral he desires. Elpenor does not die a heroic death, but breaks his neck because of his own foolish, reckless actions. Consequently Heubeck sees him as a self-deluded character, whose desires are out of line with his merit or actions,

> Elpenor requests an honourable burial. The heroic language . . . highlights the incongruity of Elpenor's claim to status: his birth, station in life, achievements, as well as the manner of his death, are profoundly unheroic. . . . Elpenor's choice of words and his wishes betray a lack of self-knowledge. Cremation with

all his weapons and the raising of a σῆμα to proclaim the dead man's fame to succeeding generations are appropriate for the hero who has fallen honourably . . . The τύμβος is to be surmounted by the oar which Elpenor wielded in life—a request which reveals the reality behind Elpenor's delusion of grandeur: his heroic deeds consist of his work as a rower.[23]

Elpenor's name thus accurately suggests his wistful nature not only while alive but even more in his incongruous wishes in the underworld.

Leodes is governed by a similar wistfulness—desires incongruous with his actions, position, and attainment. In his first speech he uses three words within two lines to express his expectation and desire, ποτιδέγμενοι (21.156), μενοινᾷ (21.157), and, most tellingly, ἔλπετ᾽(21.157), the very root from which Elpenor's name derives. Leodes includes himself in the first person plural of ποτιδέγμενοι, while the following third person singular verbs, ἔλπετ᾽and μενοινᾷ, modify an indefinite pronoun (i.e., "Now when someone"), clearly meant to express both his own point of view and to a lesser extent that of the suitors. It is worth emphasizing that Leodes' use of ἔλπω here is the only instance of any suitor using the verb. The object of both ἔλπετ᾽and μενοινᾷ is γῆμαι Πηνελόπειαν, "desires and longs to marry Penelope." Whereas all of the suitors desire to marry Penelope, and it is therefore not surprising that Leodes does as well, it is one thing, I suggest, for Antinoös, Eurymakhos, or Amphinomos to presume to woo her, and quite another for Leodes, son of Oinops, to do so. Antinoös and Eurymakhos are visible, active, vocal presences, Antinoös, conspicuous for his speaking ability and display of power, Eurymakhos, smoother, a flatterer, the ladies man.[24] Amphinomos is singled out by the narrator as Penelope's favorite (16.397–98). What queen, however, especially a Penelope, would notice and be attracted to a suitor who day after day sits in a corner by the wine bowl and makes a fool of himself in a vain attempt at stringing her husband's bow? Leodes, then, is a similarly self-deluded character, displaying a false estimation of himself roughly corresponding to that evident in Elpenor.

Underscoring the chasm between his desires and his behavior, Leodes himself seems unaware of how slender are his chances of satisfying his desires. Unable to string the bow, he declares that "it is far better / to die than to go on living having failed to obtain that for which / we always gather here, hoping for [ποτιδέγμενοι] all our days" (21.154–56). Better to die than remain alive, if he has no reasonable expectation of winning Penelope. The declaration also underscores how central to his whole being is his desire for Penelope. Later, when Odysseus has killed all other suitors except him, Leodes gives further evidence of his penchant for self-delusion. Declaring that he has not participated in the suitors' excesses, and has even tried to restrain them from committing them, he concludes, "but I must fall, since there is no gratitude for past favors" (22.319). Leodes emerges as a character with extravagant hopes, who deludes himself through his fixation on those hopes. We might reapply Heubeck's assessment of Elpenor, given above, to Leodes. In his final remark, his "choice of words and his wishes betray a lack of self-knowledge."

Both characters supplicate Odysseus for something of life-or-death importance. Elpenor successfully persuades Odysseus to grant his request for a heroic burial, tactfully asking Odysseus on behalf of Penelope, Laertes, and Telemakhos (11.66–68). He has committed no wrong against Odysseus; in his lack of self-control and heroism he has only victimized himself. Leodes unsuccessfully supplicates Odysseus, begging him to spare his life. Commentators have tended to be critical of Odysseus for rejecting Leodes' supplication.[25] If, however, we apply the norms for behavior demonstrated elsewhere in the narrative, Odysseus' slaying of the diviner is revealed to be quite consistent. Yamagata notes of Leodes that "he fails to relate himself to divine protection . . . he has been consuming Odysseus' property every day, abusing the conventions of ξεινίη. Moreover, he has been the leader of all those amorous prayers to win Penelope, which, to Odysseus' eye, is another unforgivable abuse of divine authority" (1994: 167). While he has avoided joining in some of the suitors' most offensive behavior, he has taken part in actions directed against Odysseus. The suitors' incessant depletion of Odysseus' property is an open and continual violation of the norms of reciprocal behavior upon which Archaic Greek culture depends.

Secondly, his wooing of Penelope violates a pattern of behavior earlier articulated by the gods. In Zeus' programmatic first speech (1.31–43), in which Aigisthos prefigures the behavior of the suitors,[26] the ruler of the universe emphasizes that Hermes pronounced two divine interdictions to Aigisthos, "not to kill him [Agamemnon] and not to woo his wife," μήτ' αὐτὸν κτείνειν μήτε μνάασθαι ἄκοιτιν (1.39). Leodes, unlike many of the suitors, does not parallel Aigisthos in attempting to kill Odysseus, thus upholding the first interdiction. However, he is intentionally wooing Odysseus' wife (indeed, this appears to be his sole *raison d'être*), directly violating the second interdiction. In this sense he, along with all the other suitors, parallels Aigisthos, whose behavior Zeus finds offensive, and whose slaying, by Orestes, receives the gods' sanction, Athene concurring, "Let any other man who does thus perish as he did" (1.46). We noted in chapter 1 how the force of a theoxeny underlies much of the Ithakan sequence, with the disguised Athene herself expressing outrage at the excesses she personally witnesses (1.227–29, 1.253–56, 1.265–66). Odysseus offers additional justification for denying the supplication, in that Leodes must have prayed that his homecoming, the subject matter of the poem itself, would not be accomplished (22.323).

Both Serve as Frames in Parallel Ring Compositional Structures

The *Odyssey* offers perhaps the most intriguing evidence that Elpenor and Leodes function as doubles in their participation in thematically parallel ring compositional structures.[27] It has long been recognized (Whitman 288) that Elpenor serves to frame the beginning and ending of the crew's descent to the underworld, his fall from the roof and consequent death being the last episode before the descent, and his burial on Aiaia, the first incident on their return. I suggest the schema in figure 2 as an underlying structure for the *Nekuia* and adjacent episodes. The schema depicts how Elpenor functions as a framing structure surrounding the episode.[28] Elpenor serves the *Odyssey* both as entrance into the underworld and exit from it, encompassing the entire underworld episode between the mention of his death and the description of his burial. We note that Arete's declaration in the Intermezzo that Odysseus is her guest (11.338), lies at the center of the structure. I further suggest that Elpenor's appearance before Odysseus in Hades is the counterpart of the series of tormented men whom Odysseus observes: Minos, Orion, Tityon, Tantalos, and Sisyphos (11.568–600), men punished for their offenses against the gods. In this sense he further serves as an embodiment of the crew's wrongdoing, and indication of their eventual fate.

Leodes' two appearances in the poem (21.144–174, 22.310–29) are part of a similar, and parallel, ring compositional structure that encompasses the slaying of the suitors, the sequence of events and structure of which are shown in figure 3.[29] Both characters similarly frame the two episodes whose many thematic parallels were noted above. Reece argues that the complementary rings in a ring structure are not merely a sequencing device, but serve larger organizational and thematic purposes: "The rings, often multiple rings, form a terrace leading down to a central core, focusing attention on that core, foregrounding it, and highlighting it. Often this central core is the central thematic event not only of the single episode but also of a larger section of narrative, and even of an entire epic" (Reece 1995: 220). At the core of the structure which Leodes frames is Odysseus' successful handling of the bow, the symbolic winning of Penelope, and his first public declaration of his identity since returning to Ithaka.

The parallels between the two ring compositional structures are mul-

A1. Elpenor dies (10.552–60)
   B1. The crew "descend" to Hades, sailing from Kirke (10.562–11.22)
      C1. Elpenor, Teiresias, Antiklea (11.23–225)
         D1. Catalog of heroines (11.226–332)
            E. Intermezzo (11.333–84)
         D2. Male heroes (Trojan War) (11.385–565)
      C2. Punished men, Heracles, Persephone (11.566–635)
   B2. The crew "ascend" from Hades, sailing to Kirke (11.636–12.7)
A2. Elpenor is buried (12.8–15)

Fig. 2

A1. Leodes attempts to string the bow (21.144–66).
   B1. The other suitors try to do so (21.167–87).
      C1. Eurymakhos tries to string the bow (21.234–55).
         D1. Antinoös postpones further attempts (21.256–69).
            E. Odysseus successfully manages the bow, and
            reveals his identity.
         D2. Antinoös is the first suitor killed, by the bow (22.8–21).
      C2. Eurymakhos is the second suitor killed (22.44–88).
   B2. All other suitors are killed (22.89–309).
A2. Leodes is the last to die (22.310–29).

Fig. 3

tiple. Not only do the parallel figures of Elpenor and Leodes frame the sections in which they occur but the interior sections themselves display thematic correspondences, some of their common motifs having been discussed above. In a further link, I suggest that the *Odyssey* has organized the deaths and underworld visits of the two groups in another, overlapping ring sequence (see fig. 4). In terms of this figure we have been comparing the elements in and sequence of events of A1 and C2. Elpenor only exists in and immediately around A1. Leodes only exists in C2 and events serving as immediate prelude to it, both characters serving to frame these two episodes. In terms of the poem's overall structure, this pattern helps indicate parallels between Odysseus' consultation about the future with Kirke after having returned from Hades, and his recognition scene, and subsequent consultation about the future with Penelope, after having slain the suitors.

   The *Odyssey:* Structure, Narration, and Meaning

A1: The crew go to Hades (11.1–640, framed by Elpenor).
    B1: Odysseus consults with the powerful female, Kirke (12.33–141).
        C1: All of the crew perish, losing their homecoming (12.403–19).
            D. Odysseus successfully achieves his homecoming.
            (= beginning and middle of Ithakan sequence)
        C2: All of the suitors perish (22.7–329, framed by Leodes).
    B2: Odysseus consults with the powerful female, Penelope (23.166–365).
A2: The suitors go to Hades (24.1–204).
Fig. 4

Mediators between Their Comrades and Death

Why would Homer choose such characters to frame the crew's descent to the underworld and the slaying of the suitors? Both characters serve to mediate between their respective bands and certain aspects of the afterlife. Both, in terms of their depiction and function in the poem, are closely involved with sacrifice and prophecy, though given their different circumstances, the poem suggests this common ground through highly different means. Leodes is a θυοσκόος (21.145), a diviner, who inspects sacrificial victims.[30] He thus has a natural and close relationship with death, and, in a sense, can be seen as regularly mediating between the suitors and death. It is also possible that a grim irony is to be found in his role as θυοσκόος. As evident in the ring structure which he initiates, he, in some respects, leads the suitors into death and, as the last to be slain, closes the door on the whole episode.

Elpenor, though holding no such office, also mediates, in a certain sense, between the living and the dead. He is the first named member of the crew to die; the others see him dead. He is the first figure Odysseus encounters in the underworld, a figure whom Odysseus saw alive only a short time earlier. He dictates the specifics of his own burial as no other character in the *Odyssey* does (11.71–78). He not only dictates the particulars but persuades Odysseus to agree to bury him as specified. Part of his persuasion rests on his own threat to remain active "from the other world," as τι θεῶν μήνιμα, "a cause of divine wrath" (11.73). No other member of the crew is figured as having these connections with the afterlife.

Both characters, in a further parallel indicative of their connection with the afterlife, correctly prophesy the future. Elpenor, in the dialogue in Hades, embeds in his request for Odysseus to bury him a declaration about where Odysseus will go next: "for I know how, having gone from here, out of the house of Hades, / you will direct your well-built ship to the island, Aiaia," οἶδα γὰρ ὡς ἐνθένδε κιὼν δόμου ἐξ Ἀΐδαο / νῆσον ἐς Αἰαίην σχήσεις εὐεργέα νῆα (11.69–70). Kirke, in her earlier instructions on how to reach the underworld and consult Teiresias, had said nothing about a return to her island. Elpenor thus first tells Odysseus, and the poem's audience, the next stage of the voyage, an unexpected return to Aiaia.[31] Leodes twice prophesies correctly about future events, both including references to his own death. When he fails in his attempt to string the bow, he in effect prophesies death for many of the suitors: "for this bow will sunder many of the princes / from heart and soul," πολλοὺς γὰρ τόδε τόξον ἀριστῆας κεκαδήσει / θυμοῦ καὶ ψυχῆς (21.153–54). He is unique among the suitors in this respect. On a similar note of despair, when he supplicates Odysseus on the grounds that he did not take part in the suitors' excesses, he concludes by predicting his own death: "But I was their diviner, though having done nothing / I will lie down [dead], since there is no gratitude afterward for good deeds," αὐτὰρ ἐγὼ μετὰ τοῖσι θυοσκόος οὐδὲν ἐοργὼς / κείσομαι, ὡς οὐκ ἔστι χάρις μετόπισθ᾽ εὐεργέων (22.318–19).

Both characters exist in the poem primarily to die and to lead or link other members of their groups to death and the underworld. While all of both groups, crew and suitors, die, several other characters developed as individuals, Eurymakhos, Antinoös, Amphinomos, and Amphimedon, among the suitors, and Eurylokhos and Perimedes, among the crew, have considerable interaction with Odysseus, Penelope, or Telemakhos, and are not primarily concerned with death. Elpenor's passing is the poem's only instance of a named crewman whose death is described.[32] The others die namelessly whether in large groups (as at Ismaros or Thrinakia), or in smaller numbers (as the six men lost each to Polyphemos and Skylla), again underscoring Elpenor's unique ties to death.

We have observed that Elpenor and Leodes share a considerable number of distinct features absent from any other characters in the *Odyssey*. That they do is corollary to the fact that the suitors and crew share several overarching tendencies in their relationships with Odysseus. We should thus expect some individual members within those bands to parallel each other, as do Eurylokhos and Eurymakhos, rebellious leaders of each group. At the opposite end of the spectrum, Elpenor and Leodes stand out as the least heroic members of each group. They are distinguished by their excessive consumption of alcohol in a poem which, in its thematic emphasis on the disasters resulting from ἀτασθαλίαι, "culpable recklessness" (e.g., 1.7, 1.34, 22.417), takes a highly critical view of humans' lack of self-control. They are characterized by a strong sense of desire, desire incongruous with their own actions, behavior, or merit. They stand apart within their respective groups, not taking part in activities, whether rightly or wrongly. They are closely involved with death in a number of respects, and serve as intermediaries of sorts, conduits between their own respective bands and the dead. They are used to frame the beginnings and endings of two large, thematically related episodes involving the crew and the suitors in a place of death, the descent to underworld, and the slayings in Odysseus' palace. As unheroic characters they both fittingly die unheroic deaths, Elpenor drunkenly falling and breaking his neck, Leodes decapitated by Odysseus.

Leodes, or Odysseus' treatment of him, has been thought by some to serve as a foil for Phemios, the singer, and Medon,[33] the herald, who also supplicate Odysseus and are spared (22.330–77). While there may be some truth to this, since the episode is immediately adjacent to Leodes' slaying (22.326–29), the differences between Leodes, on the one hand, and Phemios and Medon, on the other, strike me as so considerable as to suggest the boundary constituting a larger seam in the plot rather than a foil relationship between characters. Leodes is a willing member of the suitors' party; the others are present only under compulsion. The one marks the end of the bloodshed in the palace, the others perhaps signal the new restoration of order. In slaying Leodes Odysseus acts as warrior and avenging husband; in sparing Phemios and Medon, as king. No one intercedes on behalf of Leodes, and his supplication of Odysseus is unsuccessful, whereas Telemakhos firmly intervenes on behalf of Phemios and Medon, both of whom successfully supplicate Odysseus and Telemakhos.

If Elpenor and Leodes are multiforms of the same essential character, why is this same figure absent from the Skherian sequence, given that the Phaiakian athletes serve as the band of abusive young men parallel to the crew and suitors? The absence of such a figure serves to indicate some of the differences in the modality and function of that portion of the *Odyssey*. As suggested in chapter 1, the Skherian sequence is the most "civilized" of the three sequences. Odysseus encounters no threatening monsters there, no physical violence. The brief flare-up between Euryalos, Laodamas, and Odysseus (8.132–240) remains only a verbal confrontation with no real danger of escalation. Euryalos himself makes amends, offering, at Alkinoös' suggestion, a fine sword to Odysseus, and apologizing for the brief confrontation (8.396–415). In all respects the Phaiakian youths are the most orderly of the three bands of young men. The civilizing tendencies of that sequence thus greatly lessen the likelihood that a character so closely tied to intoxication, so lacking in self-control, could exist, a significant violation of the decorum that otherwise prevails on Skheria. Inasmuch as Arete is married, and Alkinoös is alive and well, there is no possibility that one of the young men would center his being upon desire for the queen, as Leodes does Penelope, though this possibility is present with regard to Nausikaa. The orderliness of Phaiakian society would also seem to rule out the existence of an idler and misfit, as we see in Elpenor and Leodes. The Skherian sequence further demonstrates that the Phaiakians have more open relations with the gods than do other mortals (7.201–5). They are perhaps as a consequence less in need of the kind of mediation with "the other world" with which this figure is concerned.

The Phaiakian athletes are also on stage for a shorter amount of time than the crew or suitors, their interaction with Odysseus far more limited. They are not under his command, as are the crew, nor his subjects, as are the suitors; nor have they violated his property, as have both other groups. They have the singular position, within the poem, of having offended a deity, Poseidon, who is himself hostile to Odysseus. The crew offend Helios, who is essentially neutral regarding Odysseus, as he did not violate the cattle. The suitors offend Athene, who is closely identified with Odysseus' interests throughout the poem.

The death of the Phaiakian athletes is also handled far differently, quite mysteriously. We are there in present time for the slaying of the suitors. In the case of the crew, we receive Odysseus' authoritative, eyewitness account of when, why, and how they perished. As for the Phaiakian athletes, however, we have only the description of the ship's petrifaction:

> and the Earthshaker came up close to her,
> and turned her into stone and rooted her there to the bottom
> with a flat stroke of his hand.
>
> (13.162–64)

The actual deaths of those on board, though a necessary consequence of the ships' transformation into stone,[34] are not actually described. Such lack of specificity or anonymity is thematic through the Skherian sequence as the actual identity of the crew is similarly never specified, though the narrative pattern clearly demonstrates that they must be the athletes, the rude Euryalos, in particular. As their deaths are not explicitly depicted, and as they, unlike the crew or suitors, are wholly unaware that their death is imminent (they having done less to deserve to die), there is less need for the mediating function of an Elpenor/Leodes figure to frame and act as conduit for their passing.

The demonstrated multiformity of Elpenor and Leodes has further implications for appreciating the composition and structure of the *Odyssey*. It lends further and more particular support to Lord's observations that the structure of Homeric epic is essentially thematic.[35] As such we should expect repetition not only of scenes and sequences but of characters filling parallel roles within those scenes. The poem presents us not only with overall parallels between the two bands, the crew and suitors, but offers individual parallels in figures representing the two extremes of behavior within the two bands. In Eurylokhos and Eurymakhos (with Antinoös as co-leader) we have those individuals occupying the most violent and disruptive pole of behavior, those who lead aggressive rebellions against Odysseus. In Elpenor and Leodes we are given the opposite pole, the passive, least heroic dreamer of the group, who nonetheless serves to connect each band with the underworld through significant means.

It has been commonplace, particularly in analyst criticism, to view Elpenor as a late addition to the poem, inserted by a different composer, or as a character whose earlier function has been considerably modified until it obtained its present form.[36] However, Leodes' close replication of all of Elpenor's defining characteristics argues against Elpenor's being a late intrusion of any kind. The two characters are used in so many parallel ways that both are best seen as belonging to a common structure or deeper fabric of the poem than has been usually thought, at least in the case of Elpenor. There is no doubt that Elpenor's positioning in the poem is the result of considerable planning and organization by the composer, that he does serve as a link between different elements of the *Nekuia*, but the same is true of Leodes as he serves to involve and frame the different elements of the slaying of the suitors. If Lord and Fenik are correct in their basic assumptions about the thematic nature of Homeric composition, then there is more to be gained by treating Elpenor not as a unique and isolated occurrence in the *Odyssey*, as has usually been the case, but to recognize that the functions he serves have a thematic parallel in the character of Leodes. Perhaps the tendency to view Elpenor as completely unique has arisen from the tendency to treat the entire *Nekuia* as an alien entity violently thrust into the Apologue. But again, if Lord and Fenik are correct in their arguments on the thematic nature of Homeric composition, as I think they are, then the kind of piecemeal, ad hoc argumentation which Elpenor has usually attracted is inconsistent with what is demonstrably true of the structure of poems such as the *Odyssey*, and may obscure more than it reveals.

❧❧❧

CHAPTER THREE

Eumaios and Alkinoös

The Audience and the Odyssey

The *Odyssey* has provoked many studies of its self-consciousness, how it is aware of itself as a poetic product.[1] As is increasingly recognized, the *Odyssey* is often concerned with what Doherty calls "the reflexive quality of the work—what might be called its attention to its own reception" (1991: 146). That is, the *Odyssey* is well aware of its own relation to the greater context and continuum of poetry. Odysseus himself appropriates the language and gestures of the epic singer, functioning as an internal narrator within the greater narrative. But the interrelationships between Odysseus and Odyssean poetic performance are deep and complicated. In addition to his own poetlike performances, he evidences a firm understanding of broader poetic contexts and conventions by showing concern for the performance of other poets, entering into reciprocal relationships with both Demodokos and Phemios.[2] Odysseus is depicted as being quite conscious of how poetry will serve to bestow fame upon his deeds, attach them to a continuum. As Odysseus to some extent suggests parallels between himself and the internal poet, Phaiakian Demodokos, so the principal narrator himself identifies himself with Odysseus and vice versa. Necessarily, if an internal narrator, such as Odysseus, parallels not only certain tendencies of the principal narrator and poetic conventions greater than the poem itself, so some of the internal audiences depicted in the poem suggest parallels and connections with external audiences, even ourselves.[3]

In the *Odyssey*, telling and hearing narratives is part of guest reception. The hospitable host provides both the environment as well as the specific impetus for most of the tale telling. Most characters who function as hosts serve as audiences. Those characters not functioning as hosts, such as Eurykleia, may not serve as audience. The *Odyssey*'s hosts come in considerable variety, from deity (Aiolos) to fabulous king (Alkinoös) to lowly but loyal servant (Eumaios). All of these hosts serve as audiences for narratives from their guests, though the *Odyssey*, with its considerable ability to bestow variety upon like elements, handles each setting quite distinctly. Of Odysseus' performance for Aiolos, embedded within the Apologue itself, we are told only that it was lengthy and concerned both events at Troy and the Akhaians' homecoming (10.14–16), but the *Odyssey* does not pass on the actual narrative to us. The longest and most well known internal narratives are Odysseus' narration of his wanderings, delivered to the Phaiakians (bks. 9–12), and those the disguised Odysseus and Eumaios exchange with each other (14.192–359, 462–506, 15.390–484), all given to us in full.[4] All of these contexts are extended treatments of hospitality, in which an exchange of narratives is an element in the type-scene.[5]

For each internal narration there is also an internal audiece. Among the many internal audiences figured in the *Odyssey*, Eumaios and Alkinoös stand out in their degree of interaction with Odysseus and in prompting narratives from him. Notwithstanding their manifold differences, Eumaios and Alkinoös are multiforms of the same essential figure, both serving parallel functions in their distinct sections of the poem, the Ithakan and Skherian sequences, respectively.[6] Both characters are closely concerned with the act of narrative itself, serving to trigger lengthy narratives from Odysseus and acting as internal audiences for those narratives. Even more specifically, both describe and comment on his powers of narration as do no other characters in the poem. Isolating the similar functions of Eumaios and Alkinoös clarifies some of the parallels between the Skherian and Ithakan sequences, as well as bringing into relief some key differences in the Aiaian sequence, as it lacks any parallel for this figure. It is Eumaios' role as internal audience which results in the narrator's frequent and unique (in the *Odyssey*) apostrophes to him.

The reciprocal relationship between guest and host has much in common with the necessary reciprocity between performer and audience. The audience, like the host, can interrogate the performer and, due to its numbers and economic clout, may exert considerable influence over the performance occasion. We, the present audience of Homeric epic, are also its hosts. We welcome it into our lives, ask it where it came from, who its parents were (τίς πόθεν εἰς ἀνδρῶν; πόθι τοι πόλις ἠδὲ τοκῆες), and the like. For an archaic audience contemporary with the poem the possible parallels between hospitable reception of a guest and audience reception of a performance would have been more obvious. Though we must be utterly unlike any audience envisioned by the oral tradition, the parallelism nevertheless remains operative. Implicitly, Eumaios and Alkinoös, as both internal, critical audiences and hospitable hosts, suggest such a connection and offer possible models of mediation between Homeric epic and its (later) audiences.[7]

There is a considerable body of recent literature distinguishing between various audiences that the existence of a text presupposes: implied audience, actual historical and contemporary audience, later audience, ideal audience.[8] Doherty has written extensively on these issues in Homeric epic, in conjunction with analysis of some of the *Odyssey*'s internal audiences. Iser defines implied reader as follows:

> The implied reader . . . embodies all those predispositions necessary for a literary work to exercise its effect—predispositions laid down, not by an empirical outside reality, but by the text itself. Consequently, the implied reader as a concept has his roots firmly planted in the structure of the text; he is a construct in no way to be identified with any real reader . . . . [T]he concept of the implied reader is a transcendental model which makes it possible for the structured effects of literary texts to be described. It denotes the role of the reader, which is definable in terms of textual structure and structured acts.[9]

Whatever our conjectures may be as to the composition of an archaic epic audience, I suggest that the depictions of the internal audiences, Alkinoös and Eumaios, are closer to the concept of implied reader than they are to any actual historical audience, archaic or contemporary. Additionally, they are, in many ways, ideal audiences, in their almost boundless appreciation of narrative and their acquaintance with epic conventions.

Eumaios has only recently become a focus of critical study.[10] Though he has been dismissed as unimportant or even a flaw in the poem,[11] the length of narrative which he occupies suggests that he is a character of some importance, if we agree with the observations of Fenik and Edwards, that the length of a narrative unit correlates with its importance in Homeric epic.[12] His function in the overall architectonics of the *Odyssey* deserves closer attention. In terms of the extended narrative pattern he is one of the two multiforms of a figure who serves as a conduit between Odysseus and the respective powerful female figures, Penelope on Ithaka and Arete in the Skherian sequence. In each sequence, Odysseus first establishes a bond with this male host, winning him over. The link having been established between Odysseus and Alkinoös/Eumaios, he can proceed to the more complex negotiations necessary to enable him to win the confidence of Arete/Penelope. In both sequences the figure serves as a significant internal audience for lengthy narratives by Odysseus. In addition to his connection with the act of narrative Eumaios also serves to foreground the distinct modality of the second half of the poem.[13] He is above all a figure of mediation on a number of levels, suggesting parallels not only with the audience but with Odysseus and the principal narrator.

Eumaios and Alkinoös as Multiforms of the Same Essential Figure

Before noting how Eumaios and Alkinoös act as internal audiences, the network of extensive, if subtle, parallels they share, suggesting that they are multiforms of the same essential character in their separate sequences, should first be considered.[14] Many different structural schemes simultaneously inform the shape of the *Odyssey*.[15] The clearest such division is into halves: books 1–12 depict Odysseus absent from Ithaka, while book 13.187 through book 24 chronicle events after he has returned. In such a bipartite scheme Alkinoös and Eumaios occupy ring compositional positions. Though consecutive hosts, Alkinoös is Odysseus's last host[16] before reaching Ithaka, Eumaios his first after returning. As such each embodies the very different modalities of the two halves of the poem, and of their respective sequences. Alkinoös is the last in a series of impressive, high-status, often exotic hosts populating books 5–12, from Aiolos to Kirke, from Kalypso to the Phaiakians themselves. The second half of the *Odyssey*, however, shifts its focus decidedly, pausing at length in the humble cottage of a swineherd and continuing to observe affairs through the eyes of what appears to be a wandering beggar. In this sense Eumaios embodies and foregrounds the modality of the second half of the poem, relatively down to earth compared with books 5–12, while Alkinoös does the first: exotic, inaccessible locales, non-Greek peoples, and so on.

As hosts, both Eumaios and Alkinoös participate in that most productive of type-scenes in the *Odyssey*, reception of a guest/stranger.[17] However, they share qualities absent from most of the other hosts depicted in the *Odyssey*.[18] We noted in chapter 1 that all three of the narrative pattern's sequences are organized around Odysseus's parallel approaches to the three powerful females, Kirke, Arete, and Penelope. These three figures control access to the next phase of Odysseus's homecoming, he being able to proceed further only after reaching agreement with each of them. In the Skherian and Ithakan sequences centered around Arete and Penelope, Alkinoös and Eumaios serve as initial hosts for Odysseus. The hero has extensive dealings with these male hosts in each case establishing verbal contracts of sorts, before reaching agreement with the powerful females. Alkinoös and Eumaios thus function as intermediary figures, with whom Odysseus first establishes a relationship before forming contracts with the (structurally) more important powerful women.[19]

Both male hosts are closely attached to the powerful females, resulting naturally in intermediation for them. Alkinoös is joined to Arete both by marriage and blood relation, Eumaios to Penelope, by long service and having been raised as a virtual member of Odysseus' family.[20] Hankey observes that "Eumaios has a definite role in the action of the second half of the *Odyssey:* unknowingly he helps facilitate the meetings of Odysseus with both his son and wife, and also the entry of Odysseus into his palace" (27).[21] The climax of this intermediary function occurs when Eumaios places the bow in Odysseus's hands (21.379).

Less noticed has been Alkinoös' similar function.[22] When Odysseus, according to the instructions of both Nausikaa (6.310) and the disguised Athene (7.53, 75–77), supplicates Arete, she makes no reply (7.146–52). Instead Alkinoös takes the leading role in responding, and later that same night wishes that Odysseus would become his son-in-law (7.311–13). Through winning Alkinoös over to his side Odysseus now has a firm foothold in the palace and is an accepted presence, from which status he will more easily be able to reach Arete.

Though Alkinoös and Eumaios occupy wildly different strata in Homeric society, the one a king and the other a swineherd, their original status is identical: both are royalty by birth. Alkinoös inherits the throne from his father (6.7–12, 7.63–66), while Eumaios' father, Ktesios, is a king (15.413), making Eumaios a prince by birth and, presumably, inheritor of his father's throne.

Their native lands are both paradises. While Skheria's paradisiacal qualities are well known, Syria, Eumaios' birthplace, is implicitly a paradise as well, as he describes it to Odysseus:

> No hunger ever comes on these people, nor any other
> hateful sickness, of such as befall wretched humanity;
> but when the generations of men grow old in the city,
> Apollo of the silver bow, and Artemis with him,
> comes with a visitation of painless arrows, and kills them.
>
> (15.407–11)

The painless human existence, fruitfulness of the earth, and comfortable life free from disease are typical topoi of paradise.[23] Though both are natives of paradise, Alkinoös remains in his, whereas Eumaios's life has been severely disrupted, suggesting a greater breadth of experience.[24]

Both figures display almost familial relations with Odysseus and both have the possibility of being involved in marriages in which Odysseus himself closely figures. Alkinoös displaces his son, Laodamas, to offer

Odysseus the honored seat at the banquet (7.170–71).[25] Shortly thereafter he offers Odysseus Nausikaa's hand (7.311 ff). Eumaios, from his earlier relations with Odysseus's family, regards himself virtually as one of the family.[26] After his abduction from Syria, Antikleia raised him together with Ktimene, Odysseus's sister, being "only a little less favored" by her than Ktimene, thus having a status similar to a younger brother of Odysseus.[27] The narrator later compares Eumaios' warm reception of Telemakhos to a father, absent for ten years, receiving a son (16.17–21).[28] Odysseus, when disclosing his identity to Eumaios and eliciting his aid against the suitors, declares that he will adopt him into his family, regarding him as Telemakhos' brother (21.213–16), and will provide the swineherd with a wife— a thematic parallel to his own potential son-in-law status with Alkinoös. Again, Eumaios and Alkinoös are unique among Odysseus' hosts in this detail.[29]

Though each of their receptions of Odysseus begins with a contretemps, the two hosts' hospitality is nonetheless of a high caliber.[30] When Odysseus reaches Alkinoös' palace, he supplicates Arete, but an awkward silence follows. Only after Ekheneos admonishes Alkinoös (7.159–60) does the king respond and properly receive him. After this awkward start Alkinoös commits a few additional gaffes,[31] though largely revealing himself a sensitive host who goes to extravagant lengths to entertain his guest.[32] Eumaios enters the narrative by rescuing Odysseus from his dogs, immediately interceding on the stranger's behalf (14.32–33).[33] Provoked into action, Eumaios offers no embarrassing pause as did Alkinoös. Having saved the stranger from harm, he prepares a meal for him, and continues to offer model hospitality.[34] Though he has far less to offer, Eumaios outdoes Alkinoös, offering more exemplary hospitality.[35] It is worth emphasizing that Eumaios is unique in the poem as a servant host. None of Odysseus' (or Telemakhos') other hosts are of such low status. His position as host thrusts Eumaios into a more important role in the poem than other servants such as Eurykleia or Philoitios, who, lacking the occasion to serve as Odysseus' host, do not serve as audiences.

Eumaios and Alkinoös as Audiences

While serving as his hosts both Alkinoös and Eumaios elicit lengthy narratives from Odysseus.[36] Each asks him to give an account of himself (8.548–86, 14.185–90), Odysseus responding with substantial tales to both. In the Apologue his two long speeches punctuated by the Intermezzo (11.333–84) are the longest unbroken narratives in Homer, while his answer to Eumaios (14.192–359) is one of the longest speeches in the *Odyssey*.[37] Both accounts are ostensibly autobiographical, books 9 through 12 comprising the actual heroic deeds of Odysseus, while the account given Eumaios constitutes the more mundane and realistic but, ironically, fictional vicissitudes of a Cretan who also fought at Troy. The two narratives offer some parallels, both in content and context.[38]

Odysseus delivers both narratives with particular objectives in mind as to his immediate audience.[39] G. Most suggests that the separate episodes in the Apologue underscore the central point, "Let me go home now,"[40] arguing that the Apologue is intended to encourage the Phaiakians to send Odysseus home. Odysseus's fictitious biographical narrative to Eumaios is best interpreted, however, as intended to win pity and forge common ground between guest and host.[41] To this end commentators have suggested that Odysseus patterns this yarn on his own prior knowledge of Eumaios' biography.[42] Though Eumaios' account is given later (15.403–84), it would already be known to Odysseus, given the length of time in which Eumaios has been in his family's employ. Both narratives are thus designed to help secure Odysseus' homecoming, the Apologue by convincing the Phaiakians that their guest does not want to stay, the fictive biography to Eumaios by securing Odysseus' temporary status with the swineherd.[43]

Having served as audiences for his narratives, both hosts remark on Odysseus' storytelling abilities. Alkinoös suggests his narrative powers inspire wonder in his audience: "but go on telling your wonderful story," σὺ δέ μοι λέγε θέσκελα ἔργα (11.374).[44] Eumaios also describes Odysseus's narrative powers as charmlike (θέλγε, 14.387), repeating the depiction to Penelope (θέλγοιτο, 17.514, ἔθελγε, 17.521).

More specifically, both hosts compare Odysseus to a singer. Eumaios does so in his report to Penelope:

> But as when a man looks to a singer, who has been given
> from the gods the skill with which he sings for delight of mortals,
> and they are impassioned and strain to hear it when he sings to them,
> so he enchanted me in the halls as he sat beside me.
>
> (17.518–21)[45]

In the Intermezzo Alkinoös compares Odysseus's storytelling ability to that of a singer:

> You have a grace upon your words and there is sound sense within them,
> and expertly, as a singer would do, you have told the story
> of the dismal sorrows befallen yourself and all of the Argives.
>
> (11.367–69)[46]

Eumaios and Alkinoös are the only characters in Homer to make this comparison,[47] their observations underscoring their roles as internal audiences. Also suggesting Eumaios' capacity as audience are Odysseus' remarks on the environment for narrative performance:

> I only wish there were food enough for the time, for us two,
> and sweet wine for us here inside the shelter, so that
> we could feast quietly while others tended the work.
>
> (14.193–95)

Such a description, while containing generic elements of the setting for telling tales, suggests as well the circumstances and audience of the raconteur's previous outing on Skheria.[48] Just as lines 14.193–95 are a brief preamble to his extended narrative to Eumaios, so Odysseus' parallel comments as to a more ideal setting, at 9.5–11, are the preamble to the Apologue requested by Alkinoös:[49]

> . . . for I think there is no occasion accomplished that is more pleasant
> than when festivity holds sway among all the populace,
> and the feasters up and down the houses are sitting in order
> and listening to the singer, and beside them the tables are loaded
> with bread and meats, and from the mixing bowl the wine steward
> draws the wine and carries it about and fills the cups. This
> seems to my own mind to be the best of occasions.

Both contexts thus offer not only the extended narratives but parallel introductory comments on the ideal settings for performance. That Odysseus himself utters both descriptions of the performance setting is yet another instance of how he parallels the principal narrator both in his knowledge of and concern for the requirements of narrative.

Alkinoös and Eumaios both use the same otherwise unique expression to note the large amount of time Odysseus's narratives pleasantly occupy, νὺξ ἀθέσφατος, "a night which has no limits."[50] In the Intermezzo, as he would coax his guest into saying more about the descent into Hades, Alkinoös notes, "Here is a night that is very long, it is endless," νὺξ δ' ἥδε μάλα μακρὴ ἀθέσφατος (11.373). In response to Odysseus' request for his own story, Eumaios observes, as prelude, "these nights are endless," αἵδε δὲ νύκτες ἀθέσφατοι (15.392). The two passages are the only instances in all of Homer and Hesiod where ἀθέσφατος modifies νύξ.[51] As Ford notes, ἀθέσφατος "refers to things that are beyond mortal articulation or exhaustive definition" (183). A night that has no limits is necessary both to convey both the limitless range of experience in the narratives and to accommodate the potential enjoyment of the audience.[52]

In the same contexts Alkinoös and Eumaios make parallel observations to the effect that there is a time for sleeping and there is a time for listening, the implication being that the exchange of narratives, on these occasions, takes priority over sleep.[53] Alkinoös again makes his remark during the Intermezzo: "It is not time yet / to sleep in the palace. But go on telling your wonderful story. / I myself could hold out until the bright dawn" (11.373–75). Eumaios makes a parallel observation as prelude to his own lengthy autobiographical narrative:

> These nights are endless, and a man can sleep through them,
> or he can enjoy listening to stories, and you have no need
> to go to bed before it is time. Too much sleep is only a bore.
>
> (15.392–94)

The comparisons underscore both hosts' pleasure in serving as audiences and, in Eumaios' case, in the exchange of narratives.

Both hosts refer to Odysseus's narratives by the same term, "your sufferings," σὰ κήδεα (11.376, 14.185).[54] Alkinoös makes his remark already having heard much of the Apologue, whereas Eumaios anticipates that such will constitute his guest's story. The term suggests that both are sympathetic audiences, and in the case of Eumaios its use is part of the process Odysseus goes through in establishing a common bond with him.

To both audiences Odysseus implies that he deserves gifts for his narrative performance. On Skheria he does so through his own prior example. Hearing two songs by Demodokos, with Alkinoös also in attendance, Odysseus rewards the bard with a choice cut of meat while requesting the subject matter of his next song (8.474–98). As Odysseus himself will shortly be compared by his host to a talented singer, so he too will deserve conspicuous gifts (Doherty 1991: 147). However, Odysseus's narrative does not bring immediate results from Eumaios, who insists that some of it is a lie (14.363 ff).[55] He does respond, however, to the range of experience in the tale, closely paralleling his own life story. In this sense the tale is a key part of the process of building a bond of camaraderie between the two men, evident in Eumaios's initial response: "O sorrowful stranger, truly you have troubled the spirit in me, / by telling me all these details, how you suffered and wandered" (14.361–62). After Odysseus's second, shorter tale about the cloak at Troy (14.468–502), Eumaios agrees to see to it that Telemakhos will give the stranger a new cloak. This narrative is part of a specific reciprocity between guest and host. On a higher narrative level, there is a similar reciprocity between Odysseus and the epic narrator. It is rather startling to note that in this narrative (14.468–502) the protagonists are Odysseus' temporary beggar persona as well as the real Odysseus. For the duration of this performance Odysseus again closely resembles the principal narrator, who describes both the heroic Odysseus as well as the "beggar" before Eumaios.

The Audience of the Odyssey

As a complement to delivering narratives, Odysseus also *hears* significant narratives in both settings. Before reciting his Apologue, he is part of the audience for Demodokos' three songs which occupy much of the eighth book. His observing the Phaiakians as audiences for the three songs helps establish them as a receptive audience and might help to shape Odysseus's own narrative, inasmuch as he knows they are aware of his Trojan exploits. Further, Odysseus actively engages Demodokos in a dialogue on his art (8.474–99). As already noted, Odysseus hears Eumaios's autobiographical narrative which closely parallels his own fictional biography in many ways.[56] As a swineherd, Eumaios lacks the luxury of having his own singer, but himself serves the role filled by Demodokos on Skheria, to perform before Odysseus as audience.[57] As Odysseus had commented on Demodokos' narratives, so he briefly remarks on Eumaios' storytelling, emphasizing his ability to move his audience: "Eumaios, you have deeply stirred the spirit within me by telling me all these things, the sorrows your heart has suffered" (15.486–87).

Both sequences proceed at a leisurely pace, Odysseus staying longer than expected or necessary, partly as a result of the embedded narratives. In fact, he spends roughly the same amount of time with both hosts.[58] Each host arranges for that which the guest most desires: to proceed to the next phase of his homecoming. Alkinoös, after Odysseus has persuaded Arete that he is her guest (11.338), arranges the escort by sea, while Eumaios personally escorts Odysseus to the palace (16.201). As noted above, each is a conduit to the powerful females, Arete and Penelope, more central to Odysseus's homecoming than are these hosts.[59] Eumaios speaks with Penelope concerning his guest, provoking her desire to interview him (17.507–50).

Against these similarities, however, Eumaios and Alkinoös differ to such a degree as to hinder recognition of their many parallels. Beyond their differences in status, Alkinoös is hurt by his association with Odysseus, when the escort ship and its crew are petrified on its return to Skheria. Eumaios, however, will prosper as a result, Odysseus promising him a wife, a house next to his own, and more (21.214–16). Such divergences underscore the differences between the two halves of the poem. Odysseus appears down and out to Eumaios, but is not. He is wearing rags, appears bald, old, and run-down, while his fabulous gifts from the Phaiakians are safely hidden. On Skheria he does not appear down and out to Alkinoös, but is. Having nothing, he wears, nonetheless, palace clothing. Alkinoös is thus impressed by the appearance of a man who has nothing, whereas Eumaios is skeptical of a man with countless riches stowed nearby.

How do we interpret the observed parallels and demonstrated multiformity between Eumaios and Alkinoös? Some of the broader parallels exist as generic components in hospitality type-scenes. However, several details relating to narrative—the νὺξ ἀθέσφατος ("a night which has no limits") remarks, the comparisons of Odysseus to a singer, the comments on listening to stories as preferable to sleep—are absent from all other hospitality scenes. This figure of the host who provokes narratives may have some bearing on larger issues of performance and audience.

That Eumaios and Alkinoös function as audiences within hospitality scenes[60] suggests that the *Odyssey* associates the production and reception of narrative with hospitality. Our own word, *reception,* is appropriate both of an audience and of hospitality. The *Odyssey* makes the parallelism clear, that guest reception can be a metaphorical equivalent of reception of a narrative, in the name of the Phaiakian singer, Δημόδοκος, a compound of δῆμος and δέχεσθαι, "received by the people."[61] Archaic Greek thus uses δέχεσθαι to express both forms of reception.[62] The audience is the singer's host, then and now, and demands narrative from him, whether as listeners or readers.

I suggest that Eumaios and Alkinoös are contrasting models of an internal audience, and that, as such, they imply different connections with audiences external to the poem. We noted above that both have associations with paradise. In the case of Alkinoös, commentators have noted many parallels between Skheria and the paradisaic afterlife, Elysium.[63] Because of their paradisiac associations the Phaiakians function as a timeless, idealized audience. We first see this in Odysseus' experience as audience to Demodokos, hearing his own exploits made famous. As Murnaghan notes, Odysseus "experiences the reward that heroes die for but do not themselves normally experience: he witnesses and participates in the transmission of his own fame" (153). That Odysseus as audience is able to hear his heroic exploits being made immortal suggests an underworld or Elysian environment.[64]

Alkinoös and the Phaiakians are a privileged audience in many ways.

For Alkinoös, whose inquiry prompts the Apologue,[65] Odysseus can step off the canvas, so to speak, as a previously known epic entity, and deliver a privileged account. As does no one else in the poem, except Penelope, the Phaiakians hear from the hero's own lips the central matter of the poem itself.[66] Demodokos, the Phaiakian singer, also in the audience, gets privileged exposure to his craft. His own songs about Odysseus had referred only to Trojan exploits. There is no suggestion that he (or Phemios) is already aware of any of the deeds Odysseus will relate in the Apologue. Odysseus' narration of his exploits to an audience which includes a gifted singer thus depicts the tradition in action. That is, this is the *Odyssey*'s only portrayal of a singer being informed in his craft, hearing new instances of the subject matter of epic poetry. The motif of "the singer looks at his source," wherein a bard observes the epic protagonist at firsthand, also occurs in *Beowulf*,[67] and the *Odyssey* may implicitly offer a second instance of the motif in Odysseus' interview with Phemios (22.330–56). As the Phaiakians receive the fullest most privileged account, they are closer to the hero himself and less like us than other internal audiences. Their privileged status is evident in other ways. Alkinoös notes their special relations with the gods (7.201–6), again suggestive of paradise or a golden age environment. Yet they will never again enjoy such intimate narrative interaction, since Poseidon prevents any further access to Skheria (13.125–65),[68] and Odysseus is never represented as giving a full-scale reiteration of his exploits.[69]

Nagy (1974 and 1979) and others have suggested that a central subject and goal of Archaic Greek epic is to ensure κλέος ἄφθιτον, "imperishable fame," for its respective protagonist. Imperishable fame requires a continuum of audience; the audience, too, must somehow be eternal if this goal is to be met. I suggest that Alkinoös paradisiac associations depict him as an eternal, almost Platonic ideal of an epic audience: isolated, almost outside of the human time-continuum, yet eagerly appreciative of good narrative, indulgent, and more than generous to a narrator.

Eumaios is also a native of a paradise, and while he retains connections with that origin he occupies a more mundane human habitat. S. West notes common elements in the description of Elysium, Alkinoös' gardens, and Eumaios' Syria (1988: 227). There is even an implicit connection with the underworld, or Elysium, in his father's name, Κτήσιος, a name with recognized underworld/afterlife associations (Mühlestein 184). As Eumaios was abducted, however, his paradisiac associations are far less immediate, as is his connection with royalty, also sundered.

Eumaios is a much more intimate audience than Alkinoös. He is not as easily representative of a people as king Alkinoös. Odysseus and Eumaios exchange their narratives face to face without the backdrop of a large royal entourage. As an audience of one for Odysseus' stories,[70] he is more like a modern individual *reading* audience than is the typical internal audience in its aristocratic megaron setting. He is a more critical audience than Alkinoös, as well. There is considerable irony in the fact that Alkinoös more easily accepts the fantastic events of the Apologue than Eumaios will accept as truth the disguised Odysseus' claim that Odysseus will soon return.[71] Though Alkinoös is the sophisticate, Eumaios shows considerable, if unexpected, sophistication.

Eumaios, the Principal Narrator, and Odysseus

Both Odysseus and the principal narrator treat Eumaios with special care.[72] Odysseus spends more time with him than his low status would lead us to expect; his almost familial relation with Odysseus has already been noted. While the protagonist exhibits such close ties to Eumaios, so does the principal narrator: Eumaios is the only figure in the *Odyssey* addressed through apostrophe.[73] Block has argued that the three main apostrophized figures in Homeric epic, Menelaos, Patroklos, and Eumaios, function as special characters, more sympathetic antitheses of Agamemnon, Akhilleus, and Odysseus, respectively.[74] I suggest that a further antithesis exists, that as Odysseus is the principal internal narrator in the *Odyssey*, the use of the apostrophe helps designate Eumaios as a significant internal audience.

A recent study suggests significant patterns in the use and positioning of the name Eumaios.[75] Only the narrator and members of Odysseus' immediate family address Eumaios by his proper name, while other characters address him generically as συβῶτα, "swineherd." Such restricted use of the name suggests an affinity between the narrator and those characters sympathetic to Eumaios (Kahane 111). The same study argues that the three different metrical positions available for proper-name vocatives, verse initial, internal, and terminal, carry different semantic values. Verse initial is a default mode, and semantically neutral. The terminal position, on the other hand, is in several ways to be associated with an address to the epic protagonists. The internal position, however, that used for all thirteen apostrophes to Eumaios, is the mode "by which special attention to the addressee is revealed" (Kahane 107).

Kahane notes that the unelided form, Εὔμαιε, "is suitable for terminal positioning and can be adapted for initial positioning. However, it is in fact used internally in all twenty-six attestations" (111). Such patterned avoidance of the other two possible positions argues for careful design in the deployment of the apostrophes to Eumaios. Kahane reiterates his conclusion that the internal proper-name vocatives, including all of the narrator's apostrophes to Eumaios, reflect "the narrator's sympathetic attitude towards particular characters" (113). Concluding his argument, Kahane suggests that "Homer pays due attention to characters that are closest in disposition to most of his audience/readers" (113). Though Kahane does not touch on the issue of internal audiences, his findings offer support for viewing Eumaios in this light. For an oral, listening audience, the apostrophes would have a considerably greater impact than for our reading audience. The bard would appear to address his listeners, individually. I suggest that the bard's direct address to Eumaios embodies direct address to the external audience in performance.

The various interactions between Eumaios and Odysseus parallel other possible interactions between the bard and external audiences. This is especially evident in the mixture of fiction, nonfiction, credible, and incredible in the narratives Odysseus and Eumaios exchange. As commentators have noted, Eumaios appears to believe all of the lies in Odysseus' alleged autobiographical account (14.192–359), but not the one element of truth, the prediction that Odysseus will soon return. Though many take this as a joke at Eumaios' expense,[76] a more complex interaction may be taking place. Odysseus' inability to convince the swineherd provides some subtle comedy at Odysseus' own expense—even a bard poking fun at himself.

Contrary to a perhaps expected naïveté in the swineherd, Eumaios displays firm independence as he resists Odysseus' opening strategy. Building, perchance, on Eumaios' expressed longing for him (14.144), the beggar swears an oath that Odysseus will soon return. Not accepting a claim made under oath, Eumaios has good reasons for suspicion, as he relates how others have come by with similar tales later exposed as lies (14.378 ff.). Ironically, Odysseus' own ingenuity undoes him. He claims to have been a comrade-at-arms to Idomeneus, a detail assumed to be credible.[77] However, Eumaios notes that an earlier visitor had claimed a connection with Idomeneus (14.382), a story later found to be false, and thus for Eumaios a detail suggesting dishonesty.

Declaring that Eumaios is quite suspicious (14.391), Odysseus again attempts to maneuver him verbally, by a ῥήτρη, a verbal agreement or bargain, with his life as the stake. If his prediction of Odysseus' return proves false, Eumaios can throw him over a cliff (393–400). Eumaios, however, will not agree to the terms (14.402–6), again outmaneuvering Odysseus, since were he to fulfill it he would clearly violate basic tenets of hospitality.[78] Recalling that Hermes endowed Autolykos in oaths (19.395 ff.),[79] and how easily Odysseus forces Kalypso into a binding oath (5.177 ff.), we might conclude that it is no easy thing thus to evade Odysseus.[80] Nonetheless, Eumaios outwits Odysseus in just this matter. By so doing he thematically parallels and foreshadows Penelope's initial incredulity and outwitting of her husband in her ruse of the bed (23.174–204).[81]

In his second narrative to Eumaios, Odysseus meets with greater success, obtaining the promise of a cloak. Once again, however, Eumaios appears to be a step ahead of him. Recognizing the brief tale as an αἶνος (14.508), a narrative whose aim is to praise or be ingratiating toward a person,[82] and complimenting Odysseus on its formulation, Eumaios agrees that he should receive a cloak, but only when Telemakhos returns. As αἶνος occurs only here in the *Odyssey*,[83] and as Eumaios critiques each of Odysseus' narratives with what are almost technical terms (14.363: τά γ'οὐ κατὰ κόσμον, 14.509: οὐδέ τί πω παρὰ μοῖραν),[84] the composer appears to be painting Eumaios as a highly experienced and informed audience. Doherty notes of his comments to Penelope on Odysseus' bardic ability, that Eumaios "has obviously attended enough epic performances to make him something of a connoisseur" (1995: 72).

Eumaios, by his own admission, is entertained and moved by his guest's narratives, but in neither instance is the protagonist able to achieve his rather modest goals: belief by his audience that Odysseus is returning and immediate receipt of a cloak. As a traditional tale, much of the *Odyssey*'s overall plot is predictable. Nonetheless, within specific episodes considerable room remains for unexpected outcomes. What Odysseus as narrator most expects to accomplish is Eumaios' agreement to his prediction, and the quick receipt of a garment. As such the situation suggests a performance dilemma facing a bard: his audience's response is not always as he expects; they may not accept what he assumes they will most easily accept. Such a narrative dilemma is elsewhere explored in the poem. When Polyphemos notes that "Nobody is killing me by force or treachery" (9.408), his immediate audience does not understand his own intended meaning.

Eumaios, the more immediate audience, is more critical, his responses harder to predict than the less critical, but more timeless, Alkinoös. Though they differ, there is considerable overlap between the two as well. There are no apostrophes to Alkinoös, but there are eight proper name vocatives, perhaps the closest device. Significantly, Odysseus, the internal narrator, delivers six of these eight, three of them falling in and around the Apologue.[85] We suggested that by apostrophe the bard speaks not only to Eumaios, but through him to the external audience, whether an archaic, listening, or twentieth-century reading audience. We, like Eumaios, are the present hosts of Odysseus. That the principal narrator paints Eumaios (like Alkinoös) as once royalty, once in paradise, may serve as implicit praise of the external audience.

There are further ties between Eumaios, Odysseus, and the narrator, some of a socioeconomic nature. Within the class structure of the *Odyssey*, a singer and Eumaios have roughly the same status,[86] as does Odysseus, in some respects. The three are perceived as craftsmen. In his first scene Eumaios is fashioning himself a pair of sandals (14.23–24), even after the narrator has credited him with fashioning the enclosure housing the swine.[87] Odysseus is seen first fashioning a raft, and the climax of his recognition scene with Penelope hinges on the revelation of his construction of their marriage bed. The connection between metaphors for Greek poetry and various forms of construction is well known.[88] Consequently, as there is implicit identification between Homer and Odysseus, so may there be between Homer and Eumaios.

Eumaios further parallels Odysseus in being an only son.[89] Austin notes the rhythm, even homophrosyne that develop between swineherd and guest (7, 203–4). Farron suggests that Eumaios can be seen as Odysseus's alter ego (89). In Eumaios' account the serving woman who delivers him into slavery describes him as κερδαλέον (15.451), a word closely associated with Odysseus.[90] As Eumaios straddles several worlds, from royal birth to rural servitude to reintegration into the palace, so does Odysseus.[91] Though a king he displays talents and occupations associated with the lower classes.[92]

We will never know the composition of the audience in and for which Homeric epic evolved. The importance of Eumaios as an internal audience suggests, however, that we may have too monolithic a conception of the aristocratic megaron setting as most typical of the performance arena of Homeric epic. The detailed descriptions of Alkinoös' palace on the one hand, and of Eumaios' circumstances and activities on the other, underline the tremendous class difference that separates the two most central internal audiences in the poem and the settings in which those narratives are performed. The poem as a whole, unless we restrict our view to the Apologue and the brief poetic performances noted in passing in books 1–4, includes among its own depictions of epic conventions Eumaios, a type of audience that must also figure among the external audiences relevant to Archaic Greek epic. Despite his low economic status he is depicted as an audience having virtually a connoisseur's appreciation of epic conventions. He is singled out by the principal narrator as the sole recipient of apostrophe, a consequence of his function as internal audience. Both gestures indicate the inclusion of lower-class people among the intended audience of the poem.

One further passage exhibits all the tendencies we have noted in Eumaios. In his first words after escorting Odysseus to the palace, Eumaios denies Antinoös' charge that he invited the apparent beggar to the palace. He notes instead the type of ξεῖνοι (17.382) who are invited:

> . . . one who works for the people, either
> a prophet, or a healer of sickness, or a skilled workman,
> or inspired singer, one who can give delight by his singing.
> (17.383–85)

Eumaios, an internal audience, has escorted something of a singer to the palace, and duly gives him his due, time and again, much as we, the present audience of the poem and of its protagonist, do. As Eustathius suspects that Homer is *philodysseus*,[93] so I suggest, is he *phileumaios*.

Absence of the Same Figure in the Aiaian Sequence

If Eumaios and Alkinoös, their individual differences notwithstanding, parallel each other in so many respects, why is this figure absent from the Aiaian sequence? What does it suggest about differences between the Aiaian and other sequences, if no counterpart to Eumaios/Alkinoös is present on Aiaia? We have especially considered the functions Eumaios and Alkinoös have of eliciting narratives from Odysseus, and serving as audience for them. Both the Skherian and Ithakan sequences focus on and are considerably intrigued with the particulars of poetic performance. It is highly significant that most of the poem's key discussions of epic poetry take place in the presence of these two characters. As a consequence of their function of provoking internal narratives, discussions about poetry naturally arise around them. While the Skherian and Ithakan sequences are highly concerned with poetry in some self-conscious ways, the Aiaian sequence, however, *is* poetic performance. It is itself an internal narrative, a poetic performance Odysseus gives to Alkinoös and fellow Phaiakians. Consequently, there is less occasion within it for some of the self-conscious meditation about poetry which occurs in the other two contexts.[94] Moreover, it would be redundant to have yet another layer within Odysseus' extended internal narrative to the Phaiakians.[95] It is for this reason, I suggest, that we are not given Odysseus' internal narrative to Aiolos (10.14–16), just the brief reference to its having occurred. In the Sirens the Aiaian sequence does contain an episode devoted to poetry, or the enchanting powers of narrative. However, their function is more like that of Demodokos, if on a divine plane. They offer to sing narratives about Odysseus, not prompt narrative from him.

Were a counterpart to Eumaios/Alkinoös present, the crew's position and function would be problematic. We noted in chapter 2 that the crew's feasting in Kirke's palace parallels the suitors' situation on Ithaka. Both would seem to be appropriate, typical settings for epic recitation as well. Neither is, however. The crew themselves, unlike Odysseus' other audiences, the Phaiakians and Eumaios, have been everywhere with Odysseus. Would they then be a suitable audience, already knowing everything Odysseus might narrate? They would also necessarily be present from time to time as actors in whatever narratives Odysseus would relate. Though Odysseus is simultaneously present as an audience for narratives in which he is featured (8.73–83, 8.499–520), he is the hero of the epic. It would be quite otherwise for the *Odyssey* to offer the same treatment of the crew. Their counterpart, the suitors, are themselves a significantly flawed epic audience in that they compel the singer Phemios to be present and sing, another aspect of their violation of hospitality.[96] The Phaiakian athletes, however, apparently included in the audience for the Apologue (8.35–42, 55–56, 96–119, 421–22) and behaving themselves for its performance, do not share this trait, again articulating that the Skherian sequence is the most civilized of the three sequences.

The absence of a Eumaios/Alkinoös counterpart also helps underscore how Kirke and her isle differ from her counterparts Arete and Penelope, and their respective locales. As a powerful, formidable goddess Kirke has no need for any of the figure's various functions. Kirke has her own divine, female servants (10.348–51), and thus has no need of the masculine figure who, in Alkinoös, escorts Arete, and in Eumaios, attends Penelope's needs. Thus the figure's masculine gender would partly rule out his presence on Aiaia, exclusively inhabited by immortal females in Kirke and her divine attendants. Kirke would also present problems as a potential audience. As a goddess she would be an audience quite unlike any on Ithaka or Skheria, a being with considerably greater awareness than any mortal. She prophesies much of Odysseus' own future career, and has considerable knowledge of his past (10.330–32). She is thus perhaps too knowledgeable to serve as an appropriate audience for his narratives. She would, we assume, be capable of performing narratives herself, much like the Sirens. Odysseus' only divine audience for his narratives is Aiolos (10.14–16), himself the closest equivalent to Eumaios in the Aiaian sequence. He is a host, and a considerate one (10.14–26), as are Eumaios and Alkinoös. Indirectly, by way of the Laistrygones, he does help escort Odysseus, through his gift of the bag of winds, to the relevant powerful female, Kirke. It is perhaps significant, however, that Odysseus tells us only the generic nature of what he told Aiolos, "everything of Ilion and the ships of the Argives, and the Achaians' homecoming" (10.14–15),[97] thus avoiding, as noted above, the intricacy of having a narrative within a narrative within a narrative. The Aiaian sequence is the most otherworldly, most mythical, most heroic of the three sequences. Odysseus, though receiving Hermes' advice (as he does that of Athene in the other two sequences), must approach Kirke alone, without the help of the conduit figure. His absence, in comparison, can be seen as a further element of the isolation and otherworldiness of Kirke's abode.

CHAPTER FOUR

The Economy of Divine Antagonism, πλάζω, and the Proem

Two areas have long been problematic in secondary literature on the *Odyssey:* the poem's three divine wraths and the coherence of the opening proem. The two topics intersect, in that many commentators have criticized the proem for alleged obscurity in singling out the wrath of Helios as the only episode highlighted.[1] The differences in the divine wraths, especially what is seen as extreme behavior in Poseidon, have also attracted criticism, provoking analyst arguments, still at least partly adhered to, of inconsistencies in the poem's handling of divine wraths, or evidence for historically separate layers of composition.[2] For those not necessarily swayed by analyst views, serious flaws in the poem's divine economy are thought to be present in the wraths, which work against, if not completely rupturing, so go the arguments, the theodicy Zeus implies (1.32–43). I address these concerns by applying the constants of the narrative pattern, those typical elements repeated in the pattern's three sequences, and paying particular attention to the significant differences visible therein. I argue, against the positions referred to above,[3] that the *Odyssey* does maintain a coherent divine economy and that the differences in the separate wraths and the structure of the proem become more intelligible when considered through the lens of the narrative pattern. In particular, since the narrative pattern and the proem both assign pivotal importance to divine interdictions, any interpretation of the poem's structure and, more specifically, interpretations of the role of the subsequent divine wraths needs to address the centrality of this motif. When the three divine wraths are placed in a broader context, they can be seen to belong to a subgenre of myth in which an angered deity threatens apocalyptic disaster but is talked into exacting severe but more local destruction, the "one just man" surviving. Examples will be adduced from other archaic Greek poetry, as well as from *Gilgamesh* and the Bible.[4]

According to our analysis of the narrative pattern, the depictions of the divine wraths feature several corresponding details. We can sum these up most easily by omitting those elements of the pattern having to do with arrival and access to the powerful female figures, focusing, in effect, on the second half of the pattern: *Conflict arises between Odysseus and the band of young men. The young men abuse Odysseus in various ways and violate a divine interdiction. The leader of each band has the parallel name of Eury___. The band's consequent death, earlier prophesied, is demanded by a wrathful god. A divine consultation limits the extent of the death and destruction.* While the narrative pattern suggests that these core elements are constants, we now address the significant differences from sequence to sequence. The three wrathful gods, Helios, Poseidon, and Athene, all differ in the nature of their relationships with Zeus, have very different relationships with the bands of young men against which they direct their wrath and punishment, and have considerably different relationships with Odysseus. These differences, I suggest, account for most of the perceived inconsistencies in the poem's depiction of divine wraths. However, as the three factors just noted are not constant and the three gods themselves display different characteristics or personalities,[5] commentators should not expect exactly the same responses in each deity. It is worth emphasizing that in the Aiaian and Skherian sequences the violation of the divine interdiction and subsequent punishment by the wrathful god form the climax of the sequence. In the Ithakan sequence this same point (bk. 22) is instead followed by the full coming to terms with the powerful female figure, the lengthy recognition scene in book 23.

The Odyssey *and the Apocalyptic Narrative*

We can better appreciate the underlying dynamics at work in the narrative pattern's depiction of divine wraths by noting some other ancient myths which hinge on the same motifs. The Bible offers a relevant *comparandum* in the Lot narrative's account of the destruction of Sodom and Gomorrah, which, like the Ithakan sequence, is a theoxeny, and, like the Skherian sequence, contains petrifaction as a consequence for violating a divine interdiction. The Lot narrative (Genesis 19) and each of the narrative pattern's three sequences depict a wrathful god destroying an entire community of men who have offended him, but saving the one just man in their midst. *Gilgamesh*, in the divine council between Ishtar and Anu (VI iii–iv), features a consultation quite parallel to that which concludes each of the three sequences (*The band's consequent death, earlier prophesied, is demanded by a wrathful god. A divine consultation limits the extent of the death and destruction.*). When Gilgamesh rejects Ishtar's offer to be her lover, she becomes enraged, and, going up to heaven, meets with her father, the sky god, Anu. She demands that he give her the reins of the Bull of Heaven, or else,

> I shall set my face towards the infernal regions,
> I shall raise up the dead, and they will eat the living,
> I shall make the dead outnumber the living.[6]

Anu expresses concern that the Bull will threaten to destroy the entire city of Uruk. Ishtar counters that the city has enough grain stored up to prevent the Bull's impact from being so devastating. She then directs the Bull to Uruk, where it kills four hundred people, until Gilgamesh and Enkidu slay it.

Though the episode fulfills other purposes in *Gilgamesh* than do the divine consultations in the *Odyssey*'s narrative pattern, it is composed of largely the same elements. We can recognize Ishtar as the offended deity, Anu as parallel to Zeus, the more powerful deity who ensures that the more devastating of her threats will not be enacted, settling on the less threatening of her two angry wishes. Furthermore, we recognize in her threat of greater destruction a close parallel to Helios' threat to go down and shine in Hades (12.382–83). I suggest, then, that the second half of the narrative pattern, together with the Lot narrative and the *Gilgamesh* divine council, may be seen as a subgenre of apocalyptic narrative, depicting a "local" or partly contained version of the destruction of an entire race. A brief comparison with these Near Eastern texts can help clarify some of the present issues by placing them in a broader, well-recognized context.

However, before an investigation of both topics, divine wraths and the *Odyssey*'s proem, it is helpful to consider in some detail a key, single word in the proem, the verb πλάζω. This verb, though little discussed, is a crucial index of divine disfavor in the *Odyssey*, its use providing valuable evidence of Poseidon's behavior in particular and in the shifting fortunes of some noteworthy mortals, especially Odysseus and, to a lesser extent, the bands of abusive young men. The verb is one of the *Odyssey*'s most significant markers for indicating the target of divine hostility. In its broadest sense πλάζω depicts a mortal buffeted, or driven, by the elements, especially the sea and storm winds. In the poem's world, however, those elements are personified most concretely in Poseidon. The motif of a deity punishing Greeks for offenses they have committed against the god(s), by raising a storm against them as they attempt to return home by sea, is thematic throughout the *Odyssey*.[7] In its dramatic foregrounding of the verb's patterned behavior, we find considerable evidence that the proem coherently sketches out the poem that follows.

The verb first occurs in a highly conspicuous position, strongly enjambed in the poem's second line, Ἄνδρα μοι ἔννεπε, Μοῦσα, πολύτροπον, ὃς μάλα πολλὰ / πλάγχθη, "Tell me, Muse, of the many of many ways who / was driven." Though the positioning is surely designed for emphasis,[8] little has been said of πλάζω, either of this instance (perhaps reflecting the problematic reception of the proem) or of its occurrences elsewhere in the poem, though the verb tends to appear in highly significant contexts. As I will show, the verb, as well as its compounded and nominalized derivatives, is a significant part of the vocabulary expressing divine hostility. In the *Odyssey*, in particular, πλάζω participates in a very specific pattern of behavior,[9] generally being used to depict a god's wrath visited upon a mortal who has committed offense. Though used of several different deities and mortals in the *Odyssey*, πλάζω centrally articulates the nature of Poseidon's relationship to Odysseus. Moreover, the verb exhibits what Watkins calls the "memorative" function found in certain key words in traditional poetry: "In epic as in myth, part of the function of the root *g^when-* in Greek is 'memorative': a form of πεφνέμεν functions as a *summation*, recalling to the mind of the epic audience what it knows already. This feature is . . . the Homeric equivalent of the Pindaric 'shortcut', the οἶμος βραχύς."[10] I suggest that πλάζω has precisely this function in the *Odyssey*. It is shorthand for the poem's key instance of a god's antagonism against a mortal, that of Poseidon against Odysseus. One way or another, most other instances of the verb thematically invoke that same, or a closely parallel, dynamic.

Πλάζω as Used of the Disguised Odysseus

Before considering πλάζω in the proem, we first need to gain a better sense of the types of contexts in which the *Odyssey* tends to employ this verb and of its dynamics and function in those contexts. The verb's last occurrence in the poem conforms to its dominant pattern of behavior. When Odysseus tests his father, in the last of his Cretan lies, he accounts for his presence on Ithaka as follows:

ἀλλά με δαίμων
πλάγξ᾽ ἀπὸ Σικανίης δεῦρ᾽ ἐλθέμεν οὐκ ἐθέλοντα.

but a god
<u>drove</u> me here from Sikania, though I didn't want to come.

(24.306–7)

By the verb's dominant pattern I mean (a) it occurs line initial;[11] (b) a deity is the subject or agent;[12] (c) Odysseus is the victim;[13] (d) it implies crossing the ocean with difficulty.[14] All four conditions are met in this passage: the line-initial position; a deity, in δαίμων, is ascribed agency; Odysseus uses it of himself; and ἐλθέμεν οὐκ ἐθέλοντα implies a difficult or inopportune sea crossing, much as Odysseus is subject to in the Apologue. As such, the passage, though fictive, suggests experiences analogous to a capsule summary of Odysseus' actual experiences, as we shall see.

The verb, in fact, is thematic in Odysseus' Cretan lies, as he uses it also to Athene (13.278) and Penelope (19.187) with parallel force. To the disguised Athene, Odysseus claims to have killed a man, then taken passage on a Phoenician ship headed for Pylos or Elis (13.276–78):

> ἀλλ' ἦ τοί σφεας κεῖθεν ἀπώσατο ἲς ἀνέμοιο
> πόλλ' ἀεκαζομένους, οὐδ' ἤθελον ἐξαπατῆσαι.
> κεῖθεν δὲ <u>πλαγχθέντες</u> ἱκάνομεν ἐνθάδε νυκτός.

> But truly the force of the wind pushed them away from those places
> quite against their will, nor did they wish to deceive me.
> <u>Having been driven</u> from those places, we came here at night.

Lacking only the line-initial positioning, the verb otherwise fully conforms to the dominant pattern, if we accept that in a traditional culture as depicted in myth the strong winds must be the working of a god, even if not named. We also note an important distinction in its grammatical voice: πλάζω and compounds occur in the passive when expressing the mortal's perspective, but are used in the active voice when a deity is the subject.[15]

To Penelope the disguised Odysseus elaborates a lengthy account of how he once entertained Odysseus, whose presence on Crete he thus explains:

> καὶ γὰρ τὸν Κρήτηνδε κατήγαγεν ἲς ἀνέμοιο,
> ἱέμενον Τροίηνδε <u>παραπλάγξασα</u> Μαλειῶν·

> For the force of the wind led him down into Crete,
> <u>having driven</u> him from Maleia as he was heading for Troy.

(19.186–87)

Again the verb conforms (though compounded forms are metrically unsuited to line-initial position), if we accept the implicit connection between storm winds and divine agency. In all three lies storms at sea force lengthy detours, a form of πλάζω serving to articulate Odysseus' considerable difficulty in crossing the sea. In the reference to Maleia, which functions as a boundary in the poem, and the particular compound of πλάζω used (παρα-), the passage shares significant common ground with a pivotal passage in the Apologue (9.79–81), discussed at length below. So much for how the verb figures in the Cretan lies.

Eumaios and Alkinoös, whose considerable parallels were noted in chapter 3, both use πλάζω of Odysseus. In each instance their use of the verb is in keeping with their function as internal audiences, and it parallels how πλάζω figures in the proem. In irony typical of the poem, Eumaios, in his first words to the disguised Odysseus, uses the verb to depict his presumably *absent* master's condition:

> . . . αὐτὰρ κεῖνος ἐελδόμενός που ἐδωδῆς
> <u>πλάζετ</u>' ἐπ' ἀλλοθρόων ἀνδρῶν δῆμόν τε πόλιν τε.

> . . . But he [Odysseus], in need of finding some sustenance,
> <u>is driven</u> to some city or countryside of alien-speaking people.

(14.42–43)

Eumaios articulates his perhaps lost master's condition with πλάζω, the verb again conforming to its dominant behavior, line initial, a sea crossing and difficult circumstances implied. While no divine agency is noted, Eumaios hints at such in his previous comment, καὶ δέ μοι ἄλλα θεοὶ δόσαν ἄλγεά τε στοναχάς τε (14.39), "but the gods have given me other pains and sorrows," that is, they are to blame for his absence.[16]

Πλάζω *and Its Prooimial Associations*

When he later answers Telemakhos' query about the disguised Odysseus' presence, Eumaios again repeats the verb, but now using it of his mysterious guest:

> ἐκ μὲν Κρητάων γένος εὔχεται εὐρειάων
> φησὶ δὲ πολλὰ βροτῶν ἐπὶ ἄστεα δινηθῆναι
> <u>πλαζόμενος</u>· ὣς γάρ οἱ ἐπέκλωσεν τά γε δαίμων.

He claims by birth to be from spacious Crete
but says he has been whirled to many cities of mortals,
<u>driven</u>. For so the divinity spun his thread for him.

(16.62–64)

Again the verb behaves precisely as we have noted, with an additional frequent tendency: it is strongly enjambed.[17] The line-initial enjambment serves to emphasize the force of the verb, its responsibility for causing "Odysseus" problems. In using πλάζω, Eumaios is reacting to the narrative he heard from Odysseus, his lengthy lie (14.199–359), in which, though Odysseus did not use the verb, he painted a portrait of a man driven and harassed at sea by a violent, Zeus-sent, storm (14.301–9). The passage is in several ways reminiscent of the proem, featuring not only the parallel use of the two passives of πλάζω, πλάγχθη (1.2) and πλαζόμενος (16.64), both enjambed in line-initial position, but πολλὰ βροτῶν ἐπὶ ἄστεα (16.63) serves as a close parallel to πολλῶν δ᾽ ἀνθρώπων ἴδεν ἄστεα (1.3). The use of ἐπέκλωσεν (16.64), while conveying the expected divine agency latent in the verb's use, may also remind us of its occurrence at 1.17, in the transition out of the proem. Eumaios's use of the verb in this prooimial manner again underscores his own function as a key internal audience, particularly one who prompts narrative from Odysseus, and one to whom Odysseus' narratives have particular relevance, reminiscent of his own life. The verb here also has the memorative function mentioned earlier, serving to sum up Odysseus, even a disguised one, in a manner central to the poem and the tradition.

Eumaios' counterpart as significant internal audience, Alkinoös, who prompts the Apologue, the poem's most important internal narrative, also uses πλάζω with strong prooimial associations. At the end of book 8, after Odysseus has firmly resisted revealing his identity, Alkinoös, in the last speech before the Apologue, just as firmly presses him to disclose who he is and where he has been:

ἀλλ᾽ ἄγε μοι τόδε εἰπὲ καὶ ἀτρεκέως κατάλεξον,
ὅππη ἀπεπλάγχθης τε καὶ ἅς τινας ἵκεο χώρας
ἀνθρώπων, αὐτούς τε πόλιάς τ᾽ εὖ ναιεταούσας.

So come now tell me this and give me an accurate answer:
where you <u>were driven off your course</u>, what countries
of men you came to, the men themselves and their strong-founded cities.

(8.572–74)

This is the specific statement that prompts Odysseus' recitation of books 9 through 12, an epic within an epic. As such, we should not be surprised at the strong prooimial quality in lines 573–74, a passive of (a compounded form of) πλάζω, and references to peoples and cities to which Odysseus was driven. Again the πλάζω compound implies a sea crossing, and difficult circumstances. As for a deity responsible for his having been driven, Odysseus will shortly narrate the Polyphemos episode, and subsequent curse, which Poseidon effects, as well as the three storms which blow him off course (9.67–82, 10.47–55, 12.405–25).

Alkinoös reprises his role both as internal audience and as one who uses πλάζω with prooimial associations, in the very first words spoken after Odysseus finishes his lengthy narrative:

> ὦ Ὀδυσεῦ, ἐπεὶ ἵκευ ἐμὸν ποτὶ χαλκοβατὲς δῶ,
> ὑψερεφές, τώ σ' οὔ τι παλιμπλαγχθέντα γ' ὀΐω
> ἂψ ἀπονοστήσειν, εἰ καὶ μάλα πολλὰ πέπονθας.

> Oh, Odysseus, since you have come to my palace, high roofed
> with bronze threshold, I think you will not lose your homecoming
> nor be driven back from it again, even though you have suffered very
> much.

$$(13.4-6)$$

As constituent elements parallel to the proem, we again have a passive form of πλάζω (13.5), and μάλα πολλὰ πέπονθας (13.6) calls to mind not only ὃς μάλα πολλὰ / πλάγχθη (1.1–2), but also πολλὰ . . . πάθεν ἄλγεα (1.4).[18] It is worth emphasizing that the last words spoken before and the first words uttered immediately after the Apologue are proemlike remarks centered on passive forms of πλάζω (8.573, 13.5). Or, in terms of our structural analysis, we can say that passive forms of πλάζω introduce and conclude the internal narrative which is the Aiaian sequence.

Πλάζω within the Apologue

Having considered how instances of πλάζω serve to trigger and conclude the Apologue, it is time to analyze relevant forms of the verb within that lengthy narrative. Though the occurrences are few, the contexts in which they appear are particularly significant. I have argued that the Apologue's first episode, the sack of Ismaros, is highly thematic, and paradigmatic for the entire Apologue, in terms of the crew's reckless and rebellious behavior. The episode has other thematic tendencies as well, for, as has often been noted,[19] this first episode unfolds, in real geography, all subsequent scenes of the Apologue occurring in fabulous settings. For our purposes it is the episode's immediate aftermath that proves particularly significant. Having left Ismaros, Odysseus and crew quickly make for the coast of Greece, headed for Ithaka, until a storm raised by Zeus drives them off course:

καί νύ κεν ἀσκηθὴς ἱκόμην ἐς πατρίδα γαῖαν
ἀλλά με κῦμα ῥόος τε περιγνάμτοντα Μάλειαν
καὶ Βορέης ἀπέωσε, παρέπλαγξεν δὲ Κυθήρων.

And now I would have come home unscathed to the land of my fathers,
but as I turned the hook of Maleia, the sea and current
and the North Wind beat me off course, and <u>drove me on past</u> Kythera.

(9.79–81)

The passage forms an important pivot in the plot in a number of re-spects.[20] In that the rest of books 9 through 12 unfold in never-never land, so to speak, it is worth emphasizing that the verb which, in effect, pushes Odysseus and crew off the map is παραπλάζω. It is this passage, largely neglected in Homeric criticism, which first signals the profound difficulties Odysseus will encounter in his homecoming. Divine agency is responsible, as Zeus is described (9.67) as having roused the hurricane-force storm (λαίλαπι θεσπεσίῃ). The passage forms a backdrop to the account the dis-guised Odysseus gives Penelope in a Cretan lie (19.186–87, which also has παραπλάζω and Maleia), discussed above. Furthermore, this articulation of his difficulties offers a specific answer to Alkinoös earlier question, ὅππῃ ἀπεπλάγχθης, "where you were driven off course" (8.573).

The storm is problematic in a number of respects. First, is it actually Zeus who raises the storm? We have no way of knowing, for by Jörgen-sen's law characters other than the principal narrator regularly ascribe phenomena to Zeus or generically to *theos* or *daimôn* if they lack specific knowledge of an event.[21] Elsewhere, in a relevant parallel, Odysseus is mis-taken in assigning Zeus responsibility for another storm (5.303–5), which the principal narrator has already revealed to be Poseidon's doing (5.291–94).[22] Second, and more important, *why* does Zeus (or some other god) raise this storm?

Though the *Odyssey* treats the matter gingerly, the extra-Homeric tra-dition suggests that another storm, one roused by Athene, occupied a similar position in other accounts of the return from Troy. Though late testimony, Quintus Smyrnaeus depicts Athene scattering the Greek fleet as it leaves Troy (14.419 ff, the climax of his poem), an event the *Odyssey* perhaps points to several times (1.326–7, 3.135 ff, 13.377 ff).[23] The *Odyssey*, through the testimony of no less an informant than Hermes, appears to allude directly to that storm, as he places Odysseus' troubled homecoming in a larger perspective:

ἀτὰρ ἐν νόστῳ Ἀθηναίην ἀλίτοντο.
ἥ σφιν ἐπῶρσ᾽ ἄνεμόν τε κακὸν καὶ κύματα μακρά.

but on the voyage home they offended Athene,
who let loose an evil tempest and tall waves against them.

(5.108–9)

Athene has multiple grounds for displeasure with the Greek cause, whether Aias' rape of Kassandra in her temple (alluded to at 4.502) or the theft of the Palladium by Odysseus and Diomedes (perhaps suggested in the *Doloneia*). It would be counter to much of the poem's overall trajectory, however, were Homer so to depict her in the *Odyssey*, given the close relationship between the goddess and the hero. In terms of the overall Archaic Greek epic tradition, we may have Zeus in place of Athene as the agent provoking the Apologue's first storm. However, that still leaves open the reason why a god would be offended by the events at Ismaros, unless, as before, the episode is modeled on other accounts of the departure from Troy.

We can address this more easily, initially, by considering why the composer would have a god-sent storm. We have noted the episode's potent thematic tendencies, to which we now add a further detail. This storm, the first in the Apologue, sets the tone for all subsequent (that is chronologically later) storms in the poem, including those in the Cretan lies. We recall that in the lie Odysseus tells Penelope he uses the same compound of πλάζω, and the same pivotal boundary of Maleia (παραπλάγξασα Μαλειῶν 19.187).[24] The composer thus makes use of this storm as part of a larger, thematically related chain of similar god-sent storms, the most important of which unfolds off Thrinakia, the poem's climactic storm of divine punishment, the one singled out by the proem, and forming the climax of the Aiaian sequence. On that occasion, it is Zeus, not Helios, the offended deity, who rouses a storm and destroys the crew. In terms of overall architectonics, then, the storm following the Ismaros episode thematically introduces that which will unfold at Thrinakia. However, at Thrinakia we have a clear chain of events, the crew's violation of a god's divine interdiction leading to his wrath and their punishment. Why does a deity take offense at events at Ismaros, other than to serve the composer's larger purpose in pointing ahead to the capping sequence on Thrinakia? The episode signals the profound centrality of self-control in the dynamics of the plot.[25] When the crew's pattern of rebellion begins at Ismaros, Odysseus narrates how after their initially successful sack of the city he urged a quick flight, but they refused, νήπιοι (9.44); this is the first time the plural has been used since the proem, which so designated the crew with regard to the mutinous events on Thrinakia (1.8). Instead, the crew insist on a lavish feast, "And there much wine was drunk, and they slaughtered / many sheep and lumbering horn-curved cattle by the shore" (9.45–46). The crew's lack of self-control is twofold. They will not obey Odysseus and their consumption is reckless, both tendencies to be reiterated on a larger scale at Thrinakia.

Two highly negative consequences result from their, not Odysseus', lack of self-control. The Kikones, having time to summon allies, counterattack, killing seventy-two men, all avoidable deaths to be blamed on the crew, supporting the proem's thematic assertion of their own recklessness as cause for their death. The tempest, immediately following, is best understood as a parallel action on the divine plane. The Kikones, mortals themselves, "punish" the crew, making them suffer for their mistake. An immortal, Zeus (?), punishes them as well, signaling divine displeasure, as do perhaps all storms in myth, punishment for their actions at Ismaros. Thus a pattern is established for the later storms and deaths at sea (including the nonstorm death of the Phaiakian crew and the stormy nondeath of Odysseus in the chronologically later tempest of bk. 5), conforming to and serving as illustration for his theodicy in book 1, that mortals bring sufferings upon themselves through their own actions. We will see a fuller instance of the same dynamic below in our analysis of why Zeus supports Poseidon's wrath against Odysseus.

Underscoring the storm's pivotal importance, Odysseus again mentions the same tempest shortly thereafter, in a context crucial to the dynamics and trajectory of the plot.[26] In his first words to Polyphemos, as he begins the encounter which will bring him into confrontation with Poseidon, Odysseus uses another πλάζω compound to articulate his difficulty in crossing the sea, accounting for his presence before his monstrous host:

Ἡμεῖς τοι Τροίηθεν ἀποπλαγχθέντες Ἀχαιοὶ
παντοίοις ἀνέμοισιν ὑπὲρ μέγα λαῖτμα θαλάσσης
οἴκαδε ἱέμενοι ἄλλην ὁδόν, ἄλλα κέλευθα,
ἤλθομεν· οὕτω που Ζεὺς ἤθελε μητίσασθαι.

We are Akhaians coming from Troy, <u>driven off our true course</u>
by winds from every direction across the great gulf of the open
sea, making for home, by the wrong way, on the wrong courses.
So we have come. So it has pleased Zeus to arrange it.

(9.259–62)

Odysseus describes his present difficulty in returning home with that verb,
ἀποπλαγθέντες, which most accurately articulates just how Polyphemos'
father, Poseidon, as a result of this very episode, will later be treating him.
Again, Odysseus' description can be seen to offer a specific answer to
Alkinoös' earlier question (8.573), ὅππη <u>ἀπεπλάγχθης</u>, "where you were
driven off course," repeating the same verb. Due to the complexity of the
Odyssey's construction, the layering of the three sequences, we have already
(in the present time of the poem) seen Poseidon, back in book 5, treating
Odysseus in just the manner this verb, πλάζω, articulates.

Before beginning a consideration of Poseidon himself, and of how
analysis of πλάζω may help clarify his relationship to Odysseus, let us turn
to one final related passage in the Apologue, the description of the storm
at Thrinakia, as it forms the climax to the whole Aiaian sequence. After
the crew reject the warnings against violating Helios' cattle and have their
profane feast (a parallel both to that described at Ismaros, the first stop,
and to the excessive consumption of the suitors on Ithaka), Zeus rouses a
deadly tempest as they depart. I quote the passage at length

αἶψα γὰρ ἦλθε
κεκληγὼς Ζέφυρος, μεγάλη σὺν λαίλαπι θύων,
ἱστοῦ δὲ προτόνους ἔρρηξ' ἀνέμοιο θύελλα
ἀμφοτέρους, ἱστὸς δ' ὀπίσω πέσεν, ὅπλα τε πάντα
εἰς ἄντλον κατέχυνθ'· ὁ δ' ἄρα πρύμνῃ ἐνὶ νηῒ
<u>πλῆξε</u> κυβερνήτεω κεφαλήν, σὺν δ' ὀστέ' ἄραξε
πάντ' ἄμυδις κεφαλῆς· ὁ δ' ἄρ' ἀρνευτῆρι ἐοικὼς
κάππεσ' ἀπ' ἰκριόφιν, λίπε δ' ὀστέα θυμὸς ἀγήνωρ.
Ζεὺς δ' ἄμυδις βρόντησε καὶ ἔμβαλε νηῒ κεραυνόν·
ἡ δ' ἐλελίχθη πᾶσα Διὸς <u>πληγεῖσα</u> κεραυνῷ,
ἐν δὲ θεείου πλῆτο· πέσον δ' ἐκ νηὸς ἑταῖροι.

. . . suddenly
a screaming West Wind came upon us, stormily blowing,
and the blast of the storm wind snapped both the forestays that were
    holding
the mast, and the mast went over backward, and all the running gear

collapsed in the wash; and at the stern of the ship the mast pole
<u>crashed down</u> on the steersman's head and pounded to pieces
all the bones of his head, so that he like a diver
dropped from the high deck, and the proud life left his bones there.
Zeus with thunder and lightning together crashed on our vessel,
and, <u>struck</u> by the thunderbolt of Zeus, she spun in a circle,
and all was full of brimstone. My men were thrown in the water.

(12.407–17)

The poem has carefully prepared for this moment, from the foregrounding in the proem (1.7–9), to the sequence of thematically related storms earlier in the Apologue. The protagonist, who has exercised self-control and piety in not violating Helios' cattle, is spared. The crew, led by Eurylokhos in failing to control themselves, or respect the gods, are all killed by a furious, god-sent storm. In essence the episode is an extensively developed account of what was presented in much smaller compass in and after Ismaros. Though the passage does not include a form of πλάζω, it twice uses forms of πλήσσω, a probable cognate,[27] to depict a wrathful god punishing mortals who have committed offense by raising a storm at sea.

Πλάζω and Poseidon

As we turn to Poseidon, and consider how πλάζω is used to articulate his relation to Odysseus and his participation in the dynamics we have explored elsewhere in the poem, it is worth noting initially how the *Odyssey* uses πλάζω and its compounds to depict the dangerous workings of the sea and other bodies of water. The Clashing Rocks, about which Kirke warns Odysseus, are from the same root, again partaking of the same line-initial positioning, Πλαγκτὰς δ'ἦ τοι τάς γε θεοὶ μάκαρες καλέουσι, "The blessed gods call these the Clashers"[28] (12.61). We note the emphatic, even double layer of divine workings in this derivative of πλάζω. Kirke, a goddess, warns Odysseus about the danger the *Plagktai* represent. The threatening rocks stand as a boundary through which mortals, in the post-Jason era, may not proceed. The gods themselves, in an ancient poetic device, have a special divine word for "The Clashers," consistent with the verb's tendency to mark boundaries or limits imposed by a deity.[29]

Προσπλάζω, occurring only twice in Homeric epic, is used exclusively to describe the surging action of water.[30] In the *Odyssey* it describes the working of the pool of water tormenting Tantalos:

καὶ μὴν Τάνταλον εἰσεῖδον χαλέπ᾽ ἄλγε᾽ ἔχοντα,
ἑσταότ᾽ ἐν λίμνῃ· ἡ δὲ <u>προσέπλαζε</u> γενείῳ.

And I saw Tantalos, suffering hard pains,
standing in lake water that <u>lapped against</u> his chin.

(11.582–83)

Though not describing a storm, προσπλάζω here, as the other instances of πλάζω and its compounds previously discussed, depicts the gods punishing a mortal who has committed offense. Tantalos is being punished for his outrageous actions, divine agency implicitly underlying the working of even this body of water.

Having observed how Homeric epic employs πλάζω for various aquatic settings, expressing an underlying divine impetus, we now consider the root's natural association with the most powerful relevant deity, Poseidon. Though Poseidon has great impact on the trajectory of the poem, his actual appearances are few, carefully positioned for maximum effect. The first Olympian mentioned by name (1.20), he dominates the poem's opening as much through his absence as through his relationship with Odysseus. Before the poem mentions either Athene or Zeus, book 1.20–26 is concerned with explaining Poseidon's absence. Though absent as well from the programmatic first divine council, Poseidon is one of its chief subjects, as Zeus explains his brother's wrath against Odysseus (1.68–79).

When Poseidon first appears in the poem, Odysseus is, fittingly, attempting to cross the ocean. It should be emphasized that this is, in fact, the only time in the *Odyssey* that the two characters are on stage together. As such, the poem's presentation of their encounter may be regarded as a definitive depiction of their relationship. Poseidon's first monologue makes clear that he is well aware that Odysseus' suffering will end when he reaches Skheria (5.288–89). Knowing that he may not kill Odysseus, the god rouses a tremendous storm to harass him (5.291–96). In a parallel to the storm at Thrinakia, the mast snaps off and Odysseus is thrown from his raft (5.315–18). In a brief respite, Leukothea approaches giving him advice and her veil. Poseidon, now stirring a great wave, shatters the hero's raft, leaving a parting threat, "There now, drift on the open sea, suffering much trouble" (5.377). Poseidon's interaction complete, the narrator notes Odysseus' predicament, vulnerable on the high sea:

Ἔνθα δύω νύκτας δύο τ᾽ ἤματα κύματι πηγῷ
<u>πλάζετο,</u> πολλὰ δέ οἱ κραδίη προτιόσσετ᾽ ὄλεθρον.

> Then for two nights and two days on the heavy sea
> <u>he was driven</u>, and many times his heart foresaw destruction.
>
> (5.388–89)

So Poseidon welcomes Odysseus to Skheria, the land of the Phaiakians, a people he favors. The passage conforms in every detail to the verb's observed pattern of behavior: divine impetus, difficult sea crossing affecting Odysseus' homecoming, line-initial positioning, and strong enjambment. More important, the passage constitutes a summary miniature of Poseidon's relationship with Odysseus, the one occasion in the *Odyssey* in which we see Poseidon acting against Odysseus in the manner in which he is thematically portrayed, as provoked by Polyphemos' curse (9.528–35). Consequently, I argue that this is the poem's core articulation of πλάζω, the other instances emanating out from it, echoing and paralleling it, as it were. The verb here has the memorative function argued earlier. In Watkins's formulation, this use of πλάζω "functions as a *summation*, recalling to the mind of the epic audience what it knows already" (472–73).

Though the encounter serves as a typical, if climactic, articulation of πλάζω, in other respects the overall depiction of Poseidon harassing Odysseus is quite unique within the larger context of the *Odyssey*'s depiction of wrathful deities punishing mortals.[31] But unlike the storm Zeus sends against the crew in book 12, or Poseidon punishing the Phaiakian crew in book 13, on this occasion an angry deity attacks a lone man, quite vulnerable on the open sea.[32] The reasons for Poseidon's wrath are unique within the larger context of the *Odyssey*'s portrayal of divine wraths. Unlike the crew on Thrinakia, the suitors on Ithaka, or the Phaiakian crew, Odysseus has not violated a divine interdiction, explicit or implicit. The deed to which Poseidon takes exception, moreover, the blinding of Polyphemos and its aftermath, took place some ten years earlier. The three bands of young men, and Aias Oïliades, all perish immediately after committing offenses against the gods.

Friedrich (1991) has offered perhaps the best analysis of the reasons behind Poseidon's wrath. After Odysseus and crew sail away from Polyphemos, returning to goat island, they sacrifice to Zeus, unable to win his favor: "but he [Zeus] was not moved by my offerings, / but still was pondering on a way how all my strong-benched / ships should be destroyed and all my eager companions" (9.553–55). Friedrich regards Odysseus' description as an exception to Jörgensen's law, arguing that "the overriding thematic concern here is to give emphatic expression to Zeus' attitude: his displeasure at Odysseus and his sanctioning of Poseidon's persecution of the hero."[33] Agreeing with Fenik that Odysseus' blinding of Polyphemos was justified, Friedrich rightly notes, however, that Poseidon is in some respects a different kind of god than Zeus. The Olympians are a pantheon, allowing for diversity in their individual reactions. It is therefore not inconsistent if Poseidon, an elemental force, who appears to be more vengeful by nature, reacts differently than Zeus. The real issue, then, is not why Poseidon is angry at Odysseus, but why Zeus *validates* the sea god's anger and persecution. What has Odysseus done that not only angered Poseidon but convinced Zeus that the sea god is correct in seeking to punish him? Does Zeus' attitude here violate his own position, programmatically put forward in the opening divine council (1.32–43)?

Friedrich locates Zeus' irritation in Odysseus' own excessive actions, or hubris. Persuasively dispensing with earlier claims that the hero acts excessively in seeking to gain guest-gifts from Polyphemos, Friedrich finds *asebia*, lack of due piety, in Odysseus' taunts, not in his boast of victory but in his claim to Polyphemos that "not even the Shaker of the Earth will ever heal your eye for you" (9.525). While Odysseus has good reasons for his boasting (it concludes his own heroic revenge on the monster who earlier humiliated him), he succumbs to the passion of his own *thumos*, not only bringing on Poseidon's wrath but prompting the temporary enmity of Zeus as well.

As at Ismaros, the episode, and the greater motif of Poseidon's wrath, serve the composer's larger purpose, one consistent with the punishment of the three bands of young men. This is one of the few occasions in the poem in which Odysseus loses his characteristic self-control,[34] that element which most distinguishes him from the three bands of young men, especially his crew and the suitors. In his victory over the suitors Odysseus restrains Eurykleia from boasting in triumph (22.407–9), raising the issue of piety (οὐκ ὁσίη: 22.412), and observing the gods' involvement in their deaths (22.413). In his victory over Polyphemos he shows no such restraint, for which he pays the price described in most of the remainder of the poem: the wrath of a powerful god, the ancillary wrath of the ruler of the cosmos. I thus argue that both wraths principally serve the composer's larger purpose, illustrating the divine punishments and rewards for mortals incapable or capable of self-control.

Additional unique tendencies give the book 5 encounter great force. This is the poem's only storm that occurs in the present (unlike those in the Apologue, Telemakhy, or Cretan lies), giving the episode an immediacy perhaps lacking in the other scenes of divine punishment. Odysseus, unlike Aias or the three bands of young men, survives the encounter, an out-

The *Odyssey:* Structure, Narration, and Meaning

come carefully prepared for in the numerous earlier emphases on his destined return home alive. His survival is an important sign that his offense against Poseidon is considerably less heinous than those committed by the three bands of young men, perhaps since no violation of a divine interdiction was involved. As further evidence of the individual manner the composer bestows upon this scene, of all the instances of πλάζω we have so far examined, this is the only one not spoken in character speech but used by the principal narrator himself (though we will note additional instances below). Last, Poseidon's confrontation with Odysseus serves to initiate the Skherian sequence, arguably this instance of πλάζω (5.389), forming the seam itself, which topic will be covered more fully in the following chapter.

Poseidon's only other appearance in the poem, his consultation with Zeus over how to punish the Phaiakians and subsequent carrying out of that punishment, forms the end of the Skherian sequence. His punishment, the petrifaction of the crew who had escorted Odysseus home, concludes his action in the poem (13.125–87),[35] though not without some residual effects, as we shall see. As Odysseus subsequently wakens, he steps into the Ithakan sequence of the narrative pattern: *Odysseus, as earlier prophesied, arrives at an island, disoriented and ignorant of his location.* Wondering where he is and what is to become of the gifts the Phaiakians gave him, he asks, πῇ δὲ καὶ αὐτὸς / πλάζομαι, "and where am I / to be driven now?" (13.203–4). Other than in lies, whether Cretan or other falsehoods having to do with a disguised Odysseus, this is the poem's last application of the verb to the real (as opposed to the disguised) Odysseus. Henceforth, the suitors become the poem's principal target of divine wrath. Unlike the other instances, πλάζω is here (13.204) used of a sea crossing that was difficult, but less so for Odysseus. The verb's pattern of behavior holds, however, referring here, no doubt, to his near miss with Poseidon, and the god's punishment of the Phaiakian crew a few lines previous, as Odysseus, disoriented from his last sea crossing and not yet realizing his whereabouts, wakens, having safely left Poseidon's wake.

Having observed the verb's highly thematic pattern of behavior, we are now in a position to consider the poem's first two articulations of πλάζω. In the opening divine council, programmatic for the rest of the poem, when Athene wonders why Odysseus has not yet returned to Ithaka, Zeus assigns responsibility to Poseidon, angered over the blinding of Polyphemos:

ἐκ τοῦ δὴ Ὀδυσῆα Ποσειδάων ἐνοσίχθων
οὔ τι κατακτείνει, πλάζει δ' ἀπὸ πατρίδος αἴης.

For his [Polyphemos'] sake Poseidon, shaker of the earth, although he
   does not
kill Odysseus, yet <u>drives him</u> back from the land of his fathers.

                                        (1.74–75)

Zeus' formulation, informed by his unique position of authority, accurately describes Poseidon's interaction with Odysseus, both in the internally narrated retrospective account of the blinding of Polyphemos and in
the present-time account given by the principal narrator in book 5. Zeus'
enunciation of the god's relation to the hero through πλάζω in this programmatic depiction of Poseidon's behavior is highly authoritative for the
plot as a whole. Zeus uses an active form of πλάζω, conforming to the
tendency noted above by which active forms depict the punishing deity in
action.

When πλάζω first occurs in the poem's second line, in emphatic, line-
initial, enjambed position, it takes part in and *initiates* the very specific
pattern of behavior we have noted throughout the poem,

> Ἄνδρα μοι ἔννεπε, Μοῦσα, πολύτροπον, ὃς μάλα πολλὰ
> <u>πλάγχθη,</u> ἐπεὶ Τροίης ἱερὸν πτολίεθρον ἔπερσε·
> πολλῶν δ' ἀνθρώπων ἴδεν ἄστεα καὶ νόον ἔγνω,

> Tell me Muse, of the man of many ways, who was
> <u>driven</u> far journeys, after he had sacked Troy's sacred citadel.
> Many were they whose cities he saw, whose minds he learned of . . .

By virtue of πολλὰ δ' ὅ γ' ἐν πόντῳ πάθεν ἄλγεα (1.4), πλάζω explicitly
refers to difficult sea crossings. By virtue of the reference to Troy, it evokes
the more specific genre of difficult homecomings of the Akhaians.

Implicitly, πλάζω in the proem *alludes* to the unnamed Poseidon, the
deity designated by the poem as hostile to Odysseus, most responsible
for driving him away from his home, as specified by Zeus, πλάζει δ' ἀπὸ
πατρίδος αἴης (1.75). The proem does not name Odysseus but defines him
through his chief qualities and exploits. The proem similarly does not
name Poseidon, but evokes him through emphatic use of πλάζω, the root
that best articulates the specific nature of his interaction with Odysseus.

For an audience hearing a traditional tale, the proem not only looks
forward, forecasting the tale that has just begun, but also looks *back* to, and
partakes of previous performances of the same myth, and an even larger
set of related myths in which the same hero may figure. As such πλάγχθη
(1.2) is the composer's shortcut for pointing to Poseidon in precisely the

way he figures in this poem, yet maintaining the *Odyssey*'s, and its proem's, thematic tendency of withholding names. Like the passive form in book 5, this instance in the proem has Watkins's memorative function, it "functions as a *summation*, recalling to the mind of the epic audience what it knows already."

Πλάζω *and the Suitors*

Before turning to further consideration of the proem, we note two last instances of πλάζω which support the assertion made above, that in the Ithakan sequence the suitors, being the principal target of divine wrath, replace Odysseus as the victims designated by this verb. Much as Akhilleus' wrath, directed primarily at Agamemnon for the first sixteen books of the *Iliad*, takes on a new trajectory, redirected at Hektor after the slaying of Patroklos, so the *Odyssey* depicts a change of focus in the target of divine hostility. In the Aiaian sequence, Helios, the offended god, insists on the crew's deaths for violating his cattle. In the Skherian sequence, Poseidon slays the crew of the ship that ferried Odysseus out of his grasp. In the Ithakan sequence, Athene in book 1 witnesses the suitors' outrageous behavior and, in the dynamics of the underlying theoxeny, becomes the wrathful deity who will insist on their death (see her comment at 13.394–96). We noted in chapter 1 how Athene plants suggestions in Telemakhos' mind of a scenario much like that which will unfold when the suitors are slain (1.113–16, 1.253–56, 1.265–66). The principal narrator also carefully plans for that eventuality early in the poem. Having, in her Mentor disguise, provided Telemakhos with ship and crew, she further smooths his path by now incapacitating the suitors in a manner quite suggestive of events in book 22:

βῆ δ'ἴμεναι πρὸς δώματ'Ὀδυσσῆος θείοιο·
ἔνθα μνηστήρεσσιν ἐπὶ γλυκὺν ὕπνον ἔχευε,
<u>πλάζε</u> δὲ πίνοντας, χειρῶν δ'ἔκβαλλε κύπελλα.

She went on her way, into the house of godlike Odysseus,
and there she drifted a sweet slumber over the suitors,
<u>and struck</u> them as they drank, and knocked the goblets from their hands.

(2.394–96)

As our investigation suggests, πλάζω is not a neutral term in the *Odyssey*, but is marked vocabulary expressing divine antagonism against a mortal who has provoked the particular deity. While Athene's immediate purpose is to help Telemakhos slip out of Ithaka unnoticed, the composer intends additional purpose, a brief foreshadowing of the slaying of the suitors. Antinoös, the first suitor slain, is struck by Odysseus while he is drinking, his goblet then falling from his hand (22.8–18). As Archaic Greek culture finds close parallels between death and sleep (e.g., ὕπνος . . . θανάτῳ ἄγχιστα ἐοικώς, *Od.* 13.79–80), 2.394–96 functions as a very accurate, if brief, anticipatory echo of the scene developed at length in book 22.

The poem offers further support that in the Ithakan sequence πλάζω depicts Athene's opposition to the suitors in a second passage, the highly charged transition to Theoklymenos' prophecy of the suitors' death. Much of book 20 is concerned with omens, from Zeus' confirmational thundering (20.102–4) to the mill woman's prayer (112–19), and Philoitios' propitious arrival (185–237). Shortly after the suitors enter the palace that day, Ktesippos, in the last act of violence against the disguised Odysseus, hurls an ox-hoof at the hero, an act which shocks even the suitors.[36] In this tense atmosphere, Athene again manipulates the suitors, much as in the previous passage:

> μνηστῆρσι δὲ Παλλὰς Ἀθήνη
> ἄσβεστον γέλω ὦρσε, παρέπλαγξεν δὲ νόημα.
> οἱ δ'ἤδη γναθμοῖσι γελώων ἀλλοτρίοισιν,
> αἱμοφόρυκτα δὲ δὴ κρέα ἤσθιον· ὄσσε δ'ἄρα σφέων
> δακρυόφιν πίμπλαντο, γόον δ'ὠΐετο θυμός.

> In the suitors Pallas Athene
> stirred up uncontrollable laughter, and addled their thinking.
> Now they laughed with jaws that were no longer their own.
> The meat they ate was a mess of blood, their eyes were bursting
> full of tears, and their laughter sounded like lamentation.

> (20.345–49)

Theoklymenos' prophecy of their death immediately follows (20.351–70).

It should be emphasized that the principal narrator articulates both descriptions of Athene acting against the suitors through πλάζω (2.396, 20.346), not, as in most other instances of the verb and its compounds, characters in character speech. Consequently, these instances carry the greater authority found in the other two cases where the narrator employed the verb, in the proem (1.2) and the definitive encounter between Poseidon and Odysseus (5.389).

Πλάζω and the Coherence of the Proem

To sum up the argument thus far, in the *Odyssey* πλάζω participates in a very particular pattern. The verb and its compounds depict the actions of a deity directed against mortals who have offended him, whom he subsequently punishes, most often through provoking a storm at sea. The verb has particular reference to Odysseus, sometimes serving a memorative function in which it evokes a summary depiction of his troubled sea-crossings, at the heart of which difficulty lies the wrathful Poseidon. The poem's definitive instance occurs in the only scene in which Poseidon and Odysseus share the stage, in which the principal narrator depicts Odysseus driven by the storm Poseidon rouses while at sea heading for Skheria (5.389). In the poem's first, highly programmatic, divine council, Zeus uses the verb to articulate how Poseidon is the chief cause preventing Odysseus' return home (1.75). The verb appears in a number of significant contexts serving to establish key dynamics of the plot in various sections of the poem. The Apologue's first episode concludes with a storm featuring the verb (9.81) as it drives Odysseus and crew off the map, serving as a boundary between the real Ismaros and the never-never land in which the remainder of the Aiaian sequence unfolds. Significantly, instances of πλάζω appear to mark the beginning (5.389) and ending (13.204) of the Skherian sequence, that section of the poem in which Poseidon acts as the offended deity. Similarly, as Alkinoös uses the root immediately before (8.573) and after (13.5) the Apologue, the verb can be seen to frame the Aiaian sequence. The poem's two most significant internal audiences, Alkinoös and Eumaios, who serve to elicit lengthy narratives from Odysseus (Alkinoös prompting the recitation of the Apologue), both use the verb in contexts which serve to recall the proem (8.573, 16.64). The proem itself uses πλάζω in a programmatic and memorative manner to sum up the difficulties Odysseus encounters on his return home. Thus the proem's use of πλάζω accurately forecasts the verb's behavior throughout the poem. I take this as one of many indications that the proem does coherently, if subtly, address the contents of the poem.

Having observed the importance of one key word in the proem, and how it accurately refers to dynamics and mortal/immortal relationships central to the rest of the plot, we now address the manner in which the proem as a whole attempts to do the same. If the extended narrative pattern forms a skeletal structure underlying the majority of the plot, might our awareness of the narrative pattern help understand the proem's function? Is the proem itself aware of the narrative pattern? Does the proem conform to the pattern?

In our discussion of πλάζω we noted many aspects of the proem's first sentence (1.1–5), encountering two proemlike sentences with similar structure (8.572–74, 16.63–64). This first sentence, in its invocational reference to Odysseus as the sacker of Troy—a summary portrait suggesting his breadth of experience and stressing his attempt to return home and to secure the homecoming of his crew—has proven less problematic to commentators than the second.[37] It is the second sentence, which highlights the crew eating Helios' cattle, that has attracted the most criticism. The second sentence emphasizes several differences between Odysseus and his crew: he could not save them (he implicitly remains alive), nor was it his fault; they perished through their own recklessness, eating Helios' cattle:

ἀλλ᾽ οὐδ᾽ ὣς ἑτάρους ἐρρύσατο, ἱέμενός περ·
αὐτῶν γὰρ σφετέρῃσιν ἀτασθαλίῃσιν ὄλοντο,
νήπιοι, οἳ κατὰ βοῦς Ὑπερίονος Ἠελίοιο
ἤσθιον· αὐτὰρ ὁ τοῖσιν ἀφείλετο νόστιμον ἦμαρ.

Even so he could not save his companions, hard though
he strove to; they were destroyed by their own wild recklessness,
fools, who devoured the oxen of Helios, the Sun God,
and he took away the day of their homecoming.

(1.6–9)

Commentators have argued, especially in modern times, that the proem is obscure in singling out Thrinakia.[38] Because of this perceived obscurity, it has become commonplace to suggest, along analyst lines, that the proem was composed for an *Odyssey* other than the one we have.[39]

The Narrative Pattern and the Proem

The narrative pattern, and the patterned behavior of πλάζω, provide parameters by which the proem's function and accuracy can be gauged. We have already seen that the proem accurately predicts the patterned behavior of πλάζω. It is highly unlikely that "a later hand" was so aware of this verb's significant properties in the poem at large that he could insert the opening πλάζω in a manner utterly consistent with its function in books 5, 8, 9, 13, and so on. By this single, yet significant, criterion, the proem's first sentence accurately initiates dynamics central to the rest of the plot, and coherently predicts significant relationships and episodes.

Does awareness of the narrative pattern help answer criticism of the proem's second sentence? For a poem with the length, complexity, and episodic quality that the *Odyssey*'s plot features, considerable selectivity is essential to the success of a proem which, by nature, must be succinct. Within the constraints of such brevity, the proem contains a large number of the most important constituent elements of the narrative pattern. It refers to Odysseus, one of the bands of abusive young men (the crew), one of the three offended deities (Helios), and an implicit violation of divine interdiction in the reference to their consumption of his cattle. The proem also offers *hints* of the dynamics that will govern each sequence: Odysseus' self-control and piety (he did not consume the cattle, nor offend Helios), the crew's own lack of same, his success, their failure. At the same time, other elements of the narrative pattern are absent. None of the powerful females is suggested, nor the youthful divine helper.

In the short space to which it is limited, the proem has selected those elements of the pattern which highlight conflict, implicit conflict between Odysseus and the band of young men, explicit conflict between the band of young men and the gods. Though there are hints of some of the underlying tensions (the differences in temperament already apparent between Odysseus and crew), the proem omits any reference to the complications which will cause these conflicts to break out, stating only the final form that those conflicts will take. The proem thus focuses on the pattern's treatment of the most heroic and ethical issues, consequently omitting Odysseus' delicate negotiations with the powerful females. As the proem cannot be expected to allude to all three of the sequences, it is clear that *it has selected the dynamics of one sequence, the Aiaian, to stand for all three* as well as the brief instances of the pattern such as Zeus' immediately following summary of Aigisthos (1.32–43). I conclude, then, that the proem does point to, is informed by, the underlying pattern in a manner that emphasizes the potential for conflict and inherent recklessness in the abusive band of young men.

Why would the proem select the Aiaian sequence over the other two, and why would it highlight only the final episode of that sequence? Foley has argued that it is in the nature of the language of oral epic to exhibit a *pars pro toto* function (1991: 10). A smaller part often sums up or stands for a larger entity (much as we have observed in how πλάζω can sum up the overall relationship between Poseidon and Odysseus). That the narrative pattern *repeats* itself in three sequences also encourages a *pars pro toto* relationship between proem and larger plot. In other words, though the Aiaian sequence may be that sequence explicitly singled out by the proem, it can, in various degrees, stand for and point to parallel elements in the other two sequences.[40]

We have established, then, that it would be cumbersome, if not impossible, for the proem to point to all three sequences, or even to enumerate all of the motifs of any single sequence. But why does the Aiaian sequence better serve the proem's purposes than either of the other sequences? Epic is an essentially heroic genre, centering on larger-than-life heroes who struggle with the boundaries of mortality itself. The epic hero, in his capabilities, his relations to the gods, and his suffering, is situated somewhere between mortals and immortals. Of the three sequences, the Aiaian sequence is clearly the most heroic. In the descent to the underworld and in Odysseus' triumph over a powerful monster, Polyphemos, the Aiaian sequence features two of mythology's most traditional heroic motifs, gestures which establish Odysseus as a top-caliber hero. Though Odysseus performs acts which can be considered heroic in both of the other sequences,[41] the proem, in singling out the Aiaian sequence, selects that sequence whose dynamics best fit the requirements of this heroic genre.

Conversely, the Skherian sequence, being the least heroic and most civilized, is the least likely to be singled out in any length by an epic proem. It is worth emphasizing, however, that that part of the Skherian sequence which does qualify as heroic, Odysseus' encounter with the wrathful Poseidon on the high seas (which serves to initiate the sequence), is precisely that part to which the proem's first sentence does allude in its patterned, programmatic use of $\pi\lambda\dot{\alpha}\zeta\omega$.[42] In heroic potential the Ithakan sequence falls somewhere in between. Lacking the fundamentally heroic motifs found in the Aiaian sequence, it does nonetheless have more of what might be called an element of machismo than is evident on Skheria. In selecting the Aiaian sequence to stand, in some way, for all three sequences, the proem thus makes the selection which is most suitable for the heroic tendencies central to epic.

If we can agree that the proem's selection of the Aiaian sequence makes sense within the generic demands of heroic poetry, why does it *not* select the triumph over Polyphemos or the descent to the underworld as the episode to highlight? It has long been recognized, even since antiquity, that the *Odyssey*'s plot has a certain moral thrust and focus, a central fact omitted, however, by most modern analyses of the proem.[43] By selecting the Thrinakian episode over some of the more swashbuckling encounters, the proem signals that the plot's chief overall trajectory will highlight ethical or moral dilemmas within the broader context of heroic engagements.[44] The proem succinctly accomplishes this by highlighting the crew's violation of the divine interdiction.[45]

The larger poem, in the opening divine council, immediately takes up and furthers the proem's interest in the dynamics of mortal/immortal rela-

The *Odyssey:* Structure, Narration, and Meaning

tions as expressed in a divine interdiction. Zeus, in remarks generally recognized as programmatic for the poem, depicts a cosmos in which humans themselves bear the responsibility for what sufferings they may encounter. He does this (1.34) by emphasizing mortals' culpability, emphasizing that they have pains beyond their expected allotment (ὑπὲρ μόρον) because of their own recklessness (σφῇσιν ἀταθαλίῃσιν). In so doing he closely reiterates the principal narrator's phrase about the crew's responsibility in violating Helios' divine interdiction, and the consequences they suffered. They perished "by their own recklessness" (σφετέρῃσιν ἀτασθαλίῃσιν). Even within the formular nature of Homeric diction, this echo, especially in such an authoritative mouthpiece as Zeus, constitutes a significant restating of a central theme.

More to the point, even, Zeus, in his programmatic exemplum, in which Aigisthos serves to support his general thesis about moral culpability and recklessness, complains that this reckless man broke not one but two divine interdictions:

> ἐπεὶ πρό οἱ εἴπομεν ἡμεῖς,
> Ἑρμείαν πέμψαντες, ἐΰσκοπον ἀργειφόντην,
> μήτ' αὐτὸν κτείνειν μήτε μνάασθαι ἄκοιτιν.[46]

> For we ourselves, having sent
> Hermes, the mighty watcher, Argeïphontes, had told him
> not to kill the man, nor court his lady in marriage.
>
> (1.37–39)

We have, then, in rapid succession, the proem highlighting the crew's reckless violation of a divine interdiction as the sole representative episode of the plot, closely followed by Zeus, complaining in a broad exemplum in which his reckless, but culpable, mortal violates two divine interdictions. While most take his repetition of ἀτασθαλίῃσιν as thematic, I argue further that his repetition of the motif of divine interdiction is also thematic, and programmatic. While Zeus's example of Aigisthos is understood by most commentators to serve as programmatic parallel for the suitors' behavior,[47] I argue that, as in the proem, the composer intends this authoritative statement of a brief version of the narrative pattern to refer to all three sequences. In repeating the proem's emphasis on mortal recklessness as leading to the violation of a divine interdiction, Zeus' formulation supplies the key missing component in the proem's use of the extended narrative pattern, the female. In chapter 1 we noted that his exemplum is a brief instantiation of the pattern, with Aigisthos as the band of abusive young men, Hermes as divine helper, and Klytaemnestra as the powerful female. Zeus' paradigmatic formulation of Aigisthos' failings looks back on and reaffirms what the proem sketches out, as well as suggesting outcomes in the other sequences.

According to our analysis the proem selects the Aiaian sequence and its climax on Thrinakia as part of a coherent strategy to highlight the most heroic of the three sequences and simultaneously point to the poem's particular focus on ethical issues. Nonetheless, as part of the *pars pro toto* tendency noted above, close parallels between the Aiaian and Ithakan sequences, absent in the Skherian sequence, enable the proem to suggest some of the pivotal events in the Ithakan sequence. Of the three bands of abusive young men, the crew and the suitors share parallels absent from the Phaiakian athletes.[48] The crew and the suitors are both repeatedly singled out for excessive, even unlawful consumption, a failing not visible in the Phaiakian athletes, and out of place in the generally civilized, decorous atmosphere that prevails on Skheria. The crew's violation of the divine interdiction, rooted in an act of consumption, eating Helios' forbidden cattle, with the failing being a specific loss of self-control, has powerful thematic importance in the plot.[49] The suitors are frequently singled out for excessive consumption, noted by such observers as Athene, Penelope, and Telemakhos, and this tendency constitutes a key ingredient in their violation of hospitality.

As the proem's use of line-initial enjambment serves to emphasize πλάζω (1.2) as a key term for Odysseus, the same technique serves to emphasize κατὰ . . . ἤσθιον, "they devoured" (1.8–9) as a key index of the crew.[50] The crew are fully aware that they are committing wrong when they consume the forbidden cattle (12.348–51). The suitors knowingly violate hospitality, and do violence against guests in the palace (17.483–87, 18.414–17 = 20.322–25). The degree, then, to which these two bands of young men are abusive, even impious, is far greater than the offense committed by the Phaiakian athletes. The crew and suitors *knowingly* engage in behavior offensive to the gods. The Phaiakian crew is unaware that Poseidon will be offended by their ferrying Odysseus home. By virtue of these parallels, the proem, by pointing to the death of the crew at the end of the Aiaian sequence, can be seen to suggest the destruction of the suitors in book 22, one of the climaxes of the Ithakan sequence.

The Subgenre of Myth to Which the Odyssey May Belong

We can better appreciate why the *Odyssey* has so organized its proem, and the narrative pattern, if we place the poem in the larger context of myths which depict the breaking of a pivotal divine interdiction and the attendant destruction of a large body of people.[51] While critics often categorize the *Odyssey* as a "return" myth,[52] a classification that the poem itself may be seen to encourage in its mention of the returns of other Greeks in addition to Odysseus, such analyses omit reference to the key elements around which the narrative pattern is organized, especially the role of the divine interdiction and the subsequent wrath of a god. Narratives that feature the breaking of a pivotal divine interdiction are not frequent in Greek myth, the most notable example being Hesiod's account of the joint failings of Epimetheus (in forgetting Prometheus' injunction against accepting gifts from Zeus) and Pandora (in breaking the interdiction against opening the jar).[53] Perhaps most well known in Western culture is the divine interdiction in the Genesis account of the tree of knowledge (Genesis 2.16–3.19). Parallels with those in Hesiod are many, as both are creation myths, and the mortals' violations of the interdictions, about which they were given specific warning, account for the sundering of once close relations between gods and mortals. Other Old Testament narratives frequently cast divine interdictions in a central role, the account of the Ten Commandments being a further prominent example (Exodus 34). Among this larger group, however, the Lot narrative, a theoxeny with a climactic violation of a divine interdiction followed by an angry god destroying a large population, offers significant parallels with the *Odyssey*'s narrative pattern, being particularly close to the Ithakan sequence.

I summarize the account as follows: Two angels come to Lot as he sits by the city gate (19.1).[54] Unaware that they are angels, but displaying exemplary hospitality, he invites them into his house that they may bathe their feet, and, preparing a meal for them, insists that they spend the night (19.2–3). Before the guests lie down to sleep, however, all the men of Sodom gather outside the house demanding that Lot allow them to have intercourse with his guests (19.4–5). Lot refuses to surrender his guests, instead offering them his two daughters (19.6–8). Incensed, the mob attempts to break into his house (19.9). The angels, however, pull Lot inside the house and blind all those attempting to enter (19.10–11). Telling him to gather his family, they order him to leave immediately, as God has sent them to destroy the city because of the citizens' behavior (19.12–13). Lot then urges his sons-in-law to depart, but they do not heed him (19.14). At dawn the angels lead Lot, with his wife and daughters, to safety outside the city. They tell him to flee to the hills, bidding him not to stop or look back, or he will be destroyed (19.15–17). Worried that he cannot reach the hills in time, Lot persuades the angels to allow him to reach Zoar instead (19.18–22). When they reach Zoar safely, God destroys Sodom and Gomorrah by raining down fire and brimstone (19.23–25). Lot's wife, however, then looks back, and is turned into a pillar of salt (19.26).

I should emphasize that I am not arguing for influence between the *Odyssey* and the biblical account, nor a common source. Rather, I suggest that as both accounts share a considerable number of motifs, a similar "grammar" underlies each myth. Though the Lot account contains details having little to do with the *Odyssey*'s narrative pattern, and, conversely, some elements from the Ithakan sequence of the *Odyssey*'s pattern are absent, we can, nonetheless, discern the following common sequence[55] underlying both narratives: *A pious man* (Lot/Odysseus) *is surrounded by wicked people who have taken over his entire city* (inhabitants of Sodom / the suitors). *Divine helpers* (angels/Athene), *having first tested his own household to see how well it exercises hospitality, aid him, the just man and his family passing the hospitality test. The divine helpers, themselves personally witnessing the improper behavior of the people, foretell the destruction of all the unjust citizens as sanctioned by the principal deity* (God/Zeus). *While the people utterly violate the sanctity of hospitality, they also misbehave sexually* (attempted rape / suitors have sex with the maidservants), *their forced entrance into the just man's house being a symbolic rape of it.*[56] *The just man attempts to warn some people of the coming destruction, but they* (Lot's sons-in-law / Amphinomos, and other suitors) *ignore him, making no attempt to flee the coming destruction. All of the wicked perish.*[57] *Further punishment and destruction await those who violate a divine interdiction* (Lot's wife / the suitors' servants).

Significant differences notwithstanding, both narratives belong to a genre of myth that might be thought of as a minor apocalypse, or local but large-scale destruction at the hands of a wrathful deity, sparing the "one just man" in the community's midst.[58] There is no doubt that such is the case in the Lot narrative, in that the subsequent account of how his two daughters get him drunk in order to have sex with him (Genesis 19.31–38) suggests the need to repopulate the world, two entire cities having been destroyed. Perhaps the best *comparandum* in Archaic Greek poetry is Hesiod's account of the passing of the earlier ages and especially of the breakdown of morality in the Iron Age. Whereas the Golden Age comes to a peaceful conclusion, *The Works and Days* describes the failings of the race of the Silver Age in terms similar to those the *Odyssey* uses of the suitors:

ἄλγε᾽ ἔχοντες
ἀφραδίης· ὕβριν γὰρ ἀτάσθαλον οὐκ ἐδύναντο
ἀλλήλων ἀπέχειν.

they suffered pains
from foolishness, for they could not keep themselves away
from violence and recklessness against each other.

(133–35)

Because of their wicked behavior, an offended and angered Zeus destroys the entire race (137–78), τοὺς μὲν ἔπειτα / Ζεὺς Κρονίδης ἔκρυψε χολούμενος. It is worth emphasizing that Hesiod's account here specifies the faults of this entire race in ἀτάσθαλος, "culpable recklessness," the same key, thematic word applied to all three of the narrative pattern's bands of abusive young men (1.7, 8.166, 10.68, 22.416).

In the Iron Age, Hesiod depicts an utter breakdown in human and religious institutions, including hospitality:

οὐδὲ πατὴρ παίδεσσιν ὁμοίιος οὐδέ τι παῖδες,
οὐδὲ ξεῖνος ξεινοδόκῳ καὶ ἑταῖρος ἑταίρῳ.

And father has nothing in common with children, nor children with father,
Nor guest with host, nor comrade with comrade.

(182–83)

These mortals do not fear the gods (οὐδὲ θεῶν ὄπιν εἰδότες: 187). Hesiod emphatically offers his grim prediction: Ζεὺς δ᾽ ὀλέσει καὶ τοῦτο γένος μερόπων ἀνθρώπων, "Zeus will destroy even this race of mortal men" (180).[59] Though Hesiod's accounts of a wrathful god destroying an entire race are not specifically theoxenies (though *Works and Days* 183 may imply such), Greco-Roman myth has another prominent example of a theoxeny of apocalyptic proportions in Ovid's account of Baucis and Philemon (*Metamorphoses* 8.618–724), in which a thousand homes are destroyed (628–29). An underlying divine interdiction informs all theoxenies: do not mistreat guests or abuse hospitality (lest they be god/angels in disguise).[60] The Lot narrative includes a further specific divine interdiction, one that is common enough in Greek myth,[61] which Lot's wife fails to uphold. The punishment, petrifaction, is the same as that visited upon the Phaiakian crew and ship for violating Poseidon's implicit divine interdiction.

Having established that Archaic Greek hexameter poetry has the relevant genre, an apocalyptic portrayal of an angry god destroying a wicked or impious race, we now briefly consider how appropriate such a classification may be for the narrative pattern's three sequences. The Aiaian sequence offers the most explicit instance of the band of young men violating a divine interdiction. There is no gray area in a mortal's response to a divine interdiction. One either upholds or fails to uphold such a test. It is through precisely such a light that the *Odyssey* views most of its characters: they are prudent and, knowing the gods' behests, possess the requisite self-control with which to uphold them; or they are foolish, lacking self-control, and, acting out of recklessness, find ways to ignore divine proscriptions. Eurylokhos, his words eerily prescient, is fully aware of what Helios's reaction must be to the violation of his cattle:

> But if, in anger over his high-horned cattle,
> he wishes to wreck our ship, and the rest of the gods stand by him,
> I would rather gulp the waves and lose my life in them
> once for all, than be pinched to death on this desolate island.
>
> (12.348–51)

Helios does react in anger (12.376): αὐτίκα δ' ἀθανάτοισι μετηύδα χωόμε- νος κῆρ, "and angered at the heart he spoke forth among the immortals"; the other gods do stand by him, especially Zeus, who personally exacts the punishment Eurylokhos expects. Helios' threatened course of action, should the crew go unpunished, to descend into Hades and shine among the dead, is fully apocalyptic in the severity of the rupture he threatens to cause in the fabric of the cosmos. To be alive in Homeric epic is to see the light of the sun (e.g., *Od.* 10.498). The dead, conversely, are to be hidden. The inversion or sundering of normal relations that would result, were Helios to act on his threat, is typically apocalyptic, a life (or death) in which everything is backward, in which the primary signs of order are absent. The sense of apocalypse is furthered by the absence of any other mortals present on Thrinakia. All mortals in the vicinity perish, much as in Genesis 19, except the one man who upholds the divine interdiction. It should be emphasized that Helios, in his specific demand that the crew be punished (12.378–79), bears no wrath against Odysseus, their relationship being essentially neutral.

In the Skherian sequence the scope of the punishment is the same as at Thrinakia: a ship's entire crew, earlier described as the best of the

Phaiakians (8.36), perishes. Again a destruction suggesting a small-scale, contained apocalypse takes place. This sequence considerably increases the apocalyptic possibilities inherent in Poseidon's destructive wrath in the emphatic fourfold repetition of his threat of stronger, more devastating consequences, that he will cover the entire city with a mountain (13.152, 158, 177, 183).[62] Were he to effect this threat, the result would be parallel to the account of Sodom and Gomorrah, obliteration of an entire city (cf. Ishtar's greater threat in *Gilgamesh* VI iii–iv).

Though the episode conforms to our thesis, that the end of each sequence suggests contained but apocalyptic destruction, in several respects Poseidon's wrath is quite different from the narrative sequence's other instances of divine wrath. Unlike both the Aiaian and Ithakan sequences, the offended deity is angered primarily at Odysseus, whom he may not destroy, and only secondarily angered at the band of young men. Odysseus, moreover, unlike the others who provoke divine wrath in the *Odyssey*, has not broken a divine interdiction in his deeds. His boasting to Polyphemos (9.525) that "not even the Shaker of the earth will ever heal your eye for you" does constitute what may be considered a verbal violation of an implicit divine interdiction, roughly akin to that in Mosaic law, against speaking ill of the gods.

The behavior of the Skherian "abusive band of young men" differs substantially from its counterparts in the other sequences, requiring further comment. The Phaiakian athletes are far less unruly than the suitors or crew. They do not exhibit the excessive consumption so central to both other bands. They are only abusive in the flare-up at the athletic games, after which Euryalos apologizes and makes amends for his actions. Although they do violate Poseidon's implicit divine interdiction, "Do not ferry someone [Odysseus] home or I will either turn the offending ship to stone or cover the city with a mountain," suggested in the prophecy Alkinoös relates (8.564–69), they do not *intentionally* do so. The prophecy does not name Odysseus (perhaps thematically keeping alive his "No-man" identity from the Polyphemos encounter). The interdiction does not involve the physical goods of a god, as with Helios' cattle, or the violation of a central institution, as with the suitors' violation of hospitality in the opening theoxeny. This divine interdiction only exists because of Odysseus.

However, divine interdictions allow only two options, observance or violation. Intent, or extenuating circumstances, as in the crew's hunger, the serpent's wiliness, or even the Phaiakian athletes' ignorance, may complicate, but do not ultimately lessen mortals' responsibility. Quite unlike both other sequences, Poseidon has something of a personal relationship with the band of young men. In his angry complaint to Zeus (*A divine consultation limits the extent of the death and destruction*), Poseidon sees their offense as even worse than it otherwise would be, for they "are of my own blood" (13.130). Earlier the poem traces the Phaiakians' lineage (7.56 ff), revealing Nausithoös, the source of the prophecy of Poseidon's wrath and father of Alkinoös, to be Poseidon's own son. Elsewhere the disguised Athene tells Odysseus that Poseidon has endowed the Phaiakians in their nautical supremacy: "They, confident in the speed of their running ships, cross over / the great open water, since this is the gift of the Earthshaker / to them" (7.34–36). Poseidon thus takes offense not only at the Phaiakian crew's violation of his implicit interdiction against ferrying Odysseus home, but in the additional violation of his ancestral relation and the abuse or misuse of his special gift to them.

The poem further suggests that the Phaiakians have a close relationship not only with Poseidon but with the gods in general, Zeus declaring (5.35) "the Phaiakians who are near the gods in origin." Nausikaa in her portrait of her people affirms that the Phaiakians "are so very dear to the immortals" (6.203). Alkinoös offers the fullest articulation of a remarkably close relationship between his people and the immortals:

> for always in time past the gods have shown themselves clearly
> to us, when we render them glorious grand sacrifices,
> and they sit beside us and feast with us in the place where we do,
> or if one comes alone and encounters us, as a wayfarer,
> then they make no concealment, as we are very close to them.
>
> (7.201–5)

Such a relationship is so close that it precludes even the possibility of a theoxeny. Such a relationship, especially the sharing of the feast, generally betokens the relationships that prevail in a golden age, an era when both races, mortals and immortals, trust each other fully.[63] In that case, the breaking of Poseidon's implicit divine interdiction especially parallels those broken by Epimetheus and Pandora, and Adam and Eve, as it results in the sundering of once close relations between a whole race of mortals and the gods. The conclusion of the sequence implies a further profound sundering of relations. The Phaiakians, never again to ferry mortals across the waters, are themselves now cut off from the outside world. Inasmuch as Poseidon will apparently never again trust the Phaiakians as before, they will lose a key part of their golden-age status, becoming more remote from the gods, more like most other mortals.

The Ithakan sequence, as already noted, offers the fullest parallels with the Lot narrative. Since the suitors have taken over the city, holding sway by force and threat, relations between mortals and immortals are now so precarious that a theoxeny is merely the final test before the gods will precipitate action against the impious. While the opening theoxeny serves to illustrate Telemakhos' piety and civility, much as with Lot, it serves the deeper purpose of rousing Athene's wrath (1.252–56, 265–66). Like the angels in the Lot narrative, she, in the guise of a guest in Odysseus's household, personally witnesses their abuse of the sacred institution of hospitality. The suitors, in addition to violating the implicit interdictions upholding hospitality, attempt to violate the two interdictions found in Zeus' exemplum of Aigisthos, "not to kill the man, nor court his lady in marriage" (1.39). Unique among the narrative pattern's wrathful gods, however, she has a particularly close relationship with Odysseus (much like the care the angels bestow on Lot), so close that we might regard it as symbiotic. She repeatedly tests Odysseus, whether in the teasing dialogue when he first returns (13.228–328), or in the additional abuse she provokes among the suitors (18.346–48, 20.284–86). She sees him as a protégé, as a mortal version of herself (13.296–99). He, having passed all these tests, earns her considerable aid, again much like Lot. Aware that he has the support not only of Athene but Zeus as well (16.260), when disguised in his own palace he now plays a role similar to that of the god in a theoxeny, keeping tabs on the behavior of the wicked and offering the wavering another chance to cease offensive behavior and leave.

Theoklymenos' prophecy (20.351–70) offers further evidence of the apocalyptic tone of the context. His vision of the land of the dead superimposed upon the living, in which "The sun has perished out of the sky" (20.356–57), eerily parallels Helios' own apocalyptic threat to invert the order of the cosmos. Theoklymenos' function, the most vivid instance of the pattern's having a prophet foretell the abusive band's destruction, is very like biblical prophets predicting apocalypse. Isaiah offers a pertinent parallel: "The day of the Lord is coming, that cruel day of wrath and fierce anger, to reduce the earth to desolation and destroy all the wicked there. The stars of heaven in their constellations will give not light, the sun will be dark at its rising, and the moon will not shed its light" (13.9–13). Theoklymenos' prophecy is partly prompted by the suitors' fiendish feasting, itself the result of Athene having addled (παρέπλαγξεν) their thinking:

> They laughed with jaws that were no longer their own.
> The meat they ate was a mess of blood, their eyes were bursting
> full of tears, and their laughter sounded like lamentation.

> (20.347–49)

The stark incongruities are in keeping with the topsy-turvy violation of norms that preclude the apocalypse, human behavior gone so awry that it must be terminated. The sustained emphasis on the suitors' excessive, even unlawful consumption serves as a fundamental link with the crew, whose unlawful consumption was the means by which they violated the divine interdiction.

Just as Helios and Poseidon considered more cataclysmic action, Athene asks Zeus if violent destruction might not now engulf the entire people: "Will you first inflict evil fighting upon them, and terrible / strife, or will you establish friendship between the two factions?" (24.475–76). As in all three sequences, however, the consultation with Zeus serves to contain the threatened obliteration, resulting in the lesser of the two options, preventing a full apocalypse.

In addition to her uniquely close relationship with Odysseus, Athene differs from the other wrathful deities in ways that signal her greater importance in the poem. She is more aware of "the big picture" than Poseidon or Helios. She is fully cognizant of the events of the Skherian sequence, for instance, and of Poseidon's role in it (13.341–43). Though personally offended by the suitors' behavior, she nonetheless has less of a personal stake in the offensive behavior than either Poseidon, whose own son was blinded and whose personal gift to the Phaiakians was abused, or Helios, whose goods or property were destroyed. In her consultation with Zeus (24.472–86) she does not declare the destructive options under consideration, as do both Helios and Poseidon, but asks Zeus which he prefers. In all of these respects, she is perhaps the least "elemental" and most "modern" (also perhaps evident in her connections with technology) and ethical of the narrative pattern's three wrathful deities.

Our analysis suggests, then, that the proem's selection of the incident at Thrinakia is hardly capricious, but forms the logical choice for a narrative with a central interest in the relations between mortals and immortals. The *Odyssey* selects divine interdiction, a test with stark, black or white options, success or failure, as the motif or type-scene which best illustrates what is at stake in behaving piously or impiously. The poem's three divine wraths all result from the failure, by the band of young men, to uphold divine interdictions. The proem, in keeping with required brevity, selects one of the extended narrative pattern's three sequences to illustrate the central and general dynamic of a large group of mortals being unable to uphold the interdiction because of their own recklessness and lack of self-control. The proem selects the version presented in the Aiaian sequence, as it is the most heroic of the three sequences, and because in both the Aiaian and Skherian sequences the violation of the divine interdictions are immediately followed by the destruction of the band of abusive young men, thus forming the climax and conclusion of the sequences. The selection of the violation of Helios' cattle is thus evidence of a coherent if subtle design behind the proem's composition.

If I am correct in grouping the *Odyssey* with the Lot narrative and Hesiod's account of the passing of earlier ages, both well-known, easily available texts, why has no earlier commentator advanced a similar argument before? The poem itself is partly to blame. Because the seductive charms of the Apologue are considerable, most studies of the poem's structure and meaning give undue importance to these four books, merely one-sixth of the narrative. The disobedience at Thrinkia, though highlighted by the proem and the climax of the Apologue, is thus obscured as most commentators and audiences remain charmed by the Siren song of the poem's more exotic and/or swashbuckling encounters. The Ithakan sequence, however, as it comprises more than half of the poem, should be taken as the best indicator as to what the poem itself regards as important. In books 13–24, Odysseus has already returned, diminishing the likelihood that the poem places any particular weight on a "return song" categorization. Instead the entire second half focuses on the topsy-turvy state of affairs on Ithaka resulting from the suitors' having taken over the city, holding sway by force and threat, relations between mortals and immortals now so precarious that the gods will precipitate action against the impious.

CHAPTER FIVE

೪೨೪೨೪೨

Kalypso and the Function of Book Five

In this final chapter we apply the extended narrative pattern to a consideration of the structure and function of the *Odyssey*'s fifth book. The book has long been criticized for its divine council (5.3–42),[1] seen as unnecessary and derivative of the opening divine council (1.26–95). Kalypso, onstage only here, and whose role is key to any analysis of the book's structure, has also attracted a variety of interpretations.[2] While I do not fully agree with the conclusions drawn by previous criticism of the divine council or of Kalypso, as is often found, the existence of so many critical arguments is a sign that something unusual is present in the poem's structure.

I suggest that book 5 is unique in the *Odyssey* in a number of respects. Most notably, the first half (5.1–261)[3] exists outside of the narrative pattern (and thus has nothing in common with the sequence of motifs with which we have been concerned). The reader may have noted that I have not yet mentioned Kalypso, or dealt in any way with the events of the book's first half. However, though it is not part of the narrative pattern, I argue that this section has nonetheless been composed in reaction, or counterpoint, to the pattern. Second, I argue that book 5 as a whole is the most highly wrought of any in the poem, by which I mean that it is a tour de force on the part of the composer, featuring the highest density of narrative techniques such as similes, dramatic monologues, divine intervention, pivotal contrafactuals,[4] and the like. I suggest that book 5 exhibits these qualities because part of its function is to insert Odysseus into the narrative pattern, a considerable feat, in many respects. We can best begin our analysis of Kalypso and of how book 5 serves this by noting the number of ways in which the Ogygian goddess differs from Kirke.

Homeric scholars usually lump Kalypso and Kirke close together.[5] Previous scholarship, while bringing to light significant similarities, has tended to suffer from a preoccupation with parallels to the exclusion of differences between the two goddesses, too often regarding them as interchangeable multiforms of the same basic character.[6] Commentators who have equated the two goddesses have observed *generic* similarities, but have, I suggest, ignored key differences in their functional relationships. Discussions of the two goddesses have further suffered from an obsession with priority. As they are so similar, go the arguments, the composer must have derived one goddess from the other.[7] The two goddesses display considerable similarities, to be sure. Both island-dwelling, chthonic goddesses entertain Odysseus for lengthy periods of time, have sex with him, swear oaths not to harm him, and offer advice, provisions, and a wind on his departure. In both episodes, Hermes intervenes for Odysseus' sake. Nagler, Crane, and others[8] have demonstrated both that these features have much in common with Near Eastern figures such as Siduri and Ishtar and that they involve motifs common to depictions of the afterlife. Scholars have perhaps been further encouraged to view the two goddesses in a similar light inasmuch as Odysseus himself twice glosses over differences between them (9.32, 10.489). However, I argue that in those instances, both in the Apologue, he has particular reasons for manipulating his immediate audience by equating the two deities.

Despite these generic similarities, the narrative pattern, as we will see, reveals Kalypso and Kirke to be virtual opposites in their relationships with Odysseus. As both goddesses are present in the poem only insofar as they interact with the protagonist, this is a fundamental distinction. In their involvement with Odysseus the two goddesses reveal strongly opposing qualities, evident in the degree of solitude in which their encounters develop, their initial attitudes toward him, their subsequent emotional engagement, their reactions as he departs, and the degree of help they offer. Kalypso is an antitype to the powerful females in the pattern, Kirke in particular. Odysseus' relations with the two goddesses can be understood as progressing through five phases, presented here in the order through which Kirke passes: (a) goddess threatens the hero, (b) Hermes intervenes on the hero's behalf, (c) goddess swears an oath protecting the hero, (d) hero and goddess make love, (e) goddess helps the hero. On Ogygia, however, these same phases unfold in almost exactly reversed order. Kalypso is at her most accommodating (e) when Odysseus first arrives. They make love (d) for the entire seven years, with the suggestion that in the early phases of the relationship Odysseus is not averse to having sex with her. Hermes intervenes on the hero's behalf (b). Odysseus, suspicious of Kalypso's motives, requires her oath (c). As he would depart, Kalypso withholds considerable information about the present and future, and her clothing almost drowns Odysseus (a).

Their relationships with Odysseus thus run in opposite directions, almost in chiastic order. Kirke, as with the narrative pattern's other power-ful female figures, moves from a hostile and threatening figure to a help-ful, considerate being who seems to have Odysseus' best interests at heart. Kalypso moves from a helpful, nurturing figure to a potentially threaten-ing being who is more concerned with her own interests than with what is best for Odysseus. Kirke is most dangerous and hostile on the hero's ap-proach but most accommodating and helpful on his departure. Kalypso is most helpful and accommodating to the hero on his approach, but more difficult and less accommodating on his departure.

A similar reversal holds for Odysseus' behavior in the two sequences. He is active and aggressive at the outset in his encounter with Kirke, as a successful hunter and a leader who rescues his men. Having achieved these tasks, however, he becomes almost entirely passive, needing a re-minder that it is time to move on. Conversely, on Ogygia Odysseus is passively bewailing his fate as the narrative finally locates him, but be-comes quite active once receiving Kalypso's assurance that he may leave. His vigorous industry in building the raft is the counterpart of his initial aggressive approach on Aiaia.

Furthermore, the composer uses the Kalypso section in order to de-pict Odysseus in a heroic context utterly unlike any encountered in the extended narrative pattern. Kalypso offers Odysseus life without conflict, life that is eternal, everlasting, and distant from humanity. Odysseus can accept or reject her offer. While he is with her, the offer still open, Odys-seus is, in effect, between everything, between the states of mortal and immortal, between the heroic wanderings and the return to Ithaka. In terms of our structural analysis, while he is with Kalypso he is between the end of the Aiaian sequence (which has concluded) and the beginning of the Skherian sequence (which has yet to begin), part of neither.

Ogygia is entirely static as far as the advancement of the narrative is concerned. Kalypso, living up to her name, not only hides the hero but threatens to conceal the plot as well. The *Odyssey* twice makes use of the epic motif "the singer looks at his sources,"[9] in that two epic bards, Demo-dokos on Skheria and Phemios on Ithaka, both meet the hero face to face, and consequently will be able to pass on authoritative accounts about him to the subsequent tradition. Though the *Odyssey* mentions several songs sung by the two bards, none of the songs touches on Odysseus' exploits after the Trojan War. Not until Demodokos hears from the hero's own lips an account of those heroic exploits described in books 9 through 12 do they become part of the tradition, capable of being passed on. Similarly on Ithaka, Phemios comes face to face with Odysseus and personally wit-nesses his slaying of the suitors. Kalypso is therefore concealing Odysseus from the tradition itself by keeping him from encountering Demodokos, and eventually, Phemios. To stay with Kalypso, therefore, would mean no epic is possible, that there would be no outside knowledge of any of the Aiaian sequence, Odysseus' most heroic accomplishments. The subject matter of the *Odyssey* would be known only by deities.

Let us then consider a thematic analysis of Kalypso and Kirke's interactions with Odysseus, in terms of the five-step sequence noted above. Since Kirke, firmly woven into the fabric of the extended narrative pattern, conforms to the poem's dominant vision of Odysseus' relations with powerful females, we consider the sequence from her point of view, allowing Kalypso's differences to appear in contrast.

Kalypso, Alone with Odysseus

It should be emphasized at the outset that though the two goddesses have generically similar islands, equipped with divine attendants (5.199, 10.350–51), Odysseus' solitary circumstances when with Kalypso, as opposed to his being accompanied by his crew when with Kirke, dictate fundamentally different dynamics in his involvement with the two goddesses. Odysseus' solitary state on Ogygia is the first of many radical departures from his encounters with the narrative pattern's powerful females. There is no abusive band of young men on Ogygia counterpart to the crew, the Phaiakian athletes, or the suitors. Whatever will complicate the relationship between Kalypso and Odysseus, they will not encounter friction from any other males present. With no abusive band of young men present, book 5 further lacks all subsequent motifs of the narrative pattern in which the band takes part, particularly the violation of a divine interdiction, the punishment of which forms the climax of both the Aiaian and Skherian sequences. This is the first of many signs that in book 5 the *Odyssey* presents us with a fundamentally different type of mythic narrative than that present elsewhere in the poem.

Not only is Odysseus alone with Kalypso, with no other mortals present; Kalypso is a far more isolated figure than Kirke in other ways. Hermes, who regularly traverses vast distances, complains to Kalypso about how inaccessible her island is (5.99–102), how remote from humankind (101–2). Odysseus reiterates Kalypso's isolation, "nor does anyone, either god or mortal, associate with her" (7.246–47).[10] Kalypso's more solitary existence extends to the animal life on the respective islands. Ogygia is not said to house any fauna except birds (5.65–67). Aiaia, however, teems with animal life, whether the lions and wolves hovering about

Kirke's palace (10.212–19) or the stag Odysseus catches before meeting the goddess (10.158). Though some of the Aiaian animals are transformed men, their presence is a further sign of greater traffic on Aiaia.

Differences in Odysseus' Arrivals to Aiaia and Ogygia

Odysseus' respective arrivals to the two islands and goddesses could hardly be more different. Coming to Aiaia, he has a ship, and is accompanied by his crew (10.133 ff). He comes to Ogygia alone, clinging to the keel of his wrecked ship, his crew having perished (5.130–34, 7.249–53). At Aiaia, his approach to Kirke is quite complex, as is the approach to the powerful female figure in all three sequences of the narrative pattern. Initial contact is postponed as Odysseus first goes by himself to hunt for food. His hunting is thematic in some respects, as discussed below, depicting him as an active leader as he begins his stay on the goddess' island. His brief separation from the crew as he looks after their best interests anticipates the thematically parallel separation on Thrinakia, at the end of the sequence. Having feasted on the stag, the crew divides into halves, Eurylokhos' half drawing the lot to investigate the island. After Eurylokhos returns unsuccessful (Kirke having turned half of the crew into swine), Odysseus begins to approach the goddess. Before encountering her, however, Hermes encounters him: *A divine helper appears, advising him how to approach a powerful female figure.* As a result, a forewarned Odysseus now approaches Kirke.

First Contact with Kalypso

On Ogygia, in a complete inversion of the narrative pattern, Odysseus does not approach the goddess; Kalypso comes to him, finding him alone, helpless, and near death. Unlike Kirke, who initially attempts to drug him, perhaps intending to kill him, Kalypso clearly harbors no hostility whatsoever toward Odysseus, instead taking pains to nurse him back to health (5.130, 135). On Ogygia the narrative has none of the lengthy, complicated, even deadly approach to the powerful female that is prominent in all three sequences. Unlike the trio of Kirke, Arete, and Penelope, Kalypso is not *a figure who is initially suspicious, distant, or even hostile toward him.* Though we lack a full account of their first meeting,[11] it is clear enough that Kalypso immediately welcomes Odysseus into her midst. Consequently, all but one of the other motifs in the narrative pattern relating to the powerful females are either missing or inverted in Kalypso's case: *She imposes a test on him, whereupon Odysseus, having successfully passed the test, wins her sympathy and help, obtaining access to the next phase of his homecoming. Their understanding is made manifest in her hospitable offer of a bath. Furthermore, Odysseus is now offered sexual union and/or marriage with the female.*

As far as we can tell, Kalypso imposes no test on Odysseus. She offers him help from the outset, and has considerable sympathy for his predicament. They do enter into a sexual relationship, but even this appears quite different from the relationship with Kirke, as discussed below. What Odysseus does not obtain from Kalypso, until the very end of the seven-year stay, and then only by intervention of Zeus, is *access to the next phase of his homecoming.*

Hermes Intervenes at Opposite Points

Though Hermes comes to each island out of concern for Odysseus, his role and mission differ considerably. On Aiaia he plays that role, recognizable in all three sequences of the narrative pattern, of the god in a youthful form who warns Odysseus about how to approach the powerful female, noting future difficulties involving the abusive band of young men. On Ogygia every facet of his mission is different. He does not take the youthful form required of this divine helper in all three sequences (10.278–79, 7.19–20, 13.222–23). *He does not even encounter Odysseus,* who is elsewhere on the island for the full duration of his visit. Since his errand to Ogygia brings him there only after Odysseus has been in Kalypso's company for seven years, he therefore has none of the advice which the divine helper gives to the hero in the narrative pattern's three sequences. Rather, he serves here to help Odysseus *leave,* not approach, a powerful female. Hermes' function on Ogygia is thus more like that of the cherubim in Eden supervising the hero's expulsion from Paradise (Genesis 3.24), than of the other divine helpers depicted in the *Odyssey.* In the narrative pattern, the youthful divine helper does not usually meet with the powerful female, but the hero himself.[12] On Ogygia, however, Hermes' meeting is solely with Kalypso. Hermes' motivation also differs in the two episodes. On Ogygia, he expressly conveys the command of Zeus to Kalypso, while on Aiaia he is given no specific motivation for intervention (Crane 40). In both episodes Hermes intervenes at that point at which each goddess offers the greatest threat to Odysseus, Kirke at the beginning of the encounter, but Kalypso at the end.

Both goddesses, at Odysseus' request, swear oaths not to harm him

(10.342–46, 5.184–89). Again, however, in function the oaths are more different than alike. Book 5 gives us Kalypso's full oath, whereas with Kirke, Odysseus merely reports that "she at once swore me the oath, as I asked her" (10.345), not retelling the oath's particulars. On Aiaia, the oath, sworn while Odysseus is still in the initial difficult stages of negotiating his agreement with Kirke, serves to protect him when he has sex with her. It marks the beginning of an agreement of trust reached between the hero and goddess. On Ogygia, the oath, in effect, signals the conclusion of their time together, and comes only after a lengthy sexual relationship.

Kalypso as More Intimate Than Kirke

Though commentators appear to equate the sexual relationships Odysseus has with each goddess, the text suggests significant differences, springing again from the more solitary environment found at Ogygia. Kalypso has a far more intimate relationship with Odysseus than does Kirke, an intimacy permitted both by the isolation that typifies her island and the greater length of their time together. Because Odysseus is accompanied by his crew when he is with Kirke, his stay on Aiaia is permeated by that most epic of type-scenes, the feast.[13] At Kirke's behest Odysseus and crew eat and drink until they regain their spirits (10.456–70). A whole year passes in feasting at Kirke's palace. Ogygia, lacking the requisite number of participants for a feast, lacks the type-scene. Instead, the episode offers a scene closer to a romantic date, with Kalypso and Odysseus the sole participants (5.194–227).

Because of Odysseus' lack of attendants and her own solitary circumstances, Kalypso's relationship with the hero is far more intimate and more overtly sexual than Kirke's. The narrative repeatedly stresses that Kalypso and Odysseus are having sex regularly (5.119–20: εὐνάζεσθαι / ἀμφαδίην; 5.129: βροτὸν ἄνδρα παρεῖναι; 5.154–55: with frequentative ἰαύεσκεν). These retrospective accounts, all of which emphasize an ongoing relationship by virtue of frequentatives or continual aspect of present-tense verbs (εὐνάζεσθαι, παρεῖναι) are capped by a final episode of lovemaking, which occurs in the present, the night before Odysseus begins to fashion the raft which will take him away from Kalypso (5.226–27). Kalypso is the sexual aggressor in the relationship, evident in both her own account and the narrator's (5.154–55).

On Aiaia, as Odysseus is accompanied by his own crew, a less intimate atmosphere prevails, and sex is rarely mentioned. The text only *once* mentions Odysseus sleeping with Kirke: "and then I mounted the surpassingly beautiful bed of Kirke" (10.347). Commentators tacitly generalize on the basis of this single mention that Odysseus has sex with Kirke regularly during the whole year.[14] It must be kept in mind that Odysseus has sex with Kirke because Hermes, a god, commands him to do so (10.297). Neither Hermes' injunction nor the text suggests repeated occurrences. How does the year pass? Kirke bids them to restore their spirits (10.456–65), the next lines describing the passing of the year precisely in accord with the goddess' instructions: "Then for all the days until a year had come to pass / we sat feasting on unlimited meat and sweet wine" (10.467–68). On the day that marks the end of the year, they again feast all day (10.476–78), Odysseus approaching the goddess at sunset. A variant of "and then I mounted the surpassingly beautiful bed of Kirke," the sole mention of their having sex a year before, recurs at 10.480, but it is immediately followed by "I supplicated her by her knees." This time the formula does not suggest sex, but the urgency with which Odysseus consults the goddess on how to leave.

On Odysseus' return from the underworld, the same sequence of motifs occurs, again without sex. Again the goddess bids the crew to eat and drink to refresh themselves after their ordeal (12.23–24). When the sun sets, Kirke sits Odysseus down apart from the crew (12.33–34) and then tells him of the upcoming obstacles. No sex is involved. Though the text does not offer conclusive evidence one way or the other, the evidence suggests that Odysseus only has sex on the one occasion when Hermes instructs him to do so. On that occasion, as Hermes instructs, Odysseus is the sexual aggressor, opposite his status with Kalypso. The *Odyssey*'s larger reception has, I suggest, distorted the nature of his relationship with Kirke, perhaps as a result of early allegorization of the episode into a hero's encounter with temptation.

Kalypso is portrayed as having a much deeper emotional relationship with Odysseus than does Kirke. Odysseus stays on Ogygia for seven years, which allows for considerable intimacy to develop between the goddess and the hero, unencumbered by his crew. Kalypso has a deep emotional investment in Odysseus as she rescues him, nourishes him back to health (5.130–35), shares intimate meals with him, and loves him; "and I gave him my love and cherished him," τὸν μὲν ἐγὼ φίλεόν τε καὶ ἔτρεφον (5.135; cf. 12.450). Because Kalypso loves Odysseus without initially remaining aloof, or subjecting him to any tests, as do all other females in the narrative pattern, she is quite opposite to them. As a further index of Kalypso's close emotional tie to Odysseus, the poem emphasizes that she not only is aware of Penelope (5.209–10), but sees her as a rival:[15]

οὐ μέν θην κείνης γε χερείων εὔχομαι εἶναι,
οὐ δέμας οὐδὲ φυήν.

I declare that I am not inferior to her,
not in form and not in beauty.

(5.211–12)

While it is dangerous for a mortal to declare rivalry with an immortal, and perhaps that is partly why Odysseus himself does not mention Penelope at this point, it is quite unusual for a goddess to put herself in the converse position, of having to justify her own beauty by mentioning a woman's. The unique moment well underscores how close Kalypso is to Odysseus, and lives up to her characterization as foregrounded at the opening of the poem, that she desires Odysseus as her husband (1.15).

Kirke, however, has little discernible emotional attachment to Odysseus. For the year he spends with her, Odysseus eats not alone with Kirke, but attended by his crew. The narrative firmly emphasizes this in his refusal to eat with Kirke before she restores the crew to their human form (10.375–87). Furthermore, considerable tension develops between Odysseus and his crew while on Aiaia: *conflict arises between Odysseus and the band of young men*. Such tension complicates the stay with Kirke, placing the emphasis on Odysseus as captain over his crew rather than on any intimate or romantic relationship between Kirke and Odysseus. Such complications are noticeably absent on Ogygia, which increases the focus on the emotional relationship between Kalypso and Odysseus. Kirke neither mentions Penelope nor shows any interest in possible female rivals, unconcerned with how attractive she herself may appear to Odysseus.[16]

The Goddesses' Different Reactions When Odysseus Departs

Both goddesses offer Odysseus help on his departure, but again differ significantly in the degree of aid they offer and in their reactions to his desire to depart.[17] The narrative repeatedly emphasizes that Kalypso is keeping Odysseus against his will (1.14, 1.55, 4.557–58 = 5.14–15, 5.154–55; note the emphatic frequentatives in 5.154–58, 7.259–60, 23.334–37). On Aiaia, however, there is only one passing suggestion that Kirke keeps Odysseus and crew there against their will: "no longer remain in my palace against your will" (10.489).[18] Nonetheless, events in book 10 do not depict the men as remaining against their will,[19] but as living up to Kirke's suggestion that they feast until they reclaim their spirits (10.460–65).

The goddesses have opposite reactions to his departure. Kalypso lets him leave only under Zeus' threat, though she tries to dissuade him and still desires him as husband. As Odysseus prepares to leave, Kalypso becomes a greater potential threat than before. He suspects her motives when she claims that he is free to go, and manipulates her into an oath guaranteeing she has no ulterior motive. When the storm later strikes Odysseus at sea, Kalypso's clothing threatens to drown him (5.321).[20] Kalypso thus becomes increasingly dangerous as Odysseus attempts to leave, while Kirke offers more help, is far more forthcoming as to the future, makes no attempt at keeping Odysseus, and provokes no suspicion as to her motives. In full contrast to Kalypso, when Odysseus asks Kirke how to leave, she says, in effect, "Fine, here's how you do it." In a further inversion to events on Ogygia, Odysseus is not in any way suspicious of the help Kirke offers him on his departure.

Both goddesses, if they wish, are capable of offering Odysseus considerable help through their prophetic powers, their advice about future obstacles he will encounter on the next phase of his homecoming. For Nagler, this is perhaps the central function of the two figures as suggested in their shared epithet, $\delta\epsilon\iota\nu\grave{\eta}$ $\theta\epsilon\grave{o}s$ $a\vec{\upsilon}\delta\acute{\eta}\epsilon\sigma\sigma a$, "dread goddess who talks with mortals" (of Kirke: 10.136, 11.8, 12.150; of Kalypso: 12.449).[21] As with every other aspect of the two goddesses, however, a generic similarity masks a functional difference. The distribution of the epithet, three to one in Kirke's favor, may suggest that it applies more centrally to her. Both are beguiling singers (5.61, 10.221, 227), but in the case of Kalypso, only Hermes is actually depicted as hearing her sing, whereas Kirke's singing is one of the qualities attracting the crew to what would have been their doom. Kirke's singing thus takes on darker overtones in its narrative context than does Kalypso's.

The central thrust of $\delta\epsilon\iota\nu\grave{\eta}$ $\theta\epsilon\grave{o}s$ $a\vec{\upsilon}\delta\acute{\eta}\epsilon\sigma\sigma a$, however, lies in the goddesses' shared ability, as immortals, to foresee the future, and so to advise Odysseus. In this sense the phrase again applies more accurately to Kirke and is suppressed or stifled in Kalypso's case. Kirke twice offers lengthy, detailed accounts of what Odysseus must do and where he must go to obtain access to the next phase of his homecoming (10.488–540, 12.37–110, and 12.116–41). She names every stop he will encounter, noting place names and names of particular mortals and immortals he will meet. She openly proclaims that such is her function: "but I will point out the way [$\delta\epsilon\acute{\iota}\xi\omega$ $\acute{o}\delta\grave{o}\nu$] and I will indicate [$\sigma\eta\mu\alpha\nu\acute{\epsilon}\omega$] each detail" (12.25–26). As such, $\delta\epsilon\iota\nu\grave{\eta}$ $\theta\epsilon\grave{o}s$ $a\vec{\upsilon}\delta\acute{\eta}\epsilon\sigma\sigma a$ is most operative at 11.8, when Odysseus would act upon the instructions just given in her first monitory speech, and at

12.150, when he will do so after the conclusion of her second.[22] By so advising, Kirke fully lives up to the powerful female's climactic function in the extended narrative pattern, providing Odysseus *access to the next phase of his homecoming.*

By contrast, Kalypso, true to the meaning of her name, conceals much of what she knows about the future as it pertains to Odysseus. She declares to Hermes that she will not help Odysseus depart: "I, at any rate, will not preside over his departure," πέμψω δέ μιν οὔ πῃ ἐγώ γε (5.140). This remark would be utterly out of character in any of the narrative pattern's powerful females.[23] To Odysseus she hints at dangers awaiting him should he leave (5.206–8), but does not spell them out. She says he will reach his home unscathed, "only if the gods consent" (5.168). But in so doing she suppresses a number of points. Hermes had told her how Zeus has declared Odysseus will not die away from home, but is fated to return (5.113–15). She herself has told Hermes that she will advise Odysseus so he will return unscathed, and that she will conceal nothing (οὐδ' ἐπικεύσω, 5.143–44). But when she is said to be devising his escort home (5.233), she merely provides him with tools with which to build his raft, and shows him where the best trees grow. As she sees him off (5.263–68), she offers him a bath, clothing, various provisions, and a wind. Though Kalypso does give Odysseus some particular advice on how to navigate, we are not given her advice firsthand, only through Odysseus' brief allusions. Again, however, Kalypso conceals as much as she reveals. Only after he is well at sea do we learn that she gave him advice as to celestial navigation (5.273–77). She does not, however, tell him the name of his destination, Skheria, though it is well known to both Poseidon (5.288–89) and Leukothea (5.345), and, presumably, to Kalypso as well. Kirke, who carefully named every danger and destination he would face, is far more forthcoming about the future, offering Odysseus inestimable help not once but twice.

Kirke is also more forthcoming about the roles of the gods. She immediately tells Odysseus, on recognizing him, that Hermes has earlier told her the hero would come (10.330–32). Kalypso, the "concealer," says nothing about either Hermes' visit, though it occurs while Odysseus is on the island, not in the past, or his message from Zeus.[24] Though described as δεινὴ θεὸς αὐδήεσσα, Kalypso clearly does not live up to the expected stereotype of the goddess who tells the hero everything he will encounter, as does Kirke (and Leukothea: 5.339–50).

The formula, δεινὴ θεὸς αὐδήεσσα, may more accurately apply to Kalypso in her tendency to utter charming, winning words. Athene emphasizes this aspect of Kalypso in the opening divine council:

αἰεὶ δὲ μαλακοῖσι καὶ αἱμυλίοισι λόγοισι
θέλγει, ὅπως Ἰθάκης ἐπιλήσεται,

but always with wheedling and winning words she
charms him, so he will forget Ithaka.

(1.56–57)

Athene's characterization accurately holds for all of Kalypso's speeches
to Odysseus in book 5. The description serves as a summary depiction of
the extent to which Kalypso departs from the role of the poem's powerful
females, who neither try to restrain Odysseus from departing nor converse
with him in such an indirect, oblique manner.

Other of the goddesses' epithets further underscore how greatly they
differ and the opposite orders in which they behave in their treatment of
Odysseus. Kirke's epithets emphasize that she poses the greatest threat on
Odysseus' first approach. Before the possibility of confrontation ends by
reaching an agreement, and Odysseus *wins her sympathy and help*, (10.345–
47), the narrative describes her in uniquely threatening terms, "with evil
thoughts in mind," κακὰ φρονέουσ' (10.317). As she is both a goddess and
a host, the poem depicts her in terms more appropriate to a monster,
or that type of evildoer whom the hero, in Greek myth, is destined to
kill for violating hospitality.[25] While maneuvering Kirke into swearing an
oath by Styx, Odysseus refers to her as δολοφρονέουσα (10.339), "planning
treachery." Her drugs are described as κακὰ φάρμακ' (10.213), φάρμακα
λύγρ' (10.236), "evil" and "woeful." Odysseus describes her intelligence or
motives as ὀλοφώϊα δήνεα (10.289), "malign wiles." None of these quite
negative terms is used of Kirke *after* she and Odysseus reach their agreement. We noted in chapter 1, that Arete, in some respects, best exemplifies
the changes the powerful females undergo, becoming kindly disposed to
Odysseus, in Athene's words, φίλα φρονέῃσ' ἐνὶ θυμῷ (7.75).

The epithet, δολόεσσα, "wily," used of both Kirke (9.32) and Kalypso
(7.245),[26] applies to the goddesses in opposite order. Kirke is δολόεσσα on
Odysseus' approach but loses this quality after swearing an oath by Styx.
Significantly, δολόεσσα is only used of Kalypso by Odysseus himself, not
the principal narrator, and only after Odysseus leaves her. The term applies accurately to her behavior in the later stages of their relationship,
when he tries to leave, and when he is at sea between Ogygia and Skheria.

These distinctions in their respective behaviors with Odysseus may suggest deeper differences in the goddesses' powers and identities. The *Odyssey* provides a number of other means, in addition to the narrative pattern, by which such differences are evident. Both the principal narrator and Kalypso herself suggest she has much in common with Eos, a sexually aggressive goddess, whose tendency to abduct mortal lovers is often alluded to in Homeric epic.[27] Eos' other principal function in Homeric epic is to mark time, to begin each day, to mark the narrative itself into sections.[28] Kalypso shares both traits.

The narrator suggests parallels between Kalypso and Eos by opening book 5, the only section in which Kalypso is onstage, with a dawn formula unique in the *Odyssey:* "Eos stirred from the bed of handsome Tithonos" (5.1–2). Austin (67–68) argues that the narrator departs from the usual formula to call greater attention to a specific day, in this case, the day on which Odysseus will first appear in the poem, the day on which Kalypso will be made to let her captive mortal lover go. It is no coincidence that the only daybreak formula to emphasize Eos' tendency to have a mortal lover occurs only here in the *Odyssey.* This opening reference to the sexually aggressive Eos establishes one of the principal themes of book 5. Of the several other formulas which could be used,[29] the narrator has selected the one phrase paralleling Kalypso's own circumstances, an amorous goddess with her mortal lover.

Kalypso herself continues the parallel in her complaint to Hermes over having to surrender Odysseus. Noting other mortal/immortal couplings to which the gods have objected, she compares herself to Eos, with another mortal lover, Orion:

> ὡς μὲν ὅτ' Ὠρίων' ἕλετο ῥοδοδάκτυλος Ἠώς,
> τόφρα οἱ ἠγάασθε θεοὶ ῥεῖα ζώοντες.

> So once rosy-fingered Eos took Orion for herself,
> until the gods, living at ease, resented her.

> (5.121–22)

Homeric epic offers numerous instances of mortal/immortal couplings. That the principal narrator opens book 5 by depicting Eos with a mortal lover, and that Kalypso selects Eos as paradigmatic for her circumstances shortly afterward, reiterates and solidifies the thematic parallels between Kalypso and Eos.

There is a sinister side to the amorous propensities Kalypso shares with Eos, rarely discussed by commentators. In a third mention in the *Odyssey*, Eos is described as abducting yet another mortal lover:

ἀλλ' ἦ τοι Κλεῖτον χρυσόθρονος ἥρπασεν Ἠὼς
κάλλεος εἵνεκα οἷο.

But Golden-throned Eos snatched Kleitos away
because of his beauty.

(15.250–51)

Kalypso does not abduct Odysseus; he has washed up on her shores. However, a similar violence, parallel to Eos' behavior, colors the episode. Odysseus is not only Kalypso's prisoner, as the poem repeatedly emphasizes, she forces him to have sex with her against his will:

ἀλλ' ἦ τοι νύκτας μὲν ἰαύεσκεν καὶ ἀνάγκῃ
ἐν σπέσσι γλαφυροῖσι παρ' οὐκ ἐθέλων ἐθελούσῃ.

By night he would lie beside her, forced to,
in the hollow caves, against his will for she willed it.

(5.154–55)

Kalypso is a rapist by this description. However, after Kalypso has sworn the oath, and, making one last but unsuccessful attempt to persuade him to stay, they make love a last time (5.227: τερπέσθην φιλότητι παρ' ἀλλή-λοισι μένοντες), Odysseus apparently participating willingly.[30]

In her response to Hermes, Kalypso also singles out Demeter as having had an interrupted affair with a mortal lover. Again she selects a goddess as paradigmatic for her circumstances:

ὡς δ' ὁπότ' Ἰασίωνι ἐϋπλόκαμος Δημήτηρ
ᾧ θυμῷ εἴξασα μίγη φιλότητι καὶ εὐνῇ
νειῷ ἔνι τριπόλῳ.

So once fair-tressed Demeter having yielded
to her desire came together with Iasion in intercourse
in a thrice-plowed fallow field.

(5.125–27)

Inasmuch as Demeter's amorous pursuits are not central to her character, Kalypso probably has in mind parallels with her more dominant traits, the ultimate nurturing, maternal figure, alluded to here in the "thrice-plowed fallow field." As she further specifies the nature of her relationship with Odysseus, her subsequent remarks reveal that she sees herself in a Demeterlike role in *nurturing* him back to health after finding him near death:

Τὸν μὲν ἐγὼν ἐσάωσα . . .
τὸν μὲν ἐγὼ φίλεόν τε καὶ ἔτρεφον, ἠδὲ ἔφασκον
θήσειν ἀθάνατον καὶ ἀγήραον ἤματα πάντα.

Him I saved . . .
him I cherished and nourished, and I always said
I'd make him immortal and ageless for all days.
(5.130–36)

The same motifs, a goddess nourishing and attempting to make a mortal immortal, recur in the *Homeric Hymn to Demeter*, where Demeter nurses Demophon, the same vocabulary and formulas being employed.[31] Metaneira interrupts Demeter's attempt at making the mortal immortal, the ultimate stage of being nourished by such a figure; in the *Odyssey* Hermes intrudes. Among the many goddesses who have had relations with mortals,[32] in Eos and Demeter Kalypso selects goddesses with whom she exhibits close parallels.

Kalypso also depicts herself in opposition to another deity. It is Artemis who killed Orion, ending Eos' affair with him (5.123–24), Artemis who punishes unchaste behavior.[33] In Kalypso's brief paradigm, and elsewhere in Greek myth, Artemis is perhaps the one goddess in strongest opposition to her own intimate behavior with mortals.

Neither the principal narrator nor Kirke draws parallels between herself and other goddesses, but in several respects she has much in common with Artemis, Kalypso's opposite. The emphasis on hunting and animals on Aiaia, neither of which is mentioned on Ogygia, firmly aligns Kirke with the Mistress of Beasts, Artemis' epithet at *Il.* 21.470. Several earlier scholars have argued that Kirke is based on the *Potnia Thêrôn* figure.[34] Odysseus approaches Kirke only after successfully hunting a stag (10.144–84), an animal repeatedly linked and sacred to the *Potnia Thêrôn* (cf. *Od.* 6.102–4).[35] A *Homeric Hymn* refers to Artemis as the hunter of stags (27.2). Odysseus' successful credentials as a hunter implicitly permit him to approach Kirke, a goddess with an Artemis-like retinue of beasts. The only deer hunted in the *Odyssey* thus makes a fitting introduction to the entire Aiaian sequence.

While the goddesses share many generic epithets,[36] two which are not shared underscore key differences in how Kalypso and Kirke function in the larger plot. Only Kalypso is explicitly ἀγήρως (5.218), "unaging," which emphasizes both her seductive offer of immortality to Odysseus, and again aligns her with both Eos, as a marker of time and a deity who offers immortality to chosen lovers, and Demeter, who can nurture select mortals to the same status. Only Kirke is πολυφάρμακος, "having many drugs," which underscores her ability to change men into animals and aligns her with Medea, never named in Homeric epic but perhaps hinted at in the *Odyssey*'s multiple allusions to the Argonautic myth.[37]

Why Odysseus Briefly Equates the Two Goddesses

There are two passages which are inconsistent with the distinctions argued above, ones which blur the differences between the two goddesses. At the beginning of the Apologue Odysseus describes both goddesses as "desiring me as husband," λιλαιομένη πόσιν εἶναι (9.30 of Kalypso, 9.32 of Kirke). The poem consistently depicts Kalypso in just this way, but nowhere portrays Kirke as having the intimate emotional interest in the hero that the formula suggests.[38] In the account of his wanderings that Odysseus narrates to Penelope, he more accurately again describes Kalypso with the same phrase (23.334), but not Kirke. The principal narrator also uses the formula authoritatively of Kalypso at the beginning of the poem (1.15), when first mentioning her and establishing her key characteristics, but never uses it of Kirke.

Is this (9.32) a narrative inconsistency, a formula which accurately applies to Kalypso but is one time carelessly applied to Kirke? Perhaps, though an equally valid interpretation is that Odysseus, the crafty speaker, is, as often, exploiting his immediate audience. Doherty has shown that significant features of the Apologue result from Odysseus' tailoring much of it specifically for Arete, queen of the Phaiakians,[39] singled out both by Nausikaa (6.303–15) and the disguised Athene (7.53–77) as that Phaiakian whose favor is most essential to Odysseus' homecoming. Odysseus thus uses his account of his wanderings to win Arete's favor. This tactic is most evident in the lengthy catalog of heroines (11.225–332) which is immediately followed by Arete's declaration that he is her guest (11.338), and by her command that the other nobles should offer him additional gifts (11.339–41). Another detail suggesting Odysseus manipulates his narrative to appeal to Arete as a female audience is the prominence given his interview with his mother, lengthier than his dialogue with Teiresias, the purported motivation for the descent to Hades.

Odysseus, in referring to both Kalypso and Kirke as λιλαιομένη πόσιν εἶναι, can also be seen as making a calculated appeal to his female audience. Odysseus increases his own stature by suggesting that not only one but two goddesses desired him as husband.[40] Emphasizing that he turned both goddesses down can be calculated to increase Arete's own possible intrigue with him, while also reiterating that he has no interest in Nausikaa, whom Alkinoös earlier implicitly offered to him in marriage (7.311–14). Attractive to females though he may be, Odysseus simply wants to return home to his own wife, to whom he has slyly made reference in the dialogue with his mother (11.224).

A similar explanation may lie behind another inconsistency noted above, Kirke's injunction, "no longer against your will remain in my palace" (10.489). Though the poem never depicts Kirke acting in such a manner, it serves Odysseus's purposes to claim that she does. He thereby provokes greater sympathy in his audience by suggesting that he was a captive, and, as before, helps to emphasize his own desirability to the opposite sex before his present female audience, Arete. As such, both inaccuracies (9.32, 10.489) work as convincing details in his subtle manipulation of Arete, for which his brilliantly exploitative speech to Nausikaa (6.149–85), with its careful emphasis on flattery, chastity, piety, and marriage, can be seen as an anticipatory echo.

Additional Differences

The *Odyssey* offers further evidence of consistent, thematic differences between the two goddesses in how it structures mention of them in those sections of the narrative in which they are offstage. The poem thoroughly prepares us in advance for Kalypso, emphatically foregrounding her in the beginning of the poem (1.14, 1.51), and continuing to refer to her (4.557) in ways that accurately anticipate her role in the plot. The gods themselves discuss her in two divine councils (1.49 ff, 5.13 ff). Kirke, however, is not mentioned until 8.448, a brief reference that reveals nothing about her role in the poem. Except for Odysseus' brief and, as noted above, inaccurate reference to her at the beginning of the Apologue (9.31), she is not otherwise mentioned until Odysseus lands on Aiaia (10.135).

The stay with Kalypso, or rather its conclusion, occurs in the present time of the narrative and is narrated by the principal narrator, whereas Odysseus' encounter with Kirke occurs in the past and is narrated by the hero. On the other hand, the poem does not describe the first meeting of Odysseus and Kalypso,[41] except in truncated, retrospective accounts (5.130–36, 7.244–66, 12.448–50), whereas we are given the full beginning and ending of his relationship with Kirke.[42] This lacuna, Odysseus' approach to and first seven years on Ogygia, the nature of his relationship with Kalypso, is the largest in our information about Odysseus between Troy and Ithaka.[43] Of Odysseus' many interactions with females on his voyage home, with Kirke, Kalypso, Nausikaa, and Arete, it is only his relationship with Kalypso which is not presented from beginning to end. Furthermore, Kalypso is the only female to receive significant mention far in advance of her actual appearance.

In a final difference, both goddesses represent or articulate important, but distinct, tests for Odysseus. Though both have been seen as embodying temptation, the goddesses pose more crucial tests, tests typical of myths set in the golden age. It is through Kirke's lips that Teiresias' earlier warning against violating Helios' cattle becomes specifically a divine interdiction. Odysseus will uphold the interdiction, thus earning the gods' favor. Though he remains against his will with Kalypso for seven years, his success in obeying divine will at Thrinakia is partly responsible for the considerable aid later given him by Athene and Zeus. Once back on Ithaka, Athene appears to him often and even openly, somewhat reminiscent of the Golden Age relations that used to hold between the Phaiakians and the gods (7.201–5).

As Crane suggests (154), Kalypso can be seen as a reward Odysseus earns for successfully passing the test on Thrinakia, upholding the divine interdiction. According to one vein of Greek myth, one visible in the *Odyssey*'s account of Menelaos' afterlife (4.561–69) and the non-Homeric afterlife of Akhilleus, the hero is rewarded with a paradisiacal existence on an island at the end of the earth, with a female companion along the lines of Helen, Medea, or, in this case, Kalypso. Homeric epic, however, generally ignores a "positive" afterlife in favor of an emphasis on the hero's mortality, an epic trait reaching back at least as far as *Gilgamesh*. Consistent with the usual Homeric emphasis, then, Odysseus, a much fuller character than Menelaos or Akhilleus, passes this disguised test as well. Outside of Homer, Kalypso might not have been a test, but a deserved reward. In the Genesis creation myth, Adam, if obedient, could have stayed in Eden, and, perhaps, eaten of the tree of life. Adam is driven out of paradise as punishment, whereas Odysseus deliberately chooses to leave. Inside Homeric epic, Kalypso and Ogygia are demonstrably not suitable for Odysseus, and therefore she is a test.

Thus we see considerable thematic differences between Kalypso and

Kirke. From a number of perspectives Kalypso is the more distinctive figure, an antitype to the other females Odysseus encounters on his voyage home. But because the audience encounters Kalypso first, sequentially, and because she shares considerable *generic* similarities with Kirke, we have greater difficulty in perceiving how different she is, and perhaps tend to see her as more like Kirke than she really is. The poem seems fashioned with an eye to deceiving us as to how different the Ogygian goddess is. As she departs so consistently from the other powerful females, she is a variation manipulated by the composer against a dominant pattern. In this sense she is "later." That Homer offers us the exception first is not only contrary to his usual practice, by which typically he offers a smaller version incorporating the same themes later stated at greater length, but one of the most unique features of the *Odyssey*'s complex architectonics.

The Function of the Second Half of Book Five

We have established that events on Ogygia are not part of the extended narrative pattern which appears to underlie almost every other episode in the poem. What we have not addressed is why this may be so. I earlier suggested that book 5 in its entirety is the most highly wrought book of the poem. For the book's first episode, Odysseus on Ogygia, I argue that such is the case in the composer's elaborate inversion of the narrative pattern's usual motifs and sequence of events. When the poem's larger structure is considered there is thus a tension that exists between the first episode's very different subject matter and the more dominant matter of the narrative pattern.

Let me here document what might be thought of as the narrative density of book 5's second episode. In a relatively short span of narrative (5.282–493) the composer utilizes a number of special narrative techniques unparalleled in the *Odyssey* in a similar number of verses:

282:	divine intervention: Poseidon's first appearance in the poem
286–90:	Poseidon's soliloquy
299–312:	Odysseus' first soliloquy
328:	first simile, parallel to that at 368
333:	divine intervention: Leukothea's only appearance in the poem
339–50:	Leukothea's speech to Odysseus
356–64:	Odysseus' second soliloquy
366:	divine intervention: Poseidon again
368–70:	second simile

377-79:	Poseidon, addressed to Odysseus
389:	πλάζετο, line initial, strongly enjambed, the poem's central, definitive instance of the verb, thematically governing its other occurrences
394-98:	third simile; cf. 23.394-97
408-23:	Odysseus' third soliloquy
426-27:	pivotal contrafactual;[44] Athene intervenes
432-35:	fourth simile
436-37:	second pivotal contrafactual: ὑπὲρ μόρον; Athene intervenes
445-50:	Odysseus' prayer to the river god
465-73:	Odysseus' fourth soliloquy (within 174 lines)[45]
488-91:	fifth simile
491:	divine intervention: Athene sheds sleep on him

The episode's richness and density of composition have been well noted. Hainsworth makes the following observation: "The extensive elaboration, principally achieved by the introduction of divinities and the use of direct speech, makes it one of the most memorable [episodes] in the *Odyssey*."[46] Fenik has analyzed some patterns in the use of repeated elements (1974: 143-44). I think it is no accident that this section, with its considerable narrative complexity and density, is that part of the poem which both serves as transition into the Skherian sequence and inserts Odysseus into the extended narrative pattern. The seam begins, I suggest, with Poseidon's entrance (5.282), his first appearance in the poem, off the coast of Skheria. Poseidon will serve to conclude the same sequence, again off the coast of Skheria, when, after consultation with Zeus, he destroys the Phaiakian ship (13.162-64).

In that this section of the narrative initiates the Skherian sequence, and introduces Odysseus in the narrative pattern as a whole, the composer expends considerable time and care in the construction of this seam, evident in a number of ways. The seam is particularly marked by the emphatic use of several significant techniques noted in previous chapters. I call particular attention to the poem's key instance of πλάζω (5.389), occurring immediately after Poseidon's second appearance, and his parting threat to Odysseus (5.377-79). As argued in chapter 4, this verb offers a summary depiction of Poseidon directing his wrath against the hero, as described by Zeus in the first divine council (1.75), and suggested in the poem's second line. This particular instance of the verb serves Watkins' *memorative function*, "recalling to the mind of the epic audience what it knows already" about the nature of Odysseus' relationship with Poseidon.

Pivotal Contrafactuals and the Seam in Book Five

Occurring in the backwash of πλάζετο, as it were, are two significant pivotal contrafactuals (5.426–27, 436–37). Though this Homeric narrative technique has been well studied, its tendency to appear at structurally significant plot points remains underappreciated.[47] Typically Homeric epic employs this structure to confer a climax by building a section of narrative up to a point of impending disaster, then averting disaster through having a deity intervene to save an endangered hero. We noted in chapter 4 the crucial role played by a partly parallel passage at the end of the Apologue's first episode:

καί νύ κεν ἀσκηθὴς ἱκόμην ἐς πατρίδα γαῖαν,
ἀλλά με κῦμα ῥόος τε περιγνάμπτοντα Μάλειαν
καὶ Βορέης ἀπέωσε, παρέπλαγξεν δὲ Κυθήρων.

And now I would have come home unscathed to the land of my fathers,
but as I turned the hook of Maleia, the waves and current
and the North Wind beat me off course, and drove me on past Kythera.

(9.79–81)

It is this passage which first signals the profound difficulties Odysseus will encounter in his homecoming. We now take a closer look at the agency responsible in this passage. The passage comes in the aftermath of a storm which Odysseus supposed to be provoked by Zeus, though Jörgensen's law, and the larger archaic Greek epic tradition, may give us cause to suspect the accuracy of Odysseus' attribution. Elsewhere in the tradition Athene is said to have provoked a storm making the Akhaians' homecoming difficult. In any case, in this passage (9.69–71) Odysseus specifies the agency responsible for driving him off course as κῦμα ῥόος τε, "the waves and current."

Regardless of how we construct the cause and effect relationship between events at Ismaros, they appear to have provoked a god-sent storm as punishment. Intriguingly, in a poem in which Poseidon is the protagonist's chief divine adversary, we have, in κῦμα ῥόος τε, agency squarely set in Poseidon's domain, which resembles the workings of Poseidon himself. Elsewhere Homeric epic sometimes uses κῦμα, in fact, to broadly suggest the larger workings of the sea,[48] as is clearly the case here. The force of the sea, incited by storm, drives (παρέπλαγξεν) Odysseus off course, just as he rounds the Cape of Maleia, complicating an otherwise easy homecoming.

Though a common Homeric technique, in this instance the passage emphatically inverts a predominant tendency. Most often Homeric epic employs pivotal contrafactuals to depict a deity intervening to avert harm, to save a favorite hero.[49] In this instance the Poseidon-like agency intrudes to ruin and cause harm to the poem's principal hero.[50] The passage well conveys, with considerable pith, the sea's potential power and savagery. However ambiguous or deliberately vague the workings of that important first storm, which forces the entire Apologue on its indirect course, they suggest the workings of Poseidon, though he would not yet seem to have reason to act against Odysseus in this manner.

What does any of this have to do with Odysseus' approach to Skheria? Just as the pivotal contrafactual at 9.79–81 serves to initiate the problems Odysseus faces in the Aiaian sequence, the composer here employs the same technique, two more pivotal contrafactuals, linked in several ways with the passage at 9.79–81, to help mark the beginning of the Skherian sequence. Shortly after Poseidon leaves, having destroyed Odysseus' raft with his storm, the hero, vulnerable on the open sea, as depicted by the poem's central instance of πλάζετο (5.389), twice faces near disaster attempting to make landfall on Skheria:

῟Ηος ὁ ταῦθ' ὅρμαινε κατὰ φρένα καὶ κατὰ θυμόν
τόφρα δέ μιν μέγα κῦμα φέρε τρηχεῖαν ἐπ' ἀκτήν.
ἔνθα κ' ἀπὸ ῥινοὺς δρύφθη, σὺν δ' ὀστέ' ἀράχθη,
εἰ μὴ ἐπὶ φρεσὶ θῆκε θεὰ γλαυκῶπις Ἀθήνη.

Now as he was pondering this in his heart and spirit,
meanwhile a great wave carried him against the rough face,
and there his skin would have been taken off, his bones crushed together,
had not the gray-eyed goddess Athene sent him an inkling.

(5.424–27)

Note that the agency responsible for Odysseus' troubles at sea is again, as at 9.79–81, κῦμα. On this occasion there is less ambiguity: it is surely the aftereffect of Poseidon himself. The position of κῦμα in the contrafactual is here reversed, however, in accordance with the narrative technique's usual deployment. Here κῦμα is not the intervening agency, as at 9.79–81, but the already present disaster threatening the hero which itself precipitates Athene's divine intervention. The passage thus presents a miniature of the poem's two opposite deities in their typical relationship, as in the opening divine council, with Athene serving to mend the harm Poseidon causes Odysseus.

Just a few lines later, the same dynamic recurs. Having temporarily saved himself by grabbing hold of a rock, Odysseus is now threatened again by the same wave's backwash:

τὸν δὲ μέγα κῦμα κάλυψεν.
ἔνθα κε δὴ δύστηνος ὑπὲρ μόρον ὤλετ' Ὀδυσσεύς,
εἰ μὴ ἐπιφροσύνην δῶκε γλαυκῶπις Ἀθήνη.

Now the great wave covered him over,
and Odysseus would have perished, wretched, beyond his destiny,
had not the gray-eyed goddess Athene given him forethought.

(5.435–37)

Again κῦμα is the agency behind the hero's near disaster; but now Poseidon's harassment threatens to disrupt the course of destiny itself (ὑπὲρ μόρον), not to mention the continuation of the poem itself. This is just the kind of climax which pivotal contrafactuals are designed to threaten, so again Athene counteracts the destructive threat posed by the sea.

At the end of the Skherian sequence, Poseidon, in effect, places a barrier around the Phaiakians, cutting them off from the rest of the world. No longer to ferry people home, Alkinoös and his people are effectively isolated by virtue of their remote location.[51] At the beginning of the same sequence, knowing that Odysseus will be safe, destined so (5.288–89) after having reached Skheria, Poseidon serves to construct something of a barrier between Odysseus and the island, making it as difficult as possible for Odysseus to obtain landfall. The two pivotal contrafactuals function as the final markers of the narrative seam that is the beginning of the Skherian sequence.[52] The two complementary gods, serving polar opposite roles in the poem, play complementary opposite roles in the two pivotal contrafactuals, κῦμα threatening to cause destruction, Athene intervening to avert it.[53]

In a further demonstration of the structural importance of these two pivotal contrafactuals, when Odysseus selectively retells the events of book 5 to Arete (7.241–86) he repeats a version of the second pivotal contrafactual as forming the climax of his hazardous approach to Skheria:

ἔνθα κέ μ' ἐκβαίνοντα βιήσατο κῦμ' ἐπὶ χέρσου,
πέτρης πρὸς μεγάλῃσι βαλὸν καὶ ἀτερπέϊ χώρῳ·
ἀλλ' ἀναχασσάμενος νῆχον πάλιν, ἧος ἐπῆλθον
ἐς ποταμόν.

but there, had I tried to set foot on the land, the rough wave
would have dashed me against tall rocks in a place that was cheerless,

had I not backed away, and swam again, until I came
to a river.

(7.278–81)

Though Odysseus is unaware of Athene's role as intervenor, again κῦμα
is assigned agency for the destructive potential, for the fourth time in a
pivotal contractual. It is infrequent in Homeric epic for a pivotal contrafactual to repeat an account earlier given in another pivotal contrafactual.
The only other instance is a similarly significant structural juncture, the
Iliad's account of Apollo intervening to prevent Patroklos from sacking
Troy (*Il.* 16.698–701 and 18.454–56).[54] In his retelling of the same climactic
incident off the coast of Skheria, the *Odyssey* perhaps suggests that Odysseus himself is aware of the significance of this boundary crossing. In any
case, the repetition should serve to make us aware of the passage's role in
the poem's overall architectonics.

To conclude, the second half of book 5 is a particularly complex section
of Homeric narrative because of the special task it has been given, both
to initiate the Skherian sequence and to insert Odysseus into the extended
narrative pattern as a whole. As a consequence, Odysseus' approach to
Skheria is by far the most elaborate and dramatic of all the island approaches depicted in the poem. This approach is quite unique in its length,
in the difficulties Odysseus faces, and in the complexity of action on the
divine plane (one deity trying to make it more difficult, two others offering
varying degrees of aid). Having broken through, so to speak, Odysseus,
after an immediate sleep, now initiates the narrative pattern's first step,
*Odysseus, as earlier prophesied, arrives at an island, disoriented and ignorant of his
location.* Only then do the narrative dynamics with which we have been
concerned throughout this study get fully under way. The process we have
been describing, Odysseus' struggle to break through to Skheria, is surely
just what Zeus has in mind in his description in book 5's divine council:

ἀλλ᾽ ὅ γ᾽ ἐπὶ σχεδίης πολυδέσμου πήματα πάσχων
ἤματι εἰκοστῷ Σχερίης ἐρίβωλον ἵκοιτο.

but he, having suffered many pains on a joined raft
might reach fertile Skheria on the twentieth day.

(5.33–34)

Finally, we should note the significant and distinct manner by which
book 5 serves to further the *Odyssey*'s agenda of focusing on key ethical
concerns. Odysseus, in the book's second episode, is thrust squarely into

what we have argued are the poem's central tests, self-control as evident in the ability both to observe a divine interdiction and uphold the gods' behests in the face of adversity. However, as much of the book exists outside of the extended narrative pattern, it here presents very different contexts in which to illustrate these important motifs. We have observed that book 5, as the poem's only episode to include Odysseus and Poseidon onstage together, offers a definitive portrait of their relationship. Odysseus is sorely tested by the god, when vulnerable on the high seas. Throughout the encounter, however, both during and after, Odysseus maintains respectful relations with the gods, even with Poseidon. The book subtly emphasizes his success by presenting us with some neat inversions of the diction elsewhere used to depict divine hostility.

In the middle of the encounter, after Poseidon's blasts have disabled his raft, and briefly hurled him from it, Odysseus receives aid from Leukothea. The goddess helps him both by informing him that it is Poseidon who has caused the turmoil, and by offering him her veil ($\kappa\rho\dot{\eta}\delta\epsilon\mu\nu o\nu$)[55] as a talisman that will keep him safe. Her parting instruction, however, calls for Odysseus, having safely reached land, to throw the veil back into the sea, having turned his face aside as he does so (5.348–50). Though she phrases her admonition as a positive command, the utterance can be interpreted as a divine interdiction, in that the encounter seems quite parallel to a widespread motif seen in the myths of Eurydike, Lot's wife, and Moses, among others.[56] It is a specific form of divine interdiction in which the deity commands a mortal not to look back upon divine workings. The divine interdiction against Pandora's opening the urn is closely related, and compare Apuleius' similar use of Venus' command to Psyche not to open the container which she retrieves from Persephone.

Though Odysseus, at this point, is rightly suspicious of all the gods' motives (5.356–64), this occurring immediately after the clothing that Kalypso had given him has threatened to drown him (5.321), he carefully observes her command. The episode offers parallels with his earlier, delicate negotiations with Kalypso. Leukothea also advises him to surrender his raft and swim for the coast (5.343–44). It is this that makes the hero suspect deception (5.356–57), as he had before with Kalypso (5.173–79), in his very first speech in the poem. As with Kalypso, he makes a considered response to the delicate dilemma presented by the necessity of obeying divine will. He will leave the raft, but only when its timbers (which he himself had cut and joined) no longer hold together. Having inserted his own modicum of control within the divine imperative, Odysseus is able to observe the goddess's behests when, after the raft does fail to hold together, and he does reach the shore by swimming, he will hurl the veil behind him into the sea (5.459–62).

However, before he can accomplish this, book 5 offers another significant index of Odysseus' relations with the gods in his interaction with the unnamed river god. Asking for pity, and declaring himself a fugitive from Poseidon, Odysseus proclaims himself a suppliant, having arrived at the river's "current" (5.449: σόν τε ῥόον). The river god immediately halts his current, ὁ δ'αὐτίκα ἑὸν ῥόον, ἔσχε δὲ κῦμα (5.451). Though ῥόον and κῦμα are, perhaps, prosaic enough words, we have noted that they figure prominently in the *Odyssey*'s vocabulary to express Poseidon's hostility against Odysseus. In the pivotal contrafactual which drove Odysseus and crew off of the map in the Apologue, κῦμα ῥόος τε (9.80) are the responsible agency. In all three pivotal contrafactuals describing the force of Poseidon's destructive storms in book 5, κῦμα (5.425, 435, 7.278) is the specific agency singled out by both the principal narrator and Odysseus himself to depict the god acting on his wrath against Odysseus. The river god, then, in a neat inversion of these terms, expresses his relation to Odysseus by removing the destructive potential from the same entities.

Book 5 thus concludes with Odysseus, having displayed considerable self-control and piety, rewarded by a deity for doing so. It is worth emphasizing that the poem shows us this side of Odysseus first, before engaging him with any of the abusive bands of young men, all on their varying courses of reckless, impious action. At the same time, then, that book 5 inserts Odysseus into the narrative pattern, it firmly depicts in him the very qualities which will enable him to survive precisely where the three bands of young men will fail, due to their own recklessness.

ᑐᑐᑐᑐ

Conclusion

My goal has been to investigate how the *Odyssey* organizes its contents. My method throughout has been to carefully avoid imposing any particular interpretive structure from without (other than chapter 4's brief comparison with other myths centered on divine interdictions and consequent wraths). To do so would be to run the risk of forcing a particular view onto the poem which may be alien to its own sense of structure. Rather, I have tried to let the evidence of the *Odyssey* itself point the way to an analysis of its form and structure, and a possible interpretation thereof. My main assumption in this investigation has been to build on the theories of Lord, Fenik, and others, that Homeric epic exhibits an essentially thematic structure, and that it is composed and organized around basic motifs or type-scenes, which are repeated, connected in series, sometimes more fully expanded or ornamented than others.

The extended narrative pattern, which we have shown to underlie a significant preponderance of the poem's plot, is something of a genetic code, a DNA, if you will, that informs, and is replicated, throughout the poem. In terms of the musical analogy used in the introduction, the narrative pattern can be thought of as the score for a complex narrative exhibiting a monumental structure which is symphonic in many respects. It is in just this sense, I assume, that Lord originally selected "theme" as his term for the motif or structural unit so central to Homeric epic.

The extended narrative pattern provides significant new information about how different portions of the poem relate to one another. For example, if various characters are seen to have parallel counterparts in different sequences, such as Elpenor in the Aiaian, and Leodes in the Ithakan sequences, then each character needs to be considered in light of this relation. Elpenor should no longer be seen as an "addition" to or "intrusion" upon the poem, but a figure whose presence is part of a deeper layer of the poem's composition and organization than usually thought, as his principal functions are replicated on Ithaka in Leodes. Leodes, conversely, should perhaps be seen as a more significant character, worthy of further study, because he replicates so many of Elpenor's salient characteristics. Perhaps additional attention to Leodes' role and function can help rescue the second half of the poem from the comparative neglect from which it has long suffered.

Similarly, the many parallels between Alkinoös and Eumaios, themselves multiforms of a parallel internal audience figure in the Skherian and Ithakan sequences, can help broaden our view of the relation between the *Odyssey* and its ancient audiences. We typically have in mind the aristocratic megaron as the original performance setting in which Homeric epic developed. However, the prominence given Eumaios as connoisseur of epic performance implies that our conception is, perhaps, too narrowly bound by preconceptions both as to class and performance setting. Again the prominence given a figure in the Ithakan sequence, parallel to one in a more frequently studied section of the poem, suggests room for considerably more research into the poem's second half.

I have argued that interpretative studies of the *Odyssey*'s meaning should pay closer attention to those specific motifs around which the narrative pattern is organized. As stated in the introduction, the selectivity the poem itself exercises in emphasizing one type of mythic vehicle over another is one of the best hermeneutic tools for eliciting meaning from the poem. I have attached far more importance than most commentators to the conclusions of each of the three sequences. Indeed, the three divine consultations (Helios with Zeus, Poseidon with Zeus, Athene with Zeus) are too often dismissed as imitations of similar scenes in the *Iliad*. In our analysis, however, as they occur as parallel elements in a thrice-repeated sequence, they should be analyzed and interpreted in terms of their correspondences with each other. Those motifs which form the conclusions of all three sequences, a reckless, impious group of mortals prompting divine wrath and their own resultant destruction, can especially help make known the *Odyssey*'s broad kinship with a specific subgenre of myth, in which a wrathful deity demands the large-scale destruction of offending mortals. In archaic Greek poetry, Hesiod suggests a similar dynamic in the account given in *The Works and Days* of the destruction of the earlier races of mortals. The pattern's concluding motif, the consultation between the offended deity and the principal god who persuades the former to enact the lesser of two destructive options, especially the Aiaian sequence's consultation between Helios and Zeus, has particular affinities with Zeus' interaction with Demeter in the *Homeric Hymn to Demeter*, and in earlier myths as far back as the divine council at *Gilgamesh* VI iii–iv, between Ishtar and Anu.

In the Ithakan sequence, many of the specific details and character functions are affected by the presence of a theoxenic story line, which throws into greater visibility the nature of the suitors' offenses as habitual violators of the sacred institution of hospitality, the character of Odysseus' disguise as a guest, and the specific motivations for Athene's wrath. The Lot narrative provides a particularly relevant comparand with the Ithakan sequence, as it too selects theoxeny as a vehicle to depict mortals' failings and their resultant large-scale destruction by an outraged deity, contrasted with the family of the one just man. Furthermore, Genesis offers a positive theoxeny immediately before the Lot narrative in the account of Abram's righteous reception of the angels (Genesis 18), much as the *Odyssey* quickly balances the skewed portrait of the suitors' behavior in Athene's presence in book 1 with Nestor's flawless reception of the same disguised deity in book 3.

The pattern also provides a lens through which to analyze difficulties in the *Odyssey*'s proem. The proem selects the events at Thrinakia because that episode is a specific instance of the pattern's own thrice-repeated climax of divine wrath and destruction prompted by the "culpable recklessness" in which the abusive bands of young men engage, the specific form their lack of self-control takes. As such, the proem's selection of Thrinakia points to the parallel outcomes of all three sequences. The proem singles out the Aiaian sequence for mention because, as the most heroic of the three sequences, it is most suitable to the generic demands of epic poetry. Through its introduction of the highly thematic verb πλάζω, the proem foregrounds a key term used to index the target of divine hostility. Odysseus himself functions as the object of Poseidon's wrath within the Aiaian sequence; Poseidon's interaction with him and, later, with the Phaiakian crew marks the boundaries of the Skherian sequence. But within the Ithakan sequence, where Poseidon's wrath does not reach, the verb designates the suitors as the victims of Athene's wrath. Consequently, πλάζω reinforces the poem's typical deployment of the polar opposition between Athene and Poseidon in their attitudes toward Odysseus.

The pattern can also help reveal significant differences between characters too often seen as virtually interchangeable, such as Kalypso and Kirke. While previous studies have made us well aware of the considerable parallels the two goddesses share, we can gain greater understanding of their functions in the poem by focusing on some of their salient differences. In this capacity the narrative pattern is a useful means by which to separate generic similarities from functional differences. Though similar in many surface characteristics, the goddesses exhibit profound differences in the ways in which they interact with Odysseus, differences thrown into clear contrast by the pattern. In terms of the pattern of behavior exhibited by the poem's other powerful females Kalypso is revealed to be an antitype. Perhaps more importantly, Kalypso is seen to exist outside of the narrative pattern, her unique circumstances affording the poem the opportunity to depict Odysseus in a dilemma quite unlike anything he encounters in any of the three sequences.

The presence of the pattern as a skeletal structure underlying, informing, and shaping the plot throughout the poem has important ramifications for theories about the transmission of the *Odyssey*'s text.[1] The pattern's existence suggests, if not demonstrates, a remarkably stable core or skeletal apparatus around which the bulk of the poem's plot is organized. The stability seen in both the pattern and its three sequences would seem to argue against any large-scale additions or subtractions of entire episodes or other substantial narrative units. The intricate, large-scale ring compositional arrangement of the three sequences further argues against any episodic view of composition or interpolation by later hands.

Regardless of such supposed factors as a Pisistratean recension, or the many other possible and conjectured vagaries of change or manipulation of the text from the eighth century (adopting Janko's dating),[2] the extended narrative pattern, in its three sequences, has enough stability to have resisted serious alteration. While some recent theorists[3] have argued that the text must have undergone considerable and continual alteration over a period of centuries, it is worth emphasizing that such arguments do not proceed from any large-scale analysis of the text or documentation of the possible changes it has undergone, but only on occasional quotations from Plato and the like, discrepancies at the level of a single word or line. In terms of larger structures, such assertions may be counter to the evidence that the pattern and its ring compositional sequences present. Most of the features we have discussed are not affected by variants of a particular word, or the absence or presence of a particular line. The succession of type-scenes may be largely "above" or "outside" of such textual issues, in that they rarely involve plot units small enough to be strongly influenced by or dependent upon a specific word that may or may not be attested in some or all of the manuscripts, or the like. Furthermore, it seems highly unlikely that interpolation, as in a rhapsode inserting an episode, could be a factor in the lengthy series of correspondences, repeated three times, which comprise the full working out of the extended narrative pattern. Equally unlikely is the possibility that the narrative pattern could underlie a "compilation" cobbled together out of a series of separate shorter "lays." In spite of attested variants, most of which, we should emphasize, are very small units, at the level of a word or brief formula, we have a text which has apparently remained quite stable in terms of many of the larger components of its plot. Although this was not my concern in conducting this study, it is now my view, on the basis of the evidence offered by the narrative pattern, that we have a poem largely shaped by one individual, though its roots stretch back far into ancient traditions.

Although Lord and his followers argue that thematic structure is evidence of orality, we know that certain literate writers also tend to organize epics around similar methods and principles.[4] I therefore do not regard the narrative pattern itself as proof of orality. I do, on the other hand, think it strengthens the possibility that the *Odyssey* is the product of an oral tradition because the pattern's existence demonstrates that one singer, aided by the underlying narrative pattern, could conceivably improvise in performance a poem of the length and complexity of the *Odyssey*.

The *Odyssey:* Structure, Narration, and Meaning

⮑⮑⮑

Notes

Abbreviations

AJP	*American Journal of Philology*
BICS	*Bulletin of the Institute of Classical Studies*
CJ	*Classical Journal*
CP	*Classical Philology*
CQ	*Classical Quarterly*
CW	*Classical World*
EEThess	Ἐπιστημονικὴ ἐπετηρίδα τῆς φιλοσοφικῆς Σχολῆς τοῦ Ἀριστοτ-ελείου πανεπιστημίου Θεσσαλονίκης, Τμήμα φιλοσοφίας
GRBS	*Greek, Roman, and Byzantine Studies*
HSCP	*Harvard Studies in Classical Philology*
JHS	*Journal of Hellenic Studies*
PCPS	*Proceedings of the Cambridge Philological Society*
REG	*Revue des études grecques*
TAPA	*Transactions of the American Philological Association*
YCS	*Yale Classical Studies*

Introduction

1. E.g., see Lowenstam's recent comment: "The most common feature in the Homeric poems is repetition. Not only are essential ideas often expressed by identical words or phrases, but similar scenes are usually depicted with the same details and patterns" (1).

2. For a history of the study of orality, see Foley 1988, and, for the earliest Homeric papers, Parry 1987.

3. Foley 1990: 5–8. See also Janko 1990 on the oral-dictated text.

4. Of the twelve published works collected in Adam Parry's edition of his father's writings, only one, a four-page review of Arend's *Die typischen Scene bei*

Homer (originally *CP* 31 [1936] 357–60 = A. Parry 1987: 404–7), deals with Homeric units larger than one line in length. His unpublished writings, however, demonstrate a growing interest in the type-scene.

5. Lord 1951. Cf. 1960: 4: "We shall come to realize the way in which themes can be expanded and contracted, and the manner in which they are joined together to form the final product which is the song."

6. E.g., "Zeus' famous speech (1.32–43) . . . is not essential to the story. It is one of the best of ornamental themes" (76). As noted in chapters 1 and 4, I place greater importance on the same speech.

7. There is considerable lack of agreement on terminology. Lord used "theme," for the same unit, apparently, that Hansen uses "sequence," Nagler, "motif," and others, "type-scene." Foley 1990 (see his index) equates "theme" and "typical scene."

8. Fenik 1968 and 1974; M. W. Edwards 1992. Cf. Krischer's study (1971) of the *aristeiai* in the *Iliad*. Nagler 1974 has explored a specific type-scene and offered comment on the techniques that underlie its employment. For more recent work, see especially Reece 1993, an analysis of the hospitality type-scene in the *Odyssey*. For a summary of the principal developments, see Foley 1990: 240–45.

9. For a summary of other relevant work, see M. W. Edwards 1992. Lowenstam and Miller do analyze lengthier structures, approaching the concerns upon which we focus here.

10. Cf. Lowenstam's discussion (2–3) of the same moment. I thank an anonymous reader who, in comments on an earlier draft of part of chapter 2, suggests the passage's relevance to the interpretive issues under discussion.

11. Translations of the *Odyssey* are those of Richmond Lattimore, though I occasionally adjust his renderings when I feel an important point has been obscured.

12. Hainsworth 359 on 8.215–18.

13. Ahl and Roisman (7–10) note the dilemma, but offer what seems to me an oversimplification of it.

14. See chapter 1, n. 4.

15. Cf. Lowenstam's open question: "However, if two distinct passages have not one but several common formulas or details, is there a point at which the literary critic should consider this phenomenon noteworthy?" (2). Cf. Mueller's notion (151–58) of "contextual surplus."

16. While I firmly disagree with Hainsworth's comment, I intend no disrespect to a scholar with whose work I am often in agreement and whom I cite frequently in this study.

17. Of readers who firmly hold to such a "localized" view of Homeric composition, perhaps I will convince few of the designs upon which I will focus. But this study may at least prove useful to them as a collection of an inordinate number of such correspondences.

18. Cook 1995 expresses similar interest: "Parallelism is one of the most pervasive and important structural features of epic narration" (125).

19. Those readers who feel writing plays a role in the poem's genesis will not

have the same qualms over the perceived existence of larger patterns of organization.

20. See Holoka 477, 480, for recent caveats against letting highly conjectural notions about the text's genesis place undue limitations on interpretative possibilities in the text itself.

21. Cf. Hainsworth on 6.232–35 and their recurrence at 23.159–62: "However, the Homeric audience were too thoroughly accustomed to repetition for any particular instance to have been significant to them" (308).

22. Cf. Lowenstam: "In short, the method is to develop and elaborate upon ideas and motifs by putting them through a series of permutations in order to perceive at the end their true value and meaning. In music, the fugue develops themes in the same way, and one can draw parallels between the literary and musical methods" (11).

23. The poem's ethical concern was often noted in antiquity; cf. Aristotle, *Poetics*, 24.3, and Longinus 9.15.

24. See Hainsworth *ad* 8.62–103. Cf. Louden 1996a.

25. The Greek text throughout is that of W. B. Stanford.

26. Cf. Nagy's interpretation, 1996a, of the variant at *Od.* 19.521, πολυδευκέα (in Aelian, *De natura animalium*, 5.38) for usual πολυηχέα φωνήν. The phrase occurs in Penelope's comparison of herself to a singing nightingale, arguably a parallel to the principal composer (on Penelope as paralleling Homer, see Felson-Rubin, 25, 42, and 156 n. 43). Nagy would render *poludeukes* as "'having much continuity' or 'having continuity in many different ways' or even 'patterning in many ways' (or 'many times'). The translation 'patterning' highlights the idea of continuity through variety. And the patterns of continuity and variety are conceived as the distinctly poetic skills of songmaking in performance" (49).

27. For a recent discussion of structural analyses of the Apologue see Cook 1995: 49–92.

28. Lord 1990: 69, cf. 81, 94. Cf. Foley, 1991: 17 and 1990: 242.

29. Perhaps first emphasized by Kearns.

30. Lowenstam 12, quoting Austin 273.

Chapter One: The Extended Narrative Pattern in the Odyssey

1. See especially Lord 1960. For analysis of the thematic structures under discussion in this chapter I have found the following particularly useful: Beye 1966, Rose 1969b, Lang 1969, Fenik 1974, Kearns, Crane, Katz, and Reece 1993.

2. As M. W. Edwards notes (1992: 285–86), such an approach is indebted to Vladimir Propp's *Morphology of the Folktale*. For distinctions between theme, type-scene, and narrative pattern see Edwards 285–86.

3. Commentators have occasionally argued for large-scale instances of ring composition, but, as with most other analyses of the poem's structure, they have usually confined their argued ring compositional schema to the Apologue. For a recent survey of such arguments see Cook 1995: chap. 2.

4. Among recent work see Rose 1969a & b, Fenik 1974, Van Nortwick, Miller 62–68, Lowenstam 145–73, Rutherford, Reece 1993: 101–21, and Katz. One of the best such discussions remains Lang 1969.

5. *Female* rather than *woman* is the necessary term to cover all such figures, since Kirke is a goddess, the others (Nausikaa, Arete, and Penelope), mortals. Curiously, a number of contemporary critics use "woman" indiscriminately for females in myth, whether human or divine. I suggest that while mortals can parallel immortals' actions to a certain extent, profound differences are always evident.

6. Demodokos' second song, the triangle between Hephaistos, Aphrodite, and Ares (8.266–366), and Zeus' paradigm of Agamemnon, Klytaimnestra, and Aigisthos (1.35–43) will be discussed below as brief versions of the pattern.

7. I suggest that the two functions of sexuality and having power over Odysseus' homecoming, which elsewhere are embodied in one female (Kirke and Penelope), are on Skheria bifurcated into Nausikaa, who bears an erotic and marital tone, and Arete, who controls access to Odysseus' homecoming. I return to this topic below.

8. Though in each instance, we receive the report of the prophecy only after Odysseus' actual arrival.

9. The Aiaian sequence begins with the first stop on the homeward voyage, Ismaros, as discussed below, with the specific motif of Odysseus having problems with a band of young men. However, as both the Skherian and Ithakan sequences begin with Odysseus' solitary approach to the powerful females, we will begin with Odysseus' approach to them.

10. The *Odyssey* offers a parallel in Hermes' visit to Aigisthos, described by Zeus at 1.38 ff.

11. Zeus first names the land and people in his prophecy at 5.34 ff.

12. Clearly there are significant differences in Odysseus' arrival at the three islands. He is accompanied by his crew when he reaches Aiaia, while he is completely alone when he makes his landfall on Skheria, his landing on Ithaka falling somewhere in between. However, each sequence has Odysseus ignorant of his whereabouts, and frustrated as a consequence. The recurring lines, 6.119–21 = 13.200–202, have been attacked in the second instance (see Hainsworth 301). However, as they are part of a lengthy, recurring complex, I find them genuine.

13. The poem gives his lineage at 15.225–56, as well as the partially suppletive information at 11.291 ff.

14. Hermes' physical form here has occasioned much comment. See Heubeck, on 10.274–79 for a brief summary of the different points of view. The debate centers on an alleged lack of motivation for Hermes' appearance as a young man when archaic iconography more typically presents him as a somewhat older male. While he assumes similar form for his intervention at *Iliad* 24.347, his youthful appearance is there thought to be more fittingly motivated by the context. Heubeck and others thus assume the Aiaian passage is modeled on *Iliad* 24. I offer a different view below. I would add in passing that there remains a distinct *Iliad*-centered bias evident in many scholars. The present study seeks to appreciate the *Odyssey*

on its own terms and does not assume specific episodes are necessarily composed in reaction to passages in the *Iliad*.

15. E.g., Hermes opens with a question to which he knows the answer, much as Athene plays with Odysseus at *Od.* 13.221 ff and Apollo teases Hektor at *Il.* 15.244–45. This is quite typical of divine intercourse with mortals; compare also God's questions of Adam at Genesis 3.9 ff. I suggest that Hermes, in ὦ δύστηνε, makes something of a play on the first two syllables of Odysseus' name, which name he never utters. For further discussion of wordplay on the name Odysseus, see Louden 1995: 34–41.

16. Cf. Cook 1995: 56: "The Kikonian episode introduces the crew in the image fixe of the suitors, feasting on boundless meat and wine."

17. See Cook 1995: 64 on the parallels between the crew's loss of self-control both on Thrinakia and in the Aiolos episode.

18. Nausikaa has also warned him at 6.273 ff. Note especially her remark, μάλα δ'εἰσὶν ὑπερφίαλοι κατὰ δῆμον (6.274).

19. ". . . but you go in with a spirit that fears / nothing. The bold man proves the better for every action / in the end, even though he be a stranger coming from elsewhere (7.50–52)."

20. Some scholars continue to question the accuracy of Athene's and Nausikaa's claims for Arete's importance. See, for instance, Fenik 1974: 105 ff. I suggest, however, that a comparison of her function with those of Kirke, Nausikaa, and Penelope reinforces Athene's (and Nausikaa's, at 6.303–15) claim.

21. The pattern, in fact, seems quite ancient and widespread. Cf. Thompson, who discusses a similar motif which appears as N716.1: "Man discovers bathing maiden." Many have discussed the motif, e.g. Fenik 1974: 33 ff, Reece 1993: 12 ff.

22. In book 13 Athene's visit is first motivated by a teasing test (as Odysseus employs in similar encounters, e.g., that with Laertes in book 24), which then gives way to the offering of advice and aid. See Reece 1993: 10 on a similar mixture of type-scenes.

23. This teasing quality is quite close to Hermes' dialogue with Priam, *Il.* 24.362 ff, perhaps more so than the dialogue between Odysseus and Hermes at *Od.* 10.281 ff.

24. Eumaios shares some parallels with Alkinoös in this respect. Each is Odysseus' first host on his respective island, until Odysseus wins over Arete/Penelope; each serves as something of a conduit between Odysseus and the powerful female; each is closely concerned with the initial storytelling that occurs in both locales. Chapter 3 explores these parallels in detail.

25. This is partly due to the different contexts. On Ithaka many people, whether loyal servants or hostile suitors, are capable of recognizing Odysseus if he is not disguised. On Skheria the cloud cover is arguably a brief element of disguise. On Aiaia, the motif is curiously reversed, as half of the crew have been "disguised," changed by Kirke into animals.

26. On this as the likely intent, see Crane 64.

27. For a study of the other passages initiated by this line see Webber.

28. Murnaghan, for instance, does not include it in her thorough analysis of Odyssean recognition scenes.

29. Hermes thus functions as a consummate mediator in this episode, as he is responsible both for advising Odysseus on how to deal with Kirke as well as having earlier advised Kirke of Odysseus' eventual arrival.

30. From a related perspective, consider Crane's comments: "The Medea of the *Argonautica* fuses in a single character aspects which the *Odyssey* distributes between Nausicaa on the one hand and Kirke/Kalypso on the other hand" (142). Many commentators have, in fact, assumed that Nausikaa is partly based on an earlier tradition of Medea's role.

31. For recent commentary on this parallel, see especially Lang 1969, Van Nortwick, and Katz 86–87, 114–15, 136–37, 141, etc.

32. See the close of Odysseus' speech to her (6.180–85), her subsequent proclamation, "If only the man to be called my husband could be like this one" (6.244), her conjectured abuse from the other Phaiakians, "Surely he is to be her husband" (277), and Alkinoös' explicit marriage offer to Odysseus (7.311 ff). There is a great deal of literature touching on this subject; see, for instance, Woodhouse, and Lattimore 1969.

33. See, for example, Fenik 1974: 127, 243, Joyce's adaptation of the scene in *Ulysses*, and Nagler 1974: 47.

34. Both Nausikaa (6.274 ff) and Athene (7.30 ff) emphasize the potential danger that awaits Odysseus as he approaches the queen.

35. Fenik 1974: 1–18, among others, has dealt at length with her delay. Though his study is a valuable one, I do not agree with his conclusions about Arete's function in the narrative (105 ff). I argue that she plays a more central role than he suggests.

36. On Ithaka, in his first interview with Penelope, Odysseus will again avoid revealing direct information about himself (19.115–22), other than his relatively recent whereabouts (19.273–82). He mentions the Thrinakia incident, final stop on the wanderings, and the stay at Skheria, instead finding opportunity to praise Penelope (19.107–14).

37. For a summary of the objections and suggested inconsistencies, see Katz 78–93.

38. On the similarities see Lang 1969 and van Nortwick.

39. On the discrepancy, see, again, Katz 78 ff, and the earlier discussions she summarizes.

40. We can also claim as parallel Kirke's duplicitous motives when she first receives Odysseus, 10.310–20.

41. See the discussion by Wohl.

42. See further, Wohl 27–29, on Nausikaa's sexual identity.

43. On the narrative problems in Odysseus' seemingly clairvoyant understanding of Penelope's motives, see again, Katz 89, 118.

44. We may have one slight trace of this tendency in Arete. At the end of Odys-

seus' first evening at court, Arete bids her servants prepare a bed for the stranger (7.335–43). This is the only occasion in Homeric epic where a host urges a guest to go to bed without a request having been made (Reece 1993: 67). This is perhaps as close as Arete comes to suggesting any sexual modality, and only distantly echoes Odysseus' making love to Kirke and Penelope.

45. That Odysseus is able to dictate the time of the interview is an indication of his subtly growing stature on Ithaka.

46. Such a procedure is inherently part of Odysseus' character, as well as his necessary reaction to the story of Agamemnon's reception by Klytaimnestra.

47. The separate acts grouped together here, though clearly present in each sequence, do not all occur in precisely the same order in each sequence.

48. We return to a fuller discussion of the nature of their sexual relations in chapter 5.

49. See Heubeck on 10.346.

50. For the most complete treatment of this topic see Reece 1993, throughout. Earlier commentators include Arend.

51. For a recent discussion, see P. V. Jones.

52. For a very different perspective on Odysseus' nakedness, see Gutglueck.

53. See Katz 177, for the view that Penelope establishes a relationship with Odysseus based more on hospitality than on marriage.

54. 6.114: "and she [Nausikaa] should be his guide to the city of the Phaiakians."

55. As Crane notes (136 ff), the offer itself is not surprising, only the swiftness with which Alkinoös makes it.

56. Such passages include *Od.* 1.43 (of Hermes to Aigisthos), 1.307 (of Athene to Telemakhos), 6.313 (of Arete to Odysseus), 7.15 (of Athene to Odysseus), 7.42 (same), 7.75 (of Arete to Odysseus), 16.17 (general, in simile, of father to child). For κακὰ φρονέων / φρονέουσα· *Il.* 16.783 (Apollo to Patroklos), *Od.* 10.317 (of Kirke to Odysseus), 20.5 (of Odysseus to the suitors). See also δολοφρονέουσα, 10.339, of Kirke before she and Odysseus make love.

57. On her intimacy, note how she delineates their lovemaking, ὄφρα μιγέντε / εὐνῇ καὶ φιλότητι πεποίθομεν ἀλλήλοισιν (10.334–35). As to her subsequent aid, consider the two lengthy sets of advice, before the Catabasis and before the resumption of his wanderings, as well as provisions and even knowledge of a particular knot (8.447–48). This topic is covered more fully in chapter 5.

58. Official recognition or conference of the status is normally a masculine role. On this see Katz 134 ff, 174. That Arete performs this role is another subtle indication of the power she wields.

59. See Doherty 1991 for a convincing analysis of how Odysseus tailors parts of the Nekuia for Arete's benefit.

60. Hainsworth on 6.181–85.

61. Note that Athene's agenda at 8.21–22, ὥς κεν Φαιήκεσσι φίλος πάντεσσι γένοιτο / δεινός τ' αἰδοῖός τε, also describes the process by which Arete becomes φίλα φρονέουσα.

62. The parallels have been noted by many. Among these, see Doherty 1991: 172–73, and Lang 1969.

63. Note her assertive "in *my* palace [ἐν μεγάροισιν ἐμοῖσι]," used of Penelope only here, and the similarly assertive 19.94, where she rebukes a rude serving maid.

64. Hainsworth, noting the repeated simile and context, suggests (on 6.232–35), "The repetition cannot have been conscious." I take a more open view, however, of the architectonics possible in oral composition. We note that not only are the lines repeated, but that they occur at the same location in each sequence of the narrative pattern.

65. *Epistle I.* 2.24–31. See Farron's brief discussion, 87. Powell 1977: 33 makes a brief parallel between the three bands of young men.

66. Excessive drinking and consumption turned the Ismaros stop into a disaster (9.43–46), while the proem heavily foregrounds the issue of excessive consumption at Thrinakia.

67. 1.365, 4.768, 17.360, 18.399, 22.21.

68. That he dies as a result of his intoxication looks ahead to the suitors' drunken state in their final day. We return to a fuller consideration of Elpenor, and Leodes, his counterpart among the suitors, in the following chapter.

69. Odysseus hunts a stag for his crew, which he catches because the μένος ἠελίοιο (10.160) has made it seek a drink in the river. Frequent mention of Helios continues (10.183, 185, 191). Functioning as something of a thematic transition, perhaps, are significant solar emphases in the previous episode with the Laistrygones (10.86).

70. Segal 1992 is perhaps too lenient, suggesting that "we feel sympathy for the doomed companions; their fault . . . seems pardonable" (509). I suggest that the poem intends us to have no more sympathy for the crew than for the suitors. Chapter 4 deals more fully with the nature of the crew's wrongdoing.

71. "[Odysseus] who beyond others / has given sacrifice to the gods" (1.66–67). Friedrich 1987: 394 accurately sums of the Thrinakian episode as "the aristeia of Odysseus' *tlemosyne*."

72. Rose 1969a remains the best account of potential conflict facing Odysseus on Skheria. For an attempted rebuttal which points out a few excesses in Rose's depiction, but nonetheless fails to overturn most of his formulations, see de Vries. See also Reece 1993: 104–7.

73. See especially 6.273–74, 7.15–17, 7.32–33, and 7.60 (the Phaiakians are descended from a "recklessly daring people", λαὸν ἀτάσθαλον).

74. Woodhouse has explored this perspective most fully, arguing that an earlier folktale version, in which Odysseus would have wooed and married Nausikaa, underlies the sequence. See also Murnaghan 97 and Reece 1993: 109 ff, and his references to the earlier literature.

75. See D. M. Jones for a useful study of ἀτάσθαλος and ἀτασθαλίαι in Homer. He translates the latter as "culpable recklessness" (21).

76. However, there is no unanimity on the subject. Cf. Hainsworth (on 8.215–

18), quoted in the introduction: "That episode [the μνηστηροφονία] does not need the support of so distant and incidental a comment as this."

77. See S. West on 4.342–44 and Russo on 17.134.

78. For further discussion of how that wrestling match reverberates in Odysseus's wider career, see Louden 1996a.

79. I am unable to find any earlier commentator having made this suggestion.

80. At 13.21 the narrator also uses ἑταῖροι of the Phaiakian crew.

81. Poseidon's punishment is analogous with the Clashing Rocks through which the Argonauts sailed (but no one since) a boundary marking off heroic deeds and times from subsequent eras.

82. In chapter 4 we return to a fuller consideration of Poseidon's wrath.

83. E.g., S. West, on 1.37 ff; "Here too the fate of Aegisthus foreshadows that of the suitors" (78).

84. See Lateiner 203–42 for an intriguing study of how the suitors' body language supports his assertion that their "behaviors present a coherent pattern that is offensive to heroic decency" (203).

85. There is no consensus as to the meanings of the three names under consideration. Though the specific elements in Eurylokhos and Eurymakhos seem unambiguous, there are different possibilities for the second component of Euryalos. Von Kamptz 71 suggests ἅλλομαι.

86. See A. Edwards 1985: 15–42 for a study of λόχος in Homer, though he does not deal with Eurylokhos.

87. Von Kamptz suggests both εὐρυ—"rich in" (89)—or ἔρυμαι (64) as possible derivations for the first element of these compounds. He does not, however, address the possibility of any relationship between the three similar names.

88. There are also traces of two leaders in the Skherian sequence, Euryalos and Laodamas. Though Euryalos has the larger and more antagonistic role toward Odysseus, there is a tight teamwork between the two as they agree to approach Odysseus (8.131–64).

89. See Fenik 1974: 198–205, for fuller discussion of differences between Antinoös and Eurymakhos.

90. Though Antinoös proposes the attempt, Eurymakhos assents to the plan, 4.663–74.

91. It is worth noting that Herakles, with whom the *Odyssey* several times parallels Odysseus, has as his principal human antagonist Eurystheus (the king, whose power over Herakles is explained at *Il.* 19.95–133), a similar compound name, and on a less important level, Eurytion. Note also that Eurystheus is Herakles' kinsman, as Eurylokhos is Odysseus' (10.441).

92. In chapter 4 I will discuss alleged problems in the proem's reference to the Thrinakia episode.

93. Polyphemos earlier curses Odysseus with approximately the same fate: "let him come late, in bad case, with the loss of all his companions" (9.534). However, inasmuch as the proem, the Ismaros incident, and the general structure of the *Odyssey* argue that the crew, not Polyphemos' curse, are themselves responsible

for their deaths, perhaps the curse is best understood as an instance of Dodds' "overdetermination," the divine causality simultaneously paralleling the human responsibility.

94. E.g., the suitors' uncontrollable laughter (345–47) and the transformation of their feast into a mess of blood (348). Fenik 1974: 242 rightly compares this last to the strange happenings on Thrinakia as the flesh of the slain cattle creeps and bellows.

95. Cf. Russo on 20.351–57: "The most eerie passage in Homer . . . the symbolism is well-nigh universal" (124).

96. The Gospels offer frequent parallels: Matthew 24.29, "The sun will be darkened, the moon will not give her light, the stars will fall from the sky." Cf. Mark 13.24–25, Luke 21.25–26, and the like. Translations are from *The Oxford Study Bible*.

97. On this see Kearns, Reece 1993: 139, 181–86, 200–201. See also Burnett 224–25 for a comprehensive list of theoxenies.

98. 1.227; 3.207; 17.245, 588; 18.381; 20.170, 370.

99. Telemakhos, 16.178–79; Penelope, 23.63–68.

100. Note especially 13.396 ff.

101. Thus the oft invoked Homeric trinity of Zeus, Athene, and Apollo (*Il.* 2.371, 4.288, 7.132; *Od.* 4.341, 6.311, 17.132, 18.235, 24.376) seem to be working in tandem.

102. For why Zeus assents so willingly, compare Hades' fear in the theomakhy at *Iliad* 20.61 ff.

103. Since antiquity, line 158 of Zeus' response has attracted much argument, as the possibilities pose very different narrative consequences. For a recent discussion see Peradotto 1990: 77–82, though I do not agree with his conclusions as to the authenticity of $\mu\acute{\epsilon}\gamma\alpha$ $\delta\acute{\epsilon}$, i.e., Zeus really recommends that Poseidon obliterate the Phaiakians. I argue that the narrative pattern in the other sequences, in which Zeus reins in the respective god's more dire threat, agreeing on a more reasonable option, the destruction of the band of young men, is persuasive against such a reading. Also against the manuscript is Friedrich 1989.

104. See Heubeck on 12.374–90.

105. Hoekstra on 13.125–87, though he does not specify which scenes he has in mind, and does not consider the parallels within the *Odyssey* itself.

106. "It is equally unmistakable that this divine scene in xxiv is based on Iliadic models" (Heubeck on 24.472–88).

107. Theoklymenos makes appearances in the palace, but is technically Eurymakhos' guest (15.513–22). As to his unexplained whereabouts between books 17 and 20, see Russo on 20.350.

108. See Thalmann 1984: 8–21 for a demonstration of the prevalence of this technique in Archaic poetry. For analysis of a specific large-scale instance of ring composition in the *Odyssey*, see Reece 1995.

109. I argue that the Skherian sequence begins when Odysseus encounters Poseidon on his way to Skheria. The preceding portion of book 5, Odysseus with

Kalypso, is a special case, not part of the extended narrative pattern. Chapter Five will focus on the singular narrative shape of the *Odyssey*'s Fifth Book.

110. The Aiaian sequence is the least human as well; consider the implied fate of the penned-in crew.

111. Though in these brief versions some elements of the pattern are missing or modified. The band of young men, for instance, is one male, Aigisthos and Ares.

112. Again some elements are lacking; e.g., Telemakhos knows his location. Crane 42 ff explores parallels between Helen and Kirke.

113. On this issue, see Rutherford 133 ff.

114. Many or all elements could clearly work for a narrative about Jason and Medea, for instance.

115. See Hoekstra, on 15.223–81, for a summary of the criticisms Theoklymenos has attracted. Lord (174) suggests he was based on an Odysseus-in-disguise theme. I argue that he is better understood as the most expanded version of the multiform of the prophet who predicts both Odysseus' homecoming and the destruction of the relevant band of young men, Teiresias, and Alkinoös' father, Nausithoös, being the other figures.

116. I do not claim that my approach resolves all alleged narrative inconsistencies, but I do argue that it provides a more useful lens with which to study them.

117. Cf. the suggestions by Lang 163 ff and Reece 1993: 116 ff that certain elements in the Skherian sequence are awkwardly modeled on particulars more comfortable in the Ithakan multiform.

Chapter Two: Elpenor and Leodes: Desire and Limitless Wine

1. Particularly true of Eurylokhos and Eurymakhos, less so of Euryalos.

2. Elpenor has attracted considerable discussion, much of it dominated by genetical discussions exploring his possible origin as: borrowed from Argonautic legend (Meuli 91), making use of the motif of meeting a deceased acquaintance in the underworld (Eisenberger 167), alluding to the possible existence of a relevant tumulus (Merkelbach 204), or as an allegedly late addition to the poem (Page 44–47), to help connect the Nekuia with the rest of the poem (Kirk 1962: 239–40). Leodes remains a comparably neglected character. Recent discussions include those by Fenik 1974: 192–96, Dimock 282–83, 306, Yamagata 1994: 167, and Reece 1995: 208–11, 221–24. I believe I am the first to argue that Elpenor and Leodes are related. Fenik 1974: 192–96 argues that Leodes is a double of Amphinomos. While there is much to be said for his argument, such a view omits several of Leodes' most salient characteristics. Furthermore, Fenik himself (194) notes an inconsistency in his analysis: "He is without physical strength . . . and without either the stature or vigor of his counterpart [Amphinomos]."

3. See again Lateiner's statement: "The suitors' behaviors present a coherent pattern that is offensive to heroic decency" (203).

4. E.g., Fenik 1974: 242.

5. Cf. Beye 1966: "The suitors, waiting for her to finish the shroud with which

she is deceiving them, are in their riotous debauchery really no different from the pigs transformed from men whom Circe has charmed" (175). Cf. Beye 1974: 97–98.

6. Aiolos feasts the crew for a month (10.14), but none of the powerful female figures is present, nor are the other key elements of the narrative pattern, the prophet, the strife between crew and Odysseus, and the like.

7. On regarding Theoklymenos' two briefly separated speeches as one, see Friedrich's analysis (1991: 23–24) of Odysseus' boasts to Polyphemos.

8. Aside from the passages noted, εἰδώλων is otherwise used in the *Odyssey* only of the dream image Athena sends to Penelope (4.796, 4.824, 4.835).

9. Not true of either of the other named crewmen, Eurylokhos, who appears throughout books 10–12, and Perimedes, appearing in the underworld episode (11.23), as well as that of the sirens (12.195).

10. Not true of a considerable number of suitors: Antinoos (1.383), Eurymakhos (1.399), Eurynomos (2.21), Leokritos (2.242), Amphinomos (16.351), Moulios, his herald (18.423), Eurydamas (18.297), Peisandros (18.299), in addition to Melanthios (17.212), all of whom are mentioned or themselves appear on earlier occasions. Of the other suitors with speaking parts, only Ktessipos (20.288) and Agelaos (20.321) are named only on their final day. Demoptolemos (22.242), Polybos (22.243), Euryades (22.267), and Elatos (22.267), all of whom do not have speaking parts, occur only in the μνηστηροφονία. Amphimedon has a speaking part in the underworld (24.103 ff).

11. See Reece 1995: 208 on the order of the suitors' attempts as implicitly linked to their importance and their likelihood at success.

12. Antinoös' reasoning is entirely specious and clearly an attempt to avoid the spectacle of his own public failure, were he to try to string the bow. See Fernández-Galliano on 21.257–62, who also notes the considerable irony in Antinoös being the first to die from the same bow.

13. Thus far the same could be said of Amphinomos, whom Fenik argues is a double of Leodes. However, Amphinomos does not replicate the other parallels shared by Elpenor and Leodes, excessive drinking and softness.

14. Fernández-Galliano (on 21.144) regards Οἶνοψ as an itacistic form, taking ἦνοψ, which does occur as a proper name at *Il.* 16.401, as the likely form of the patronymic. As he does not, however, find any contextual reason or meaning gained by this derivation, and given Homeric epic's well-known propensity for wordplay based on proper names, it seems preferable to stay with the consensus view, adopted by Stanford and others, deriving the name from οἶνος.

15. E.g., Stanford 1962 on 21.144, Dimock 282, and Reece 1995: 224. Von Kamptz renders it as "weinfarbig." Mühlestein regards it as a "nom de couleur" (21).

16. Among many studies, see especially Sulzberger, Stanford 1939, Rank, and Louden 1995.

17. Cf. Cook 1995: 45: "The Kikonian episode introduces the crew in the image fixe of the suitors, feasting on boundless meat and wine."

18. See Fernández-Galliano's note on 21.293–310.

19. Edmunds observes that the gap between Antinoös' intent and our interpretation is part of a regular pattern in Homeric epic's use of myth in which "the story has a meaning beyond the one intended by [the speaker]" (420).

20. As for the name Leodes, textual problems again make it difficult to assess its function as a significant name. Stanford 1962, however, assuming $\Lambda\epsilon\acute{\iota}\omega\delta\eta s$, renders it "Smooth," consistent with his delicate hands; cf. Reece 224, "Tender." Van Kamptz, reading $\Lambda\eta\acute{\omega}\delta\eta s$, derives it from *$\lambda a\digamma o$-$\digamma\acute{a}\delta\eta s$ (76).

21. Cf. Reinhardt 114, and Peradotto on the name as meaning "man of delusion" (107) and/or "man of desire" (167).

22. See Louden 1995: 30.

23. Heubeck, on 11.66–78 and 11.74–78.

24. See Fenik 1974: 198–205 for fuller discussion of differences between Antinoös and Eurymakhos.

25. E.g., Fernández-Galliano, who, on 22.318, refers to the "sacrilege" of his death, and (on 22.330–80) to his "cruel Fate" (276, 278).

26. E.g., S. West, on 1.37 ff: "Here too the fate of Aegisthus foreshadows that of the suitors" (78).

27. On the importance of ring composition as a structural device in archaic Greek poetry see Thalmann 1984: 8–21, Parks, and Reece 1995.

28. See Cook 1995: 65–78, for a recent attempt to apply and refine Whitman's schema, as well as bibliography on other relevant analyses.

29. Modified from Reece 1995: 221–22.

30. See Fernández-Galliano (21.145) on the likely nature of Leodes' profession.

31. Although it is not uncommon in the *Iliad* for a mortally wounded warrior, in his last moments, to see through a brief window into the future (e.g., Patroklos 16.852–54), Elpenor provides the only such instance of the motif in the *Odyssey*.

32. Other than the brief mention of Antiphos (2.17–20), who is not named, however, when his death actually occurs in book 9.

33. See Fernández-Galliano on 22.330–80.

34. Friedrich (1987: 399) argues that the Phaiakians sustain no loss of life in the ship's petrification. I have to disagree on the basis that a conjectured miraculous rescue of the crew seems a stretch, and both the narrative pattern and Poseidon's wrath argue against the Phaiakian crew's preservation.

35. See especially *The Singer of Tales,* chap. 4.

36. See, again, Heubeck's discussion on 10.551–60.

Chapter Three: Eumaios and Alkinoös: The Audience and the Odyssey

1. Recent studies include: P. Rose 145–49, Stewart 146–95, Moulton 145–53, Seidensticker, G. Walsh 3–21, Thalmann 1984: 170–84, Murnaghan, Goldhill 111, Pratt 63–94, Segal 1994: 85–109, Doherty 1991, 1995.

2. On his reciprocity with Demodokos see Louden 1996a.

3. Cf. Doherty (1995: 89): "By allowing the hero to take over . . . the narration of the poem . . . the epic narrator sets up an implied double comparison: on the

one hand, a comparison between himself and Odysseus in the narrator's role; on the other hand, a complementary comparison between the Phaeacians as internal audience and implied audience of the epic as a whole."

4. Cf. those in which Odysseus is not involved, the accounts Nestor (3.103–200, 254–328) and Menelaos (4.240–64, 351–587) give to Telemakhos.

5. Reece 1993; see his discussion of item XII in his grid, "Entertainment." The *Odyssey* offers many other internal narratives, including Phemios's first song, the songs of Demodokos, for which Odysseus himself is included among the internal audience, and Odysseus's truncated internal narrative of his wanderings related to Penelope (23.306–41).

6. On multiforms, different instantiations of the same theme or character performing the same essential function, as a typical feature of oral/mythic narrative, see, e.g., Lord 1960: 120, 198–99, 221, 1991: 102. Cf. Nagy 1979: 3, 43, 205, 42n3, Foley 1990: 10, 12, etc. Without taking orality into account, Propp presupposes the same tendency. Relevant recent Homeric studies include Lowenstam, Reece 1993, and Louden 1993a.

7. Doherty 1995 is centrally concerned with this topic.

8. See especially Iser 1974.

9. Iser 1978: 34–38. Though his textual models are more "literary" than oral, nonetheless, if we substitute audience for his "reader," the model remains useful and applicable.

10. Among recent work see Hankey, Roisman, Ramming 146–50, Segal 1994: 164–83 (see esp. his comment, "Books 14 and 15 are probably the most neglected of the *Odyssey* [164]"), and Olson 120–39. See also brief discussions by Farron 59–101, P. Rose 1975, Petropoulou, A. Edwards 1993: 60–70. For discussions of Eumaios' function as internal audience, see Thalmann 1984: 161, Goldhill 65–66, G. Walsh 5, 9, 19, and Doherty 1995: 72, 84–85, 119, 148–50, 157–59, 171.

11. E.g., Kirk 1962 asserts that book 14 is "the least satisfactory . . . of any in either poem" (360); cf. Clarke: "The time and space given to the garrulous Eumaeus seem disproportionate, and the whole is not marked by any compensating rustic charm" (73).

12. Fenik 1968: 159, M. Edwards 1987b: 47 ff.

13. By "modality" I do not necessarily mean a strict interpretation à la Northrop Frye, though his distinctions as to high mimetic, low mimetic, and so forth do capture the distinctions I have in mind. The Ithakan sequence involving Eumaios is verisimilar and contemporary by contrast with the Marchen world in which Alkinoös is situated.

14. Segal 1994: 164–65 briefly notes a few correspondences between the characters.

15. E.g., the poem neatly divides into six four-book units (1–4, 5–8, etc.). For a recent structural analysis along these lines see Tracy 1990 and 1997. The weaknesses of such an approach, however, are considerable. The book divisions postdate the poem's composition, and are thus a superimposition onto its proper narrative shape, obscuring the different chronologies at work in the three sequences

and obscuring arguably more important structural seams, such as the beginning and ending of the Skherian sequence (5.282 ff, 13.187), the ring compositional structure in which Elpenor figures, and so on.

16. Because of the ring compositional arrangement of the sequences, the Ithakan surrounding the Skherian.

17. The hospitality type-scene has been well studied since Arend. Reece 1993 has the most complete analysis and summary of earlier work.

18. As will be noted intermittently below, Menelaos, in his reception of Telemakhos, shares many of the qualities found in Eumaios and Alkinoös, but does not act significantly as an audience to Telemakhos. Rather, he delivers his own extensive narrative to him (4.347–586).

19. As Fenik (1974: 155 ff.) has shown, the structure of Odysseus's encounter with Eumaios in book 14 is closely related to his later encounter with Penelope. On Eumaios as intermediary between Odysseus and Penelope, see Ramming 149. Menelaos plays a similar role in introducing Telemakhos to Helen, though she exercises less control over his journey than the narrative pattern's powerful females do over Odysseus' passage.

20. Penelope is on very close terms with Eumaios; e.g., 17.507 ff and 17.542 ff.

21. In Eumaios' background sketch the narrator closely links him to Penelope (14.7–9).

22. Though Alkinoös dominates the Phaiakian sequence, having a considerably larger speaking role than Arete, both Athene, the epic's most important deity, and Nausikaa declare Arete's importance (7.53–77, 6.305–15). Arete's true role is most evident in the Intermezzo (11.335–45); on which see Doherty 1991 and Louden 1993a: 15–17.

23. Cf. Hesiod, *Works and Days,* 109–20. For attempted identifications of Syria see Heubeck 1989: 257. I, however, assume no real location is intended, much as with Skheria or Ogygia (though many have attempted identifications for these). Such locales are meant to be inaccessible for mortals. The *Odyssey* provides an etiology as to why no one may now reach Skheria (13.125–87). Thalmann 1984: 231 n. 7 and A. Edwards 1993: 48–49 are some of the few commentators to note Syria's paradisiacal qualities. For closer discussion and analysis of Skheria's paradisiacal qualities see Thalmann 1984: 97–106; A. Edwards 1993: 47. Dimock 1989: 83 calls Skheria "the first Utopia in Western literature"; Austin (153–62) compares Skheria and Ogygia. I do not argue that there are no distinctions between these paradises. Skheria is an elaborate utopia explored at some length, while Syria is only mentioned here, in passing.

24. Note that Menelaos also has a connection with paradise in his prophesied future in the Elysian Fields, 4.563–68. On parallels between Menelaos and Alkinoös, their opulence, the slight gaffes, and potential humor in both, see Reece 1993: 82–83, and the commentators he notes (82n.20).

25. However, Reece 1993: 21–22 notes such displacement is a typical element of hospitality.

26. See Hankey 29–31.

27. 15.363-70. Cf. Powell 1977: 61-62, Murnaghan 41, and Hankey 29. Cf. Dimock 1989: 311, with reference to 14.138-43. Note also that Eumaios refers to his master as ἠθεῖος (14.147), explained by a scholiast as properly used by a younger brother of an older brother. Cf. Stanford's comments on 14.145-46. Cunliffe lists four passages, *Il.* 6.518, 10.37, 22.229, 239, all of a brother to an elder brother, and *Il.* 23.94, Akhilleus to Patroklos (his senior). See also Hankey 29-30.

28. Furthermore this simile, 16.17-21, is thought by many to be part of a series of interlocking family-centered similes: *Od.* 5.394-97, 23.233-40. On which see Moulton 128 ff.

29. Again Menelaos offers a parallel for a host receiving Odysseus into the host's family in his offer to empty a city for Odysseus (4.174-80). Odysseus' offer extends to Philoitios as well, a partial double to Eumaios, though lacking his roles both as host and internal audience.

30. Cf. Race 1993: "The treatment of a guest . . . is the touchstone of every character's ἦθος in the *Odyssey*" (82).

31. See Reece's summary (1993: 105-6).

32. Commentators differ regarding the Phaiakians' hospitality. I side largely with G. Rose (1969). For opposing views see Reece's survey (1993: 102-16), the works cited therein, and his own explanation for the divergent opinions.

33. His entrance is dramatically underscored by a typical Homeric narrative technique, the pivotal contrafactual. For fuller discussion of the technique and of this passage see Louden 1993b.

34. Again Menelaos offers a parallel in that his hospitality, when Telemakhos arrives, is initially less than perfect (Eteoneus leaves him standing outside, 4.25-36), but then continues in an exemplary manner.

35. Cf. Lowenstam's comparison (181 n. 95). Many see in Eumaios the influence of a Baukis and Philemon and/or theoxeny story operative throughout the second half of the poem. On which see Reece 1993: 47-57, 182-84. See also Petropoulou on the sacrifice at 14.414-56.

36. As opposed to such hosts as Polyphemos, Kirke, and Kalypso, who do not. Doherty (1995, chap. 2) offers the fullest discussion to date of Alkinoös and Eumaios as internal audiences. As a specific subset of their tendency to prompt narratives from Odysseus, both Alkinoös and Eumaios make remarks which I classify as prooimial: 8.572-74, 16.62-64. I postpone discussion until chapter 4, however, because of their use of the verb πλάζω.

37. At 168 lines it is longer than the description of Akhilleus's shield (*Il.* 18.490-607) but four lines shorter than Phoinix's speech (9.434-605). The only speech in the *Odyssey* longer is Menelaos's narrative, 4.333-592.

38. See Dimock 194 ff, on the similar range of experience; Finley 136, on the capping storm in each narrative; Fenik 1974: 167-71, on other similar elements. On the structure of Odysseus's fictive biography, see Gaisser 27-31. Odysseus proclaims a fondness for arrows in the story to Eumaios (14.225), thematically part of a chain of references to his actual archery ability (e.g., 1.262, 8.215 ff, etc.); see Farron 60.

39. Most evident in his second narrative to Eumaios, an escapade with Odysseus at Troy, recognized by Eumaios as told to elicit a cloak (14.462–506).

40. Most 30. Cf. Louden 1993a: 16.

41. See Pratt 90.

42. Tracy 1990: 87; cf. Finley 174–75, Thalmann 1984: 161, Hankey 29, and Olson 129 on the similarity of their tales and similar range of experience suggested in Eumaios and Odysseus.

43. Roisman notes the "inner rapport and psychological sympathy" (218) that develops in the episode.

44. Cf. the principal narrator's description, κηληθμῷ δ' ἔσχοντο, 11.334. As Od. 1.337 describes the content of Phemios' songs as θελκτήρια, both hosts' comparable terms suggest reaction to his narratives as to those of a bard.

45. See Pratt 80–81 for a recent discussion of this passage.

46. See Pratt 67–70 for discussion of 11.367–69. "Sorrows" (11.369) renders Greek λυγρά, which can also be seen as something of a technical term as Od. 1.327 and 341 use it of song content.

47. Though Odysseus implies such a comparison, 17.418, as does the principal narrator, 21.406 ff. Odysseus further invites a comparison when he gives a gift to Demodokos (8.474–84), suggesting a reciprocal relationship between the Phaiakian singer and himself.

48. Thalmann (1984: 161) notes the similar contexts for storytelling: "And the recalling of the past with delight, which accompanies a meal, makes this scene the rustic analogue of the entertainments in aristocratic houses with their professional singers." For further evidence of generic elements, cf. descriptions in *Beowulf*, 87 ff, 494 ff, 1159 ff, etc.

49. Both passages refer to feasting (9.7, 14.195), wine (9.10–11, 14.194), and the lack of work (9.6–10, 14.195).

50. On the meaning of ἀθέσφατος, see Ford 181–83, 189–90, though he does not comment on the parallels under discussion.

51. Elsewhere in the *Odyssey* ἀθέσφατος modifies θάλασσαν (7.273), οἶνος (11.61), βόες (20.211); in the *Iliad*, ὄμβρος (3.4, 10.6); in the *Th.* ὄψ (830); in the *Op.* ὕμνος (662).

52. Odysseus also suggests that a great deal of time is necessary for the narrative he will deliver to Eumaios: "easily I could go on for the whole of a year, and still not / finish the story of my heart's tribulations (14.196–97)," roughly paralleling such bardic statements as *Il.* 2.488 ff. At 19.589 ff Penelope offers variants of the topos but without νὺξ ἀθέσφατος: οὔ κέ μοι ὕπνος ἐπὶ βλεφάροισι χυθείη, and (19.591–92) ἀλλ' οὐ γάρ πως ἔστιν ἀΰπνους ἔμμεναι αἰὲν / ἀνθρώπους. Cf. Athene lengthening the night to accommodate Odysseus and Penelope as they exchange narratives (23.241–46).

53. Cf. Joyce's description of the ideal reader for *Finnegans Wake*, "that ideal reader suffering from an ideal insomnia" (120), which passage is also a touchstone in Eco's works.

54. At 7.242 Odysseus begins his brief narrative to Arete with the same phrase,

as well as at 9.15, beginning his great narration of the wanderings. See also the narrator's ὅσα κήδε᾽ (23.306) of Odysseus' summary to Penelope. As suggested above in the case of λυγρά, κήδεα can be regarded as an aesthetic term.

55. I return to this topic below. Note that Alkinoös also raises the issue of falsehood with regard to the Apologue (11.363–67). While not accusing his guest of lying, he emphasizes the possibility of lies in such narratives. Cf. Pratt 92–93 and Thalmann 1984: 172–73.

56. Many have commented on the parallels, e.g., Thalmann 1984: 161, Doherty 1995: 149–52.

57. Though the Ithakan sequence contains a full-fledged singer in Phemios, the content of Phemios's songs is effectively ignored other than in briefest synopsis, allowing more room for both Odysseus and Eumaios to take up a bardic role.

58. On Skheria, Odysseus spends a night at the palace, a second day occupied by Demodokos's songs and the athletic games, capped by the Apologue, the Phaiakians sending him home on the third morning. On Ithaka, Odysseus spends two nights at Eumaios's hut, with Telemakhos arriving on the third morning. They spend one last night at Eumaios's hut before Odysseus proceeds to his palace on the fourth morning. If not for the meeting with Telemakhos, Odysseus would have headed to the palace on the third morning, replicating the sequence on Skheria.

59. Though the *Odyssey* treats and develops the two females quite differently. While Penelope's importance is evident, for Arete, see supra, n. 22.

60. As do all of the *Odyssey*'s internal narratives other than that delivered to Athene in book 13.

61. Von Kamptz 1982: 73, 190. Cf. Nagy 1979: 17 and Peradotto 111.

62. E.g., Odysseus' first words to Eumaios, ὑπέδεξο (14.54), as an instance of the root used to express guest reception.

63. E.g., Cook 1992: 266 asserts that "the internal evidence of the *Odyssey* suggests that we should see Scheria as an otherworldly Paradise bordering on Elysium which it also resembles." See also the earlier literature cited therein.

64. Cf. the tendency in later epic for depictions of the underworld to include poetic performances, e.g., *Aeneid*, 6.644 ff, *Paradise Lost*, 2.546 ff.

65. In chapter 4 we will note the strong prooimial connotations in his request (8.573–74).

66. And again Aiolos (10.14–16) might hear an abbreviated account up through the Cyclopeia.

67. See Creed.

68. Poseidon prevents the Phaiakians from ever again serving as escorts (see Louden 1993a: 30 and n. 88), and, consequently, ever again entertaining guests. For a recent discussion of the passage, see Peradotto 77–82.

69. The account given to Penelope (23.306–41) is truncated. Arete receives a full narration of the Aiaian sequence, because how Odysseus portrays himself is key to his coming to terms with her. In the Ithakan sequence we have a slightly different order. Odysseus has already come to terms with Penelope before he gives his narrative. Thus there is no reason for the full, expansive account.

70. His four underling swineherds are absent from the hut until 14.410. At 15.395–98, Eumaios discounts them as an audience.

71. See Doherty 1995: 123–24 and Thalmann 1984: 172 on Alkinoös' impressionable character.

72. Cf. Griffin on the narrator's comment about Eumaios at 15.556–57: "That openly laudatory comment departs widely from the normal reticence of the epic narrator" (47).

73. 14.55, 165, 360, 442, 507; 16.60, 135, 464; 17.272, 311, 380, 512, 579. For recent studies of apostrophe in Homer, see Parry 1972, Block, Yamagata 1989, and Kahane 80–113, 153–55. The use of apostrophe for Eumaios has been frequently criticized. See M. Edwards' assessment "fossilized" (1987a: 37). In support of the Eumaian apostrophes is Hankey 32.

74. Block 16, and discussion of same by Kahane 113.

75. Kahane; see esp. chap. 4.

76. His refusal to believe that Odysseus will return, however, thematically parallels Telemakhos' own conviction that Odysseus is dead, similarly expressed (14.133–36, 1.161–62).

77. Pratt 92: "His presence also adds weight and gives the mark of authenticity to Odysseus' fictions."

78. Eumaios responds with considerable irony (402–6), noted by Dekker 178–80, again belying alleged rustic naïveté.

79. Typically in Greek mythology one is emphatically the inheritor of family traits, though there are exceptions; e.g., Melanthios, gone over to the suitors' party, while his father, Dolios, is still loyal to Laertes and Odysseus.

80. See Dimock 256–57, for discussion of Autolykos's powers regarding oaths.

81. See Fenik 1974: 155 ff, on parallels in Odysseus's interviews with Eumaios and Penelope.

82. On αἶνος as a specific form of discourse, see Nagy 1979: 235 ff.

83. See Pratt 89 for a recent discussion of Eumaios' use of αἶνος.

84. Cf. Odysseus' remarks to Demodokos, κατὰ κόσμον (8.489), κατὰ μοῖραν (496).

85. Odysseus: 7.208, 8.382, 9.2, 11.355, 378, 13.38; Ekheneos: 7.159; Euryalos: 8.401.

86. See Pratt's discussion (67 ff), and Eumaios' comment, 17.381 ff.

87. See Austin 166–68 and A. Edwards 1993: 60, 62, on the initial description of Eumaios as emphasizing his craftsmanship.

88. For further discussion see Louden 1996a, and bibliography cited therein.

89. Eumaios appears to be an only child, inasmuch as no other children of Ktesios are mentioned, thus paralleling Odysseus' single line of descent (16.117 ff).

90. E.g., 6.148, 8.548; cf. κερδοσύνη 4.251, 14.31, etc.

91. The straddling is also evident in the application of heroic/aristocratic epithets to Eumaios. For a recent discussion, see Lowenstam 13–57.

92. Farron 70 ff notes that the implicit parallels between Odysseus and Hephaistos in book 8 reinforce such a view.

93. For discussion of Eustathius' remark, see Clay 1983: 34–38.

94. Clay 1994: 45 notes the absence of internal narrative on Aiaia, but suggests the reason is Kirke's lack of *thelxis*.

95. We would have a narrative within a narrative within a narrative, at this point. While that would not be uncommon in some Asian literatures, it would be utterly unique within Homeric epic.

96. Is this also why we never get to hear any of Phemios' songs?

97. The line (10.15) is a virtual one-line synopsis of Homeric epic, Ἴλιον Ἀργείων τε νέας καὶ νόστον Ἀχαιῶν.

Chapter Four: The Economy of Divine Antagonism, πλάζω, and the Proem

1. For recent studies of the *Odyssey* proem see T. Walsh, who offers a useful summary of recent arguments, Pedrick, Nagler 1990, S. West's commentary, Christidis (whose arguments I find particularly cogent), and Van Groningen, for study of the typical components in the proem, among others. Much of Cook 1995: chap. 1 and app. 1, touch on the proem. West offers a typical assessment of the alleged problem: "It [the proem] . . . gives disproportionate emphasis to a single incident" (68). For understanding the *Odyssey*'s divine wraths I have found Friedrich 1987b, 1989, and 1991 most useful.

2. See T. Walsh and Cook 1995: 171–80 for recent summaries of the respective arguments.

3. However, I find much to agree with in Nagler 1990 and Cook 1995, as well as T. Walsh's suggestion that temporal sequence is a factor in the proem's selection of Thrinakia.

4. I will not use these *comparanda* to "correct" the *Odyssey*, but to provide it with a larger context to appreciate more clearly the function of the divine interdictions and subsequent divine wraths.

5. Cf. Friedrich's reasonable assertion (1987b: 382) that we should expect variety from the different gods in a polytheistic universe.

6. Citations from *Gilgamesh* are from the translation of Dalley (80). Dalley notes that the same threat is made in the Descent of Ishtar, and in Nergal and Ereshkigal.

7. I.e., 1.326–27, 3.145, 4.499 ff, to name only a few in the opening books.

8. It is necessary, as the verb of the imbedded relative clause, to complete the sense of the first line, and it is followed by a full stop.

9. Though I will adduce a few relevant instances in the *Iliad*, the pattern of behavior that πλάζω exhibits is less prevalent in the *Iliad*, owing to key differences in the plots of the two poems.

10. Watkins 472–73, borrowing the term from K. Hoffman, *Der Injunktiv im Veda*, Heidelberg 1967. While in the broadest sense all terms in traditional oral epic can be seen as "memorative," inevitably some things are more memorative

than others. As argued below, in the *Odyssey* πλάζω serves to call before the audience the image of Poseidon driving Odysseus away from Ithaka. Cf. Foley's notion of metonymic reference (1991: 10, passim).

11. True of thirteen of sixteen occurrences (1.2; 2.396; 3.95, 106, 252; 4.325; 5.389; 13.204; 14.43; 15.312; 16.64, 151; 24.307).

12. A deity is the explicit agent only at 2.396 and 24.307, and of many compounded verb forms (e.g., 20.346). However, even if not stated, a deity is the usual implicit agent.

13. True of ten of sixteen occurrences (1.2, 75; 5.389; 6.278; 13.204, 278; 14.43; 15.312; 16.64; 24.307).

14. Again this force is sometimes more implicit than explicit. I would argue thirteen of sixteen (1.2, 75; 3.95, 106, 252; 4.325; 5.389; 6.278; 13.204, 278; 14.43; 16.64; 24.307) imply difficult sea crossings.

15. Active only at 1.75, 2.396, 9.81, 19.187, 20.346, and 24.307; passive at 1.2, 3.95 = 4.325, 3.106, 3.252, 5.389, 6.278, 13.204, 13.278, 14.43, 15.312, 16.64, 16.151.

16. While commentators, since antiquity, often take passives of πλάζω to mean "wander" (cf. the scholiast's comment, πλάγχθη: ἐπλανήθη), I suggest that a more literal passive sense, "be driven," most often captures the appropriate meaning.

17. True of nine out of sixteen occurrences in the poem (1.2; 3.95, 106, 252; 4.325; 5.389; 13.204; 15.312; 16.64).

18. The phrase μάλα πολλὰ πέπονθας is formulaic and by itself far too broad to suggest the phrases at 1.1–2 and 1.4. However, in combination with the passive of πλάζω, we have two key prooimial elements.

19. E.g., Thalmann 1992: 71.

20. For a study of the underlying syntax, see Louden 1993b; pp. 185–86 and 196–97 focus on the passage under discussion. Cf. Lang 1987, de Jong, and Morrison.

21. Jörgensen. For recent discussions see Friedrich 1987b: 386–88 and 1991: 16, and Cook 1995: app. 1.

22. See Friedrich 1987b: 385–86.

23. For the fullest exposition of the role of Athene's wrath in the *Odyssey*, see Clay 1983.

24. Furthermore, ἲς ἀνέμοιο, occurring in 13.276 and 19.186, is found immediately before the passage under discussion (9.71).

25. For a similar argument as to the thematic importance of self-control in the poem see Cook 1995: 31.

26. The poem underscores the weight of its most important storms by repeatedly mentioning them. We will discuss below how Odysseus in book 7 repeats mention of the earlier storm in book 5. In his Cretan lies, his storms appear to be modeled on those at Thrinakia and after Ismaros.

27. Pokorny 832 and Chantraine (s. v. πλήσσω) both view the two verbs as related. The *Odyssey*, however, does not manipulate πλήσσω in such a tight pattern as it does πλάζω.

28. The meaning of Πλαγκταί has been interpreted variously as "clashing" or "wandering," reflecting the same ambiguity noted above over how to translate passive forms of the root. I find "clashing" more likely on the basis of the overall argument presented here regarding πλάζω, and from the descriptions of how the Πλαγταί subsequently form an impenetrable barrier (12.66–71).

29. The figure, whether explicit or, as here, implicit, of a human term and a different divine term for the same thing also occurs at *Od.* 10.305, *Il.* 1.403–4, 2.813–14, 14.291, 20.74. See Watkins 38–39 for a brief discussion.

30. At *Il.* 12.285, it modifies κῦμα, in the aftermath of a storm raised by Zeus.

31. The language is not unique. Several formulae featured here form elements in other divinely provoked storms (e.g., 5.293b–94 = 9.68b–69).

32. The closest parallel in the *Odyssey* in this regard (but not others) is Poseidon's slaying of the lone Aias Oïliades (4.500–511), who, however, is quite unlike Odysseus in temperament or deserts.

33. Friedrich 1991: 16. This and the following paragraph summarize his argument.

34. Penelope carefully manipulates him into another loss of self-control in her trick over their marriage bed (23.182–204). That occasion, however, does not prompt a tragic chain of events.

35. Other than Odysseus' future sacrifice to him, as prophesied by Teiresias (11.119–30).

36. The scene contains further evidence of Athene's acting against the suitors as the wrathful deity of the Ithakan sequence in the formulaic lines that immediately preface Ktesippos' act: "And yet Athene would not altogether permit the arrogant / suitors to keep from heart-hurting outrage" (20.284–86 = 18.346–48).

37. Commentators (e.g., S. West 68) most often criticize this opening sentence for alleged inaccuracy in the third line's reference to ἄστεα, arguing that few are actually enumerated in the poem. See Cook 1995: 68, however, for a defense of the statement's accuracy.

38. T. Walsh: 385–92 contains a useful summary.

39. E.g., S. West: "It is a natural conjecture that this opening was composed for a poem devoted to Odysseus' wanderings. . . . It is understandable if the poet was anxious to preserve this splendid and carefully constructed proem, even though he must have realized that it no longer quite fitted a narrative which was to culminate in Odysseus' heroic vengeance" (69).

40. Compare T. Walsh's suggestion: "I suspect that the parallel between the crew members and the suitors will be an even more important subject to explore" (410). Cf. Nagler 1990: 341: "The Thrinacia story has been composed to characterize the Ithaca story in its ethical dimension." Cf. Cook 1995: 27: "Structural and verbal parallels allow the fate of one character or group to provide tacit commentary on that of another."

41. The slaying of the suitors, often compared to an Iliadic *aristeia*, would qualify.

42. To a lesser extent, it is possible that the proem's use of πλάζω also alludes to Athene's role as the wrathful deity hostile to the suitors, articulated through the same root (2.394–96, 20.345–49).

43. There are exceptions; cf. Nagler 1990 and Cook 1995.

44. See again Nagler's comment, 1990: 341.

45. In this sense the Polyphemos episode is the exception and hence far less suited to stand for the poem as a whole. In the present time of the poem Odysseus enjoys the full favor and support of not only Athene but Zeus. Were the composer to highlight the one episode that shows Odysseus losing self-control, and consequently earning divine enmity, he would not sum up the poem or point to its conclusion, but merely suggest its opening.

46. I would suggest that his heavily spondaic line (1.39) is so for emphasis.

47. E.g., S. West on l. 37 ff: "Here too the fate of Aegisthus foreshadows that of the suitors, who similarly ignore divine warnings."

48. Also noted in chapter 2, as both sequences have the Elpenor/Leodes figure, lacking on Skheria.

49. Their excessive consumption was firmly foregrounded in their inopportune feasting at Ismaros, and perhaps also hinted at in their suggestion to steal cheese from Polyphemos' cave (9.225).

50. Cook 1995: 11 and passim locates the crew/suitors' misbehavior specifically in "improper eating." While there is much to be said for his argument, I argue instead that improper eating is rather the means by which the crew and suitors demonstrate disobedience to the gods, lack of self-control, inability to uphold a divine interdiction.

51. Cook 1995: 81 ff argues that the incident at Thrinakia belongs to a family of myths devoted to the first sacrifice. While his discussion brings out some salient details in the episode, I feel that the level of destruction at the episode's conclusion rules out such a classification. However, as Eliade has argued (17–21 and passim), all myths that focus on ritual can be seen as re-creating the archetype.

52. E.g., Foley 1990: 14–15 and Thalmann 1992.

53. *Theogony* 507–616, *Works and Days* 47–105.

54. The biblical text consulted for Old and New Testament references is that of Suggs.

55. The analysis is my own. I am unaware of earlier commentators having compared the two myths.

56. Though popular interpretation of the Bible usually construes the episode as a condemnation of homosexuality, the narrative appears to be much less specific on this account. Condemnation of the violation of hospitality, and of improper sexual relations with guests, would seem to be its more likely aims. For the suitors' improper sexual relations with the maidservants, see 16.108–9, 20.6 ff, 20.318–19.

57. For the fire and brimstone falling on the city, cf. the sulfur attendant upon Zeus's destruction of the crew at Thrinakia (12.417).

58. The pattern is common in the Bible. In addition to Lot, cf. the accounts of

Noah (Genesis 6–9) and Enoch (best appreciated in Milton's depiction in *Paradise Lost* 11.655–71). Milton himself makes central use of the pattern in *Paradise Lost*. On which see Louden 1990: 115–26, 171–72.

59. The *Homeric Hymn to Demeter* also depicts a deity so angered as to consider destroying an entire race, καί νύ κε πάμπαν ὄλεσσε γένος μερόπων ἀνθρώπων (310). Zeus also intervenes on this occasion (313), as in the narrative pattern's three sequences, to assuage the offended deity.

60. Operative even in the New Testament; cf. Hebrews 13.2: τῆς φιλοξενίας μὴ ἐπιλανθάνεσθε· διὰ ταύτης γὰρ ἔλαθόν τινες ξενίσαντες ἀγγέλους, "Do not neglect to show hospitality; by doing this, some have entertained angels unawares."

61. The "do not look back" divine interdiction actually occurs in the *Odyssey* (5.350), when Leukothea so bids Odysseus. He characteristically upholds the interdiction (as is discussed in chapter 5). Cf. the parallel in the myth of Orpheus and Eurydike. The motif survives even into the ending of the film *Indiana Jones and the Raiders of the Lost Ark*.

62. None of the lines is an exact repetition, each containing ὄρος πόλει, and a form of ἀμφικαλύπτω. Stanford's remark (at 13.156–58): "The whole incident with its triple repetition . . . of the ambiguous threat is disturbing." I find this to be precisely the point of the repetition.

63. See Hainsworth's comment at 7.201. Cf. the feast attended by men and gods in the *Theogony* 535 ff, before Prometheus' deception of Zeus put an end to such intimate relations.

Chapter Five: Kalypso and the Function of Book Five

1. E.g., Page 70 ff. Cf. Hainsworth's comments 251–52. I will not be concerned with book 5's divine council, except in passing. It is unfortunate, in my view, that so many discussions of the fifth book have focused on the opening council to the comparative neglect of the other episodes.

2. See Hainsworth 253, especially, and 260–61 for a brief survey of various opinions.

3. Hainsworth (250) notes that book 5 essentially contains two episodes: Odysseus' departure from Ogygia (1–261), and his shipwreck at Skheria (262–493).

4. Pivotal contrafactuals are past contrary-to-fact conditions in which the order of the clauses is reversed, e.g., "And now X would have occurred had not Y intervened." See Louden 1993b.

5. E.g., Wilamovitz, Scully, Cook 1992: 249–50, Nagler 1996.

6. Exceptions include Woodhouse 46–53, Stanford 1961: 47–49, Segal 1968: 421–24, Austin 149–53, Marquardt 243–46, and Olson 57, 178, 181.

7. See Crane 31, for a summary of relevant research. The issue of priority is itself rooted in nineteenth-century analyst notions of Homeric composition.

8. Nagler 1996, Crane passim.

9. On the motif in *Beowulf*, see Creed.

10. Though at 12.390 we are told of another possible visit to Ogygia by Hermes.

11. In a further indication of the unique status of the Ogygian section, unlike all three sequences of the narrative pattern, events on Ogygia are not narrated from start to finish. We enter in present time only at the end of the section, lacking a full account of the beginning and earlier stages of the relationship between Kalypso and Odysseus. I return to this topic below.

12. The only exception to this is the strange retrospective mention by Kirke of Hermes' much earlier visit to her (10.330–32). He apparently appeared as himself, however, not in the youthful form that the pattern features.

13. On the *Odyssey*'s use of the feasting type-scene see Foley 1990: 265–76, Reece 1993 passim. On the type-scene as common outside of Homeric epic see especially *Beowulf*.

14. See, most recently, Olson 181: "The result is an affair powerful and satisfying enough to detain Odysseus on Aiaia for a year and make him forget everything else." This is reading a considerable amount into the text.

15. Segal 1968: 424; cf. Doherty 1995: 124 n. 84.

16. In not desiring Odysseus as her husband, Kirke parallels Arete, one multiform of the powerful female figure. Both other multiforms, Nausikaa and Penelope, however, do have a marital interest in Odysseus.

17. Cf. Stanford 1961: 47–49, Segal 1968: 421, 424.

18. The injunction parallels her earlier behest 10.457, 10.489. See Olson 57: "Unlike Kalypso, Kirke offered no overt resistance to being abandoned by her mortal lover."

19. See Clay 1994: 45 on Odysseus being under no compulsion to stay with Kirke.

20. Kahane argues (135) that, as her name is terminal in the two formulas describing her waterlogged clothing (5.312, 5.372), the positioning serves as part of a pattern that reinforces the threat she represents.

21. Nagler 1996: 148: "The traditional phrase theos audêessa invokes the life-saving ability of this goddess to report verities of the mantic world and thus induce or at least indicate the hero's return to life and light."

22. Cf. Odysseus' subsequent characterization of Kirke's warnings as θέσφαθ' (12.155).

23. Cf. Alkinoös' remark, his plural including Arete, who is by his side, τὸν ξεῖνον πέμπωμεν ἐὴν ἐς πατρίδα γαῖαν (13.52).

24. Marquardt 244. However, at 12.389–90, Odysseus notes that Kalypso said Hermes told her about the divine council between Zeus and Helios (12.374–88), an apparent contradiction of Hermes' and her remarks about his not having been to Ogygyia before. On which see Heubeck 140.

25. Such a dynamic lies behind Odysseus' punishment of the suitors; cf. most of Theseus' six exploits on the road to Athens, the Argonauts' encounter with Amykos, king of the Bebrykians, who forces ξεῖνοι to box with him (*Argonautica*, 2.1–97), and the like.

26. For discussions on the accuracy of δολόεσσα see Nagler 1996: 147 and Dirlmeier 21–22, 24, who suggests Kalypso inherits the quality from ὀλοόφρων Atlas.

27. Boedeker 67: "The tradition of the mortal lover of the Dawn-goddess is an old one; in Greek epic it is surely the most obvious aspect of Eos' mythology." The *Odyssey* mentions three of her lovers/victims, Tithonos (5.1), Orion (5.121), and Kleitos (15.250).

28. Hainsworth 254. Cf. Slatkin 29–30: "Eos brings the day into being: in a sense she creates time. . . . As she brings the day into existence, and, in effect, controls time, time controls the lives of men, by aging them; yet the goddess herself is unaging, ever-renewed. . . . From the human point of view, she is not simply immortal; she is the agent of the process by which the meaning of mortality is fulfilled." Kahane 131: "Eos is a personification of heroic time."

29. See Kirk 1984: 119 for a complete list of the many dawn formulas available, and their occurrences. See Austin 67–68 for a brief discussion of selectivity behind their deployment.

30. On Aiaia, Kirke and Odysseus make love immediately after the oath is sworn, whereas on Ogygia, Kalypso makes her last attempt at persuasion after the oath.

31. Demeter nurtures Demophon, ἔτρεφεν (235), intending to make him immortal and ageless, καί κέν μιν ποίησεν ἀγήρων τ' ἀθάνατόν τε (242); ἀθάνατόν κέν τοι καὶ ἀγήραον ἤματα πάντα (260). On the last expression, see Clay 1991–92.

32. Aphrodite and Anchises, Aphrodite and Adonis, Thetis and Peleus, and so on. See Sowa's comparison (39) of the *Hymn to Demeter* with the *Hymn to Aphrodite:* "Both tell of a fertility goddess who wants to make a man immortal, is balked in the attempt, and brings him increase instead."

33. Clay 1989: 179 n. 91 notes Artemis' unique interest in punishing certain negative behavior: "The only divinity who punishes unchaste behavior seems to be Artemis."

34. A. Lang 275–84, Patroni 321 ff, Christou 179 ff.

35. Arans and Shea 383.

36. Both are ἀθάνατος / ἀθανάτη, αὐδήεσσα, δεινή, δῖα, δολόεσσα, ἐϋπλόκαμος, θεά / θεός, νύμφη, and πότνια. Dee 16, 106–10, provides a useful summary.

37. Stanford 1962: 424 suggests 10.108, 135, 11.235, 12.3–4, 59, and 70–72 as possibly alluding to the Argonautic saga. In that her knowledge of drugs is what enables her to change men into beasts, the epithet, however indirectly, also points to her affinities with Artemis.

38. Woodhouse is one of the few commentators to note the inaccuracy of the description: "The moment he expressed a desire to be gone, Kirke was entirely willing. . . . There is thus evidently no ground whatever for the bare-faced assertion of Odysseus—'and in like manner Kirke restrained me in her halls, guileful one of Aia, eager that I should her husband be.' No such proposal was ever made by her" (50). Cf. Hogan 199: "His aim is to obtain homeward passage, and he may be stretching the facts just a bit in order to impress Alcinoos."

39. Doherty 1995: 22, 67, 78, 92–93, 99, 101n, 103–4, 112. See also the discussion above in chapter 1.

40. Cf. Woodhouse 50: "Odysseus for his own glorification willfully misrepresents her [Kirke], by ascribing to her a desire that belonged to Kalypso alone."

41. Cf. Woodhouse 51.

42. A description of the middle of their relationship is missing, but only because it was, apparently, uneventfully static.

43. See Felson-Rubin (46) on the depiction of their relationship as given only retrospectively.

44. On which see Louden 1993b, Lang 1989, Morrison 1991 and 1992, and de Jong. Morrison and de Jong do not, howver, discuss instances in the *Odyssey*.

45. Of Odysseus's six soliloquies in the poem, four occur in this short span (elsewhere at 13.198 and 20.17).

46. Hainsworth 279. Cf. 251 (also of book 5's second episode): "It is necessary to recognize the methods by which the epic poet seeks to compose a grand and impressive scene. He seeks quality through quantity, and doubles and trebles the hero's woes."

47. On this see especially the discussions in Louden 1993b of *Il.* 11.504–7 (185) and *Od.* 9.79–81 (186, 196–97).

48. See Cunliffe's second grouping of passages sub κῦμα.

49. See Louden 1993b: 184 n. 8 for totals and a list of the relevant passages. Milton, who patterns his own use of the same narrative technique in *Paradise Lost* on Homer's example, closely follows Homeric practice in this regard, having a deity intervene through pivotal contrafactuals to avert disaster in all but one instance. On which see Louden 1996b.

50. The only other instance out of sixty-one pivotal contrafactuals in the Homeric corpus in which a deity intrudes to cause harm is *Il.* 18.454–56, in which Thetis describes how Apollo caused Patroklos' death.

51. The Argonautic Clashing Rocks are essentially the same motif (*Od.* 12.65–72), never again to allow ships to sail through.

52. They are the two closest pivotal contrafactuals in the entire Homeric corpus. See again Louden 1993b: 183 n. 5 for a complete list.

53. The *Beowulf* poet uses the same construction, pivotal contrafactuals, to highlight his hero's underwater battles with monsters (1054–58, 1550–54, 1655–58). On which see Louden 1996c.

54. Louden 1993b: 194–95. The passage constitutes a significant structural turning point because it leads directly to Patroklos' death, subsequently prompting Akhilleus to reenter battle.

55. Nagler 1974: chap. 2 explores the resonances of this word in Homeric epic, though I do not agree with his assertion that in this passage "the poet makes temptation suggestively present in Ino's relinquishing of her veil" (47).

56. Hainsworth notes that "the injunction usually applies to dealing with chthonic or malevolent powers" (283) and cites parallels in Thompson 331–33.

Conclusion

1. For considerations of space I have not touched upon the transmission of the text until now. I do not mean to introduce it here gratuitously, but hope to return to a fuller treatment at a later date.

2. See Janko 1982.

3. E.g., de Vet and Nagy 1996a and b. While de Vet rightly points out some weaknesses in the application of Yugoslav oral tradition to Homeric epic, a paradigm in existence since Parry's eariest publications, the comparison she suggests in its place, to the Balinese model, strikes me as suffering from similar weaknesses due to significant cultural differences.

4. E.g., Milton, who structures *Paradise Lost* around many of the same phenomena the present study has investigated, restatement of themes, sometimes in lengthy sequence, lengthy sets of corresponding structures separated over large sections of his poem, etc. See Louden 1990: 114–26 for further discussion.

~~~~

Bibliography

Ahl, F., and H. M. Roisman. 1996. The Odyssey *Re-Formed*. Ithaca, N.Y.

Arans, O. R., and C. R. Shea. 1994. "The Fall of Elpenor: Homeric *Kirkê* and the Folklore of the Caucasus." *Journal of Indo-European Studies* 22: 371–98.

Arend, W. 1933. *Die typischen Scenen bei Homer*. Berlin.

Austin, N. 1975. *Archery at the Dark of the Moon: Poetic Problems in Homer's* Odyssey. Berkeley, Calif.

Beye, C. R. 1966. *The* Iliad, *The* Odyssey, *and the Epic Tradition*. Garden City, N.Y.

———. 1974. "Male and Female in the Homeric Poems." *Ramus* 3: 87–101.

Block, E. 1982. "The Narrator Speaks: Apostrophe in Homer and Vergil." *TAPA* 112: 7–22.

Boedeker, D. D. 1974. *Aphrodite's Entry into Greek Epic*. Leiden.

Burnett, A. P. 1970. "Pentheus and Dionysus: Host and Guest." *CP* 65: 15–29.

Chantraine, P. 1968–80. *Dictionnaire étymologique de la langue grecque*. Paris.

Christides, T. 1978–79. "The Companions in the *Prooimion* of the *Odyssey*." EEThess 19: 353–68.

Christou, C. A. 1968. *Potnia Thêrôn. Eine Untersuchung uber Ursprung, Erscheinungsformen und Wandlungen der Gestalt einer Gottheit*. Thessaloniki.

Clarke, H. 1967. *The Art of the* Odyssey. Englewood Cliffs, N.J.

Clay, J. S. 1983. *The Wrath of Athena: Gods and Men in the* Odyssey. Princeton, N.J.

———. 1989. *The Politics of Olympus: Form and Meaning in the Major Homeric Hymns*. Princeton, N.J.

———. 1991–92. "Immortal and Ageless Forever." *CJ* 77: 112–17.

———. 1994. "Sex, Drugs, and . . . Poetry." In *Epic and Epoch: Essays on the Interpretation and History of a Genre*, ed. Steven M. Oberhelman, Van Kelly, and Richard J. Golsan. Lubbock, Tx.

Cook, E. 1992. "Ferrymen of Elysium and the Homeric Phaeacians." *Journal of Indo-European Studies* vols. 20.3 and 4: 239–67.

———. 1995. *The* Odyssey *in Athens: Myths of Cultural Origins*. Ithaca, N.Y.

Crane, G. 1988. *Calypso: Backgrounds and Conventions of the* Odyssey. Frankfurt am Main.

Creed, R. 1962. "The Singer Looks at His Sources." *Comparative Literature* 14: 44–52.

Cunliffe, R. J. 1980. *A Lexicon of the Homeric Dialect*. Norman, Okla.

Dalley, S. 1991. *Myths from Mesopotamia*. Oxford.

Dee, J. H. 1994. *The Epithetic Phrases for the Homeric Gods (Epitheta Deorum apud Homerum)*. New York.

de Jong, I. 1987. *Narrators and Focalizers: The Presentation of the Story in the Iliad*. Amsterdam.

Dekker, A. 1965. *Ironie in de Odyssee*. Leiden.

de Vet, T. 1996. "The Joint Role of Orality and Literacy in the Composition, Transmission, and Performance of the Homeric Texts: A Comparative View." *TAPA* 126: 43–76.

de Vries, G. J. 1977. "Phaeacian Manners." *Mnemosyne* 30: 113–21.

Dimock, G. E. 1989. *The Unity of the* Odyssey. Amherst, Mass.

Dirlmeier, F. 1967. "Die 'schreckliche' Kalypso." In *Lebende Antike: Symposion für Rudolf Sühnel*, ed. Horst Meller and Hans-Joachim Zimmerman. Berlin.

Doherty, L. E. 1991. "The Internal and Implied Audience of *Odyssey* 11." *Arethusa* 24.2: 146.

———. 1995. *Siren Songs: Gender, Audience, and Narrators in the* Odyssey. Ann Arbor, Mich.

Edmunds, L. 1997. "Myth in Homer." In *A New Companion to Homer*, ed. I. Morris and B. Powell. Leiden.

Edwards, A. 1985. *Achilles in the Odyssey*. Beitrage zur klassischen Philologie 171. Konigstein.

———. 1993. "Homer's Ethical Geography: Country and City in the *Odyssey*." *TAPA* 123: 27–78.

Edwards, M. W. 1987a. *Homer: Poet of the* Iliad. Baltimore, Md.

———. 1987b. "*Topos* and Transformation in Homer." In *Homer: Beyond Oral Poetry*, ed. J. M. Bremer, I. J. F. de Jong, and J. Kalff. Amsterdam.

———. 1992. "Homer and Oral Tradition: The Type-Scene." *Oral Tradition* 7: 284–330.

Eisenberger, H. 1973. *Studien zur Odyssee* (Palingenesia 7). Wiesbaden.

Eliade, M. 1971. *The Myth of the Eternal Return or, Cosmos and History*, trans. W. R. Trask. Princeton, N.J.

Farron, S. G. 1979–80. "The *Odyssey* as Anti-Aristocratic Statement." *Studies in Antiquity* 1: 59–101.

Felson-Rubin, N. 1994. *Regarding Penelope: From Character to Poetics*. Princeton, N.J.

Fenik, B. 1968. *Typical Battle Scenes in the Iliad* (Hermes Einzelschriften 21). Wiesbaden.

———. 1974. *Studies in the Odyssey* (Hermes Einzelschriften 30). Wiesbaden.

Fernández-Galliano, M. 1992. "Books XXI–XXII." In *A Commentary on Homer's Odyssey*, vol. 3, ed. J. Russo, M. Fernández-Galliano, and A. Heubeck. Oxford.

Finkelberg, M. 1987. "Homer's View of the Epic Narrative: Some Formulaic Evidence." *CP* 82: 135–38.

Finley, J. H., Jr. 1978. *Homer's Odyssey*. Cambridge, Mass.

Foley, J. M. 1988. *The Theory of Oral Composition: History and Methodology*. Bloomington, Ind.

———. 1990. *Traditional Oral Epic: The Odyssey, Beowulf, and the Serbo-Croatian Return Song*. Berkeley, Calif.

———. 1991. *Immanent Art: From Structure to Meaning in Traditional Oral Epic*. Bloomington, Ind.

Ford, A. 1992. *Homer: The Poetry of the Past*. Ithaca, N.Y.

Friedrich, R. 1987a. "Heroic Man and *Polymetis:* Odysseus in the *Cyclopeia*." *GRBS* 28: 121–33.

———. 1987b. "Thrinakia and Zeus' Ways to Men in the *Odyssey*." *GRBS* 28: 375–400.

———. 1989. "Zeus and the Phaeacians: *Odyssey* 13.158." *AJP* 110: 395–99.

———. 1991. "The Hybris of Odysseus." *JHS* 111: 16–28.

Gaisser, J. H. 1968. "A Structural Analysis of the Digressions in the *Iliad* and the *Odyssey*." *HSCP* 73: 27–31.

Goldhill, S. 1991. *The Poet's Voice*. Cambridge.

Griffin, J. 1986. "Homeric Words and Speakers." *JHS* 106: 36–57.

Guntert, H. 1919. *Kalypso*. Halle.

Gutglueck, J. 1988. "A Detestable Encounter in *Odyssey* VI." *CJ* 83: 97–102.

Hainsworth, J. B. "Books V–VIII." In *A Commentary on Homer's Odyssey*, vol. 1, ed. A. Heubeck, S. West, and J. B. Hainsworth. Oxford.

Hankey, R. 1985. "Eumaeus and the Moral Design of the *Odyssey*." In *Essays in Honour of Agathe Thornton*, ed. R. Hankey and D. Little. Otago, New Zealand.

Hansen, W. F. 1972. *The Conference Sequence: Patterned Narration and Narrative Inconsistency in the Odyssey*. University of California Press: Classical Studies 8. Berkeley.

Heubeck, A. 1989. "Books IX–XII." In *A Commentary on Homer's Odyssey*, vol. 2, ed. A. Heubeck and A. Hoekstra. Oxford.

Hoekstra, A. 1989. "Books XIII–XVI." In *A Commentary on Homer's Odyssey*, ed. A. Heubeck and A. Hoekstra, vol. 2. Oxford.

Hogan, J. C. 1976. "The Temptation of Odysseus." *TAPA* 106: 187–210.

Holoka, J. P. 1991. "Homer, Oral Poetry Theory, and Comparative Literature: Major Trends and Controversies in Twentieth-Century Criticism." In *Zweihundert Jahre Homer-Forschung: Rückblick und Ausblick* (Colloquium Rauricum Band 2), ed. J. Latacz. Stuttgart.

Iser, W. 1974. *The Implied Reader: Patterns of Communication in Prose Fiction from Bunyan to Beckett*. Baltimore, Md.

———. 1978. *The Act of Reading: A Theory of Aesthetic Response*. Baltimore, Md.

Janko, R. 1982. *Homer, Hesiod, and the Hymns: Diachronic Development in Epic Diction*. Cambridge.

————. 1990. "The *Iliad* and Its Editors: Dictation and Redaction." *Classical Antiquity* 9: 326–34.

————. 1992. *The Iliad: A Commentary, Vol. IV: Books 13–16.* Gen. ed. G. S. Kirk. Cambridge.

Jones, D. M. 1954. "Ethical Themes in the Plot of the *Odyssey.*" Inaugural lecture, Westfield College, London.

Jones, P. V. 1989. "*Odyssey* 6.209–223: The Instructions to Bathe." *Mnemosyne* 42: 349–64.

Jörgensen, O. 1904. "Das Auftreten der Götter in den Büchern ι–κ der *Odyssey.*" *Hermes* 39: 357–82.

Kahane, A. 1994. *The Interpretation of Order: A Study in the Poetics of Homeric Repetition.* Oxford.

Kakridis, J. 1949. *Homeric Researches.* Lund.

Katz, M. A. 1991. *Penelope's Renown: Meaning and Indeterminance in the* Odyssey. Princeton, N.J.

Kearns, E. 1982. "The Return of Odysseus: A Homeric Theoxeny." *CQ* 32: 2–8.

Kirk, G. S. 1962. *The Songs of Homer.* Cambridge.

————. 1984. *The Iliad: A Commentary, Vol. I: Books 1–4.* Cambridge.

Krischer, T. 1965. "*ΕΤΥΜΟΣ* und *ΑΛΗΘΗΣ.*" *Philologus* 109: 161–74.

————. 1971. *Formale Konventionen der homerischen Epik.* Munich.

Lang, A. 1893. *Homer and the Epic.* London.

Lang, M. L. 1969. "Homer and Oral Techniques." *Hesperia* 38: 159–68.

————. 1989. "Unreal Conditions in Homeric Narrative." *GRBS* 30: 5–26.

Lateiner, D. 1995. *Sardonic Smile: Nonverbal Behavior in Homeric Epic.* Ann Arbor, Mich.

Lattimore, R. 1967. *The Odyssey of Homer.* New York.

————. 1969. "Nausikaa's Suitors." *Classical Studies Presented to Ben Edwin Perry. Illinois Studies in Language and Literature,* special issue 58: 88–102.

Levine, D. B. 1983. "Theoklymenos and the Apocalypse." *CJ* 79: 1–7.

Lévi-Strauss, C. 1965. "The Structural Study of Myth." Reprinted in *Myth: A Symposium,* ed. T. A. Sebeok. Bloomington, Ind.

Lidov, J. 1977. "The Anger of Poseidon." *Arethusa* 10: 227–36.

Lord, A. B. 1951. "Composition by Theme in Homer and Southslavic Epos." *TAPA* 82: 71–80.

————. 1960. *The Singer of Tales.* Cambridge, Mass.

————. 1968. "Homer as Oral Poet." *HSCP* 72: 1–46.

————. 1991. "Homer as an Oral-Traditional Poet." In *Epic Singers and Oral Tradition,* ed. A. B. Lord. Ithaca, N.Y.

Lord, M. L. 1967. "Withdrawal and Return: An Epic Story Pattern in the *Homeric Hymn to Demeter* and in the Homeric Poems." *CJ* 62: 241–48.

Louden, B. 1990. "Interactive Narrative Techniques in the *Iliad,* the *Odyssey,* and *Paradise Lost.*" Ph.D. diss., University of California–Berkeley.

————. 1993a. "An Extended Narrative Pattern in the *Odyssey.*" *GRBS* 34: 5–33.

———. 1993b. "Pivotal Contrafactuals in Homeric Epic." *Classical Antiquity* 12: 21–38.

———. 1995. "Categories of Homeric Wordplay." *TAPA* 125: 27–46.

———. 1996a. "Epeios, Odysseus, and the Indo-European Metaphor for Poet." *Journal of Indo-European Studies* 24: 277–304.

———. 1996b. "Milton and the Appropriation of a Homeric Technique." *Classical and Modern Literature* 16: 325–40.

———. 1996c. "A Narrative Technique in *Beowulf* and Homeric Epic." *Oral Tradition* 11: 346–62.

———. 1997a. "Eumaios and Alkinoös: The Audience and the *Odyssey*." *Phoenix* 51: 95–114.

Lowenstam, S. 1993. *The Scepter and the Spear: Studies on Forms of Repetition in the Homeric Poems*. Lanham, Md.

Marquardt, P. A. 1989. "Love's Labor's Lost: Women in the *Odyssey*." In *Daidalikon: Studies in Memory of Raymond V. Schoder*, ed. R. F. Sutton Jr. Wauconda, Ill.

Merkelbach, R. 1951. *Untersuchungen zur Odyssee*. Zetemata, Heft 2. Munich.

Meuli, K. 1921. *Odyssee und Argonautika*. Berlin.

Miller, D. 1982. *Improvisation, Typology, Culture, and the "New Orthodoxy": How Oral Is Homer?* Washington, D.C.

Morris, I., and B. Powell, eds. 1997. *A New Companion to Homer*. Leiden.

Morrison, J. 1991. "Alternatives to the Epic Tradition: Homer's Challenges in the *Iliad*." *TAPA* 122: 61–71.

———. 1992. *Homeric Misdirection: False Predictions in the* Iliad. Ann Arbor, Mich.

Most, G. W. 1989. "The Structure and Function of Odysseus' *Apologoi*," *TAPA* 119: 15–30.

Moulton, C. 1977. *Similes in the Homeric Poems* (Hypomnemata, xlix). Göttingen.

Mueller, M. 1984. *The Iliad*. London.

Mühlestein, H. 1987. *Homerische Namenstudien*. Beiträge zur klassischen Philologie 183. Frankfurt am Main.

Murnaghan, S. 1987. *Disguise and Recognition in the* Odyssey. Princeton, N.J.

Nagler, M. 1974. *Spontaneity and Tradition: A Study in the Oral Art of Homer*. Berkeley, Calif.

———. 1990. "The Proem and the Problem." *Classical Antiquity* 9: 335–56.

———. 1996. "Dread Goddess Revisited." In *Reading the* Odyssey: *Selected Interpretive Essays*, ed. S. L. Schein. Princeton, N.J.

Nagy, G. 1974. *Comparative Studies in Greek and Indic Meter*. Cambridge.

———. 1979. *The Best of the Achaeans*. Baltimore, Md.

———. 1996a. *Poetry as Performance: Homer and Beyond*. Cambridge.

———. 1996b. *Homeric Questions*. Austin, Tx.

Olson, S. D. 1995. *Blood and Iron: Stories and Storytelling in Homer's* Odyssey. Leiden.

Page, D. 1955. *The Homeric Odyssey*. Oxford.

Parks, W. 1988. "Ring Structure and Narrative Embedding in Homer and *Beowulf*." *Neuphilologishe Mitteilungen* 89: 127–51.

Parry, A. 1972. "Language and Characterization in Homer." *HSCP* 76: 1–22.

———, ed. 1987. *The Making of Homeric Verse: The Collected Papers of Milman Parry.* Oxford.

Patroni, G. 1950. *Commenti Mediterranei all' Odissea di Omero.* Milan.

Pedrick, V. 1992. "The Muse Corrects: The Opening of the *Odyssey*." *YCS* 29: 39–62.

Peradotto, J. 1990. *Man in the Middle Voice: Name and Narration in the* Odyssey. Princeton, N.J.

Petropoulou, A. 1987. "The Sacrifice of Eumaeus Reconsidered." *GRBS* 28: 135–49.

Pokorny, J. 1994. *Indogermanisches Etymologisches Wörterbuch.* Tübingen.

Powell, B. 1970. "Narrative Pattern in the Homeric Tale of Menelaus." *TAPA* 101: 419–31.

———. 1977. *Composition by Theme in the Odyssey.* Beiträge zur klassischen Philologie 81. Meisenheim am Glan.

Pratt, L. 1993. *Lying and Poetry from Homer to Pindar: Falsehood and Deception in Archaic Greek Poetics.* Ann Arbor, Mich.

Propp, V. 1968. *Morphology of the Folktale.* Austin, Tx.

Pucci, P. 1987. *Odysseus Polutropos: Intertextual Readings in the* Odyssey *and the* Iliad. Ithaca, N.Y.

Race, W. H. 1993. "First Appearances in the Odyssey." *TAPA* 123: 79–107.

Ramming, G. 1973. *Die Dienerschaft in der Odyssee.* Erlangen.

Rank, L. P. 1951. *Etymogiseering en Verwante Verschijnselen bij Homerus.* Assen.

Reece, S. 1993. *The Stranger's Welcome: Oral Theory and the Aesthetics of the Homeric Hospitality Scene.* Ann Arbor, Mich.

———. 1995. "The Three Circuits of the Suitors: A Ring Composition in *Odyssey* 17–22." *Oral Tradition* 10: 207–29.

Reinhardt, K. 1996. "The Adventures of the *Odyssey*." In *Reading the Odyssey: Selected Interpretive Essays,* ed. S. L. Schein. Princeton, N.J.

Roessel, D. 1989. "The Stag on Circe's Island: An Exegesis of a Homeric Digression." *TAPA* 119: 31–36.

Roisman, H. M. 1990. "Eumaeus and Odysseus—Covert Recognition and Self-Revelation?" *Illinois Classical Studies* 15: 215–38.

Rose, G. 1969a. "The Unfriendly Phaeacians." *TAPA* 100: 387–406.

———. 1969b. "The Song of Ares and Aphrodite: Recurrent Motifs in Homer's *Odyssey*." Ph.D. diss., University of California–Berkeley.

Rose, P. 1975. "Class Ambivalence in the *Odyssey*." *Historia* 24: 129–49.

Russo, J. 1992. "Books XVII–XX." In *A Commentary on Homer's Odyssey,* vol. 3, ed. J. Russo, M. Fernández-Galliano, and A. Heubeck. Oxford.

Rutherford, R. B. 1985. "At Home and Abroad: Aspects of the Structure of the *Odyssey*." *PCPS,* n.s. 31: 133–50.

Scully, S. 1987. "Doubling in the Tale of Odysseus." *CW* 80: 401–17.

Segal, C. S. 1968. "Circean Temptations: Homer, Vergil, Ovid." *TAPA* 99: 419–42.

————. 1992. "Divine Justice in the *Odyssey:* Poseidon, Cyclops, and Helios." *AJP* 113: 489–518.

————. 1994. *Singers, Heroes, and Gods in the* Odyssey. Ithaca, N.Y.

Seidensticker, B. 1978. "Archilochus and Odysseus." *GRBS* 19: 5–22.

Slatkin, L. M. 1991. *The Power of Thetis: Allusion and Interpretation in the* Iliad. Berkeley, Calif.

Sowa, C. A. 1984. *Traditional Themes and the Homeric Hymns.* Chicago, Ill.

Stanford, W. B. 1939. *Ambiguity in Greek Literature: Studies in Theory and Practice.* New York.

————. 1961. *The Ulysses Theme.* Oxford.

————. 1962. *The Odyssey of Homer.* 2 vols. London.

Stanley, K. 1993. *The Shield of Homer: Narrative Structure in the* Iliad. Princeton, N.J.

Stewart, D. 1976. *The Disguised Guest.* Lewisburg, Pa.

Suggs, M. J., K. D. Sakenfeld, and J. R. Mueller, eds. 1992. *The Oxford Study Bible: Revised English Bible with the Apocrypha.* New York.

Sulzberger, M. 1926. "*ONOMA EΠΟΝΥΜΟΝ:* les noms propres chez Homère et dans la mythologie grecque." *REG* 39: 385–447.

Thalmann, W. G. 1984. *Conventions of Form and Thought in Early Greek Epic.* Baltimore, Md.

————. 1992. *The* Odyssey: *An Epic of Return.* New York.

Thompson, S. 1957. *Motif-Index of Folk-Literature.* Bloomington, Ind.

Thornton, A. 1970. *People and Themes in Homer's Odyssey.* London.

Tracy, S. V. 1990. *The Story of the* Odyssey. Princeton, N.J.

————. 1997. "The Structures of the *Odyssey.*" In *A New Companion to Homer,* ed. I. Morris and B. Powell. Leiden.

Tsagarakis, O. 1979. "Oral Composition, Type-Scenes, and Narrative Inconsistencies in Homer." *Grazer Beiträge* 8: 23–48.

Van Groningen, B. 1946. "The Proems of the *Iliad* and the *Odyssey.*" *Medelingen Ned. Ak., Afd. Letterk.* 9: 279–94.

Van Nortwick, T. 1979. "Penelope and Nausicaa." *TAPA* 109: 269–76.

Vernant, J.-P. 1995. "The Refusal of Odysseus." Trans. Vincent Farenga, in *Reading the Odyssey: Selected Interpretive Essays,* ed. S. L. Schein. Princeton, N.J.

von Kamptz, H. 1982. *Homerische Personennamen.* Göttingen.

Walsh, G. 1984. *The Varieties of Enchantment: Early Greek Views of the Nature and Function of Poetry.* Chapel Hill, N.C.

Walsh, T. 1995. "*Odyssey* 1.6–9: A Little More Than Kine." *Mnemosyne* 48: 385–410.

Watkins, C. 1995. *How to Kill a Dragon: Aspects of Indo-European Poetics.* New York.

Webber, A. 1989. "The Hero Tells His Name: Formula and Variation in the Phaeacian Episode of the *Odyssey.*" *TAPA* 119: 1–13.

West, M. L. 1985. *The Hesiodic Catalogue of Women: Its Nature, Structure, and Origins.* Oxford.

West, S. 1988. "Books I–IV." In *A Commentary on Homer's Odyssey,* vol. 1, ed. A. Heubeck, S. West, and J. B. Hainsworth. Oxford.

Whitman, C. H. 1958. *Homer and the Heroic Tradition.* New York.

Wilamowitz-Moellendorff, U. 1921. "Homerische Untersuchungen." In *Philologische Untersuchungen.* Berlin.

Wohl, V. J. 1993. "Standing by the Stathmos: Sexual Ideology in the *Odyssey.*" *Arethusa* 26: 40–41.

Woodhouse, W. J. 1930. *The Composition of Homer's Odyssey.* Oxford.

Yamagata, N. 1989. "The Apostrophe in Homer as Part of the Oral Technique." *BICS* 36: 91–103.

———. 1994. *Homeric Morality.* Mnemosyne supplement 131. Leiden.

Yen, A. 1973. "On Vladimir Propp and Albert B. Lord: Their Theoretical Differences." *Journal of American Folklore* 86: 161–66.

Index

Homer, *Odyssey (cont.)*
   20.102–4, 88; *20.112–19,* 88;
   20.156, 39; *20.170,* 144n. 98;
   20.185–237, 88; *20.211,* 151n.
   51; *20.252–55,* 39; *20.276–*
   78, 39; *20.284–86,* 101, 156n.
   36; *20.288,* 146n. 10; *20.318–*
   19, 157n. 56; *20.321,* 146n. 10;
   20.322–25, 94; *20.345 ff,* 32, 34,
   88, 144n. 94, 157n. 42; *20.346,*
   155nn. 12, 15; *20.347–49,* 101–
   2; *20.350,* 144n. 107; *20.351–57,*
   21, 34, 88, 101, 144n. 95; *20.356,*
   34; *20.364–70,* 34, 88, 101;
   20.370, 144n. 98
  21: *21.69,* 39, *21.144,* 38, 146n. 14;
   21.144–48, 36; *21.144–62,* 35;
   21.144–74, 43; *21.145,* 45; *21.145–*
   46, 38; *21.146,* 37; *21.146–47,*
   37; *21.150–51,* 35–36; *21.153–*
   54, 46; *21.154–56,* 41; *21.156,* 41;
   21.157, 41; *21.172–73,* 36; *21.184–*
   87, 36; *21.188–244,* 36; *21.213–16,*
   55; *21.245–47,* 36; *21.257–62,*
   146n. 12; *21.258,* 39; *21.263,*
   39; *21.270–75,* 39; *21.273,* 39;
   21.293–94, 39; *21.293–310,* 146n.
   18; *21.304,* 14, 38; *21.379,* 54;
   21.406 ff, 151n. 47
  22: *22.8–18,* 88; *22.9–11,* 40; *22.21,*
   142n. 67; *22.205–309,* 27; *22.242,*
   146n. 10; *22.243,* 146n. 10;
   22.267, 146n. 10; *22.310–29,* 43;
   22.313–15, 37; *22.318–19,* 46;
   22.319, 42; *22.323,* 43; *22.326–*
   29, 47; *22.330–56,* 61; *22.330–77,*
   47; *22.407–9,* 84; *22.412,* 84;
   22.412–16, 23; *22.413,* 84; *22.416,*
   16, 19; *22.417,* 46
  23: *23.10 ff,* 13; *23.63–68,* 144n. 99;
   23.85–343, 13; *23.157–62,* 13;
   23.174–204, 64; *23.182–204,*
   13, 156n. 34; *23.206,* 152n. 54;
   23.233–40, 150n. 28; *23.241–46,*

151n. 52; *23.306–41,* 148n. 5,
152n. 69; *23.334,* 119; *23.334–37,*
112
24: *24.14,* 34; *24.103 ff,* 146n. 10;
   24.306–7, 72–73, 155nn. 11–15;
   24.376, 144n. 101; *24.472–86,*
   102; *24.472–88,* 144n. 106;
   24.473–76, 24; *24.475–79,* 102;
   24.478 ff, 23
Homeric Hymn to Aphrodite, 160n. 32
Homeric Hymn to Demeter, 118, 131, 158n.
   59, 160nn. 31, 32
Homeric Hymn 27 (to Artemis), 118
Horace, 14, 142n. 65
hospitality, 5, 6, 8, 10, 11, 13, 14, 15,
   16–17, 18, 22–23, 25, 32, 50–51,
   53, 55, 60, 63, 67, 94, 95–97, 99,
   101, 115, 132, 149n. 17, 157n. 56. *See
   also* theoxeny

Iliad-centered bias, 25, 138–39n. 14
*Indiana Jones and the Raiders of the Lost
   Ark,* 158n. 61
Intermezzo (= *Od.* 11.333–84), 9, 11–13,
   28, 43, 55–58, 149n. 22
Iser, W., 52, 148nn. 8, 9
Ishtar, 25, 70–71, 99, 105, 131, 154n. 6
Ismaros, 4, 21, 35, 46, 76–79, 84, 89,
   124, 138n. 9, 142n. 66, 143n. 93,
   155n. 26, 157n. 49

Janko, R., 133, 135n. 3, 162n. 2
Jason, 81, 145n. 114
Jones, D. M., 141n. 51, 142n. 75
Jörgensen's law, 77, 83, 124, 155n. 21
Joyce, J., 140n. 33, 151n. 53

Kahane, A., 62–63, 153nn. 73, 75,
   159n. 20, 160n. 28
Kakridis, J., 29
Kalypso, xvii, 11, 53, 64, 104–29,
   132–33, 140n. 30, 145n. 109,
   150n. 36

Nausithoös, 3, 21, 100, 145n. 115
Nekuia (= Book 11), 12, 34, 43, 49,
141n. 59, 145n. 2
Nestor, 27, 132, 148n. 4
Noah, 158n. 58

Odysseus: as archer, xii–xiii, 16, 26,
35, 54, 150n. 38; as craftsman,
65, 128; piety of, 30, 81, 91; self-
control of, 30, 38, 81, 84, 91,
128–29
Oinops, 35, 38, 39, 41
Olson, S. D., 148n. 10, 151n. 42, 158n.
6, 159nn. 14, 18
"one just man," xvii, 69–70, 96, 98,
132
oral-derived, xi
oral tradition, xi, xiv, xvi, 29, 30, 63,
91
Orestes, 19, 42
Orion, 43, 116, 118, 160n. 27

Page, D., 145n. 2, 158n. 1
Pandora, 95, 100, 128
paradise, 60–61, 152n. 62
Parry, A., xi, xiv, 135–36nn. 2, 4, 153n.
73, 162n. 3
Patroklos, 17, 29, 62, 87, 127, 141n. 56,
147n. 31, 150n. 27, 161n. 54
Patroni, G., 160n. 3
Pedrick, V., 154n. 1
Penelope, xvii, 2, 3, 6–9, 13–15, 18–
19, 25, 27–30, 33–34, 41, 42, 44,
46, 48, 52–54, 59, 61, 64, 67, 94,
108, 111, 119, 137n. 26, 138nn. 5, 7,
139n. 20, 140nn. 36, 43, 141nn. 44,
53, 142n. 63, 144n. 99, 146n. 8,
148n. 5, 149nn. 19, 20, 21, 152nn.
59, 69, 156n. 34, 159n. 16
Peradotto, J., 144n. 103, 147n. 21,
152nn. 61, 68
Perimedes, 46, 146n. 9
petrifaction, 48, 59, 70, 85, 97, 147n. 34
Petropoulou, A., 148n. 10, 150n. 35

Phaiakian athletes, xiii, xvii, 1, 2,
3, 5, 14, 16–18, 28, 47–48, 67,
83, 94, 97, 99–100; violation of
hospitality, 16–17
Phaiakians, xii, 3, 16–18, 30, 47–
48, 50–68 passim, 98–100; as
audience, 51, 53, 59, 66, 67; problematic hospitality of, 5, 8, 10,
16–18; special relations with the
gods, 48, 61, 121
Phemios, 47, 50, 61, 67, 106–7, 148n. 5,
152n. 57, 154n. 96
Philoitios, 36, 55, 88, 150n. 29
Philomeleides, 17–18
pivotal contrafactuals, 74, 77, 104, 123–
27, 129, 150n. 33, 158n. 4, 161nn.
44, 47, 49, 50, 52–54
πλάζω, xvii, 71–92, 94, 101, 123, 124,
125, 132, 150n. 36
Polyphemos, 14, 38, 46, 64, 76, 79–80,
83–86, 92, 99, 143n. 93, 150n. 36,
157nn. 45, 49
Poseidon, 17–18, 20–21, 23–25, 30, 48,
61, 69–72, 76–87, 89, 97, 99, 102,
114, 122–29, 131, 132, 143n. 82,
144nn. 103, 109, 146n. 7, 147n. 34,
152n. 68, 156n. 32
Powell, B., 142n. 65, 150n. 27
powerful female figure, xvii, 1–4, 6,
10–11, 27–29, 33, 44, 52–54, 59,
67, 70, 91, 94, 105–9, 114–15, 122,
133
Pratt, L., 147n. 1, 151nn. 41, 45, 46,
152n. 55, 153nn. 77, 83, 86
proem (= 1.1–10), xvii, 14, 20–21, 30,
69, 71–72, 74–76, 78–79, 81,
86–94, 95, 102–3, 132
Prometheus, 95, 158n. 63
prophecy, 3, 4, 18, 20–22, 33–34,
45–46, 88, 99–101, 138nn. 8, 11
Propp, V., 137n. 2, 148n. 6

Quintus Smyrnaeus, 78

Library of Congress Cataloging-in-Publication Data

Louden, Bruce, 1954–
   The Odyssey : structure, narration, and meaning / Bruce Louden.
      p.   cm.
   Includes bibliographical references and index.
   ISBN 0-8018-6058-x (alk. paper)
      1. Homer. Odyssey.   2. Epic poetry, Greek—History and criticism.
   3. Odysseus (Greek mythology) in literature.   4. Oral-formulaic analysis.
   5. Narration (Rhetoric)   6. Rhetoric, Ancient.   7. Homer—Technique.
   I. Title.
   PA4167.L68   1999
   883'.01—dc21   98-41521
                                                                             CIP